"This thoughtful book epitomizes its main themes as it weaves insights into the theology and creation of *The Saint John's Bible*. Homrighausen uses strands of spirituality, the experience of physical making, and scholarship as his warp to clothe this illuminated Bible with new insights. His added layers of meaning continue its life and impact on its readers—and even, in my case, on its creators."

—Susan Hufton, artist and scribe for *The Saint John's Bible*

"I thoroughly enjoyed reading this book. Homrighausen's writing style is both authoritative and lively—a rare combination! His research is a treasure trove of material drawn from various disciplines."

—Arthur Holder, Professor of Christian Spirituality, Graduate Theological Union, and author of *The Venerable Bede: On Song of Songs & Selected Writings*

"This thoughtful book gives the Song of Songs its due in modern Christian art, restoring visual intrigue to a religious classic in a style both enjoyable and engaging."

—George Greenia, Professor Emeritus of Modern Languages, and founder of the William & Mary Institute for Pilgrimage Studies

"Following the work he began with *Illuminating Justice* (2018), this latest offering from Jonathan Homrighausen is an embodied experience in and of itself, full of the sounds of the stylus on parchment, the rich earth of the garden from which the letters spring forth, and the journey of the eye on a pilgrimage across these pages. Homrighausen shows that matter not only matters when thinking about incarnational theology, but indeed that 'sensory experience is taken to be a sacramental embodiment of divine presence' and is as important in the exquisite contemporary performance of the art of *The Saint John's Bible* project as it was in the scribal illuminations of the medieval world. Homrighausen guides us on a journey through the page and into the sacramental imagination, and like all pilgrimages, the graces will surely continue to be revealed."

—Kathryn Barush, Thomas E. Bertelsen Jr. Associate Professor of Art History and Religion, Jesuit School of Theology of Santa Clara University, and author of *Imaging Pilgrimage: Art as Embodied Experience*

"Homrighausen's presentation of the Song of Songs as presented in *The Saint John's Bible* is, simply put, luminous. With elegance and concision, this study contextualizes *The Saint John's Bible's* distinctive, if often overlooked, visual presentation of the Song in a sweeping history of the biblical book's language and history of interpretation, even as it articulates the deeply intertextual web of biblical language that underlies the manuscript's imagery. In this volume, itself a study of the eloquence of imagery and the vividness of words, Homrighausen models the rich synergy among media with a sensitivity true to one who is both a scholar and an artist."

—Rabbi Laura Lieber, Professor of Religious Studies, Duke University, and author of *A Vocabulary of Desire: The Song of Songs in the Early Synagogue*

PLANTING LETTERS AND WEAVING LINES

Calligraphy, The Song of Songs, and *The Saint John's Bible*

JONATHAN HOMRIGHAUSEN

FOREWORD BY EWAN CLAYTON

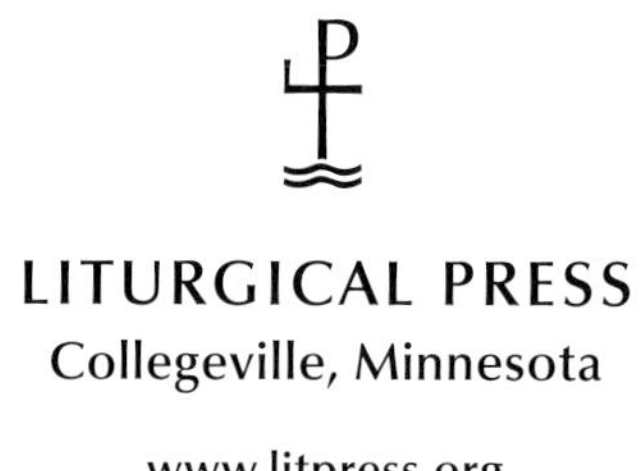

LITURGICAL PRESS
Collegeville, Minnesota

www.litpress.org

Published by Liturgical Press, Collegeville, Minnesota.
Printed in the United States of America.

1 2 3 4 5 6 7 8 9

Library of Congress Cataloging-in-Publication Data

Names: Homrighausen, Jonathan, author. | Clayton, Ewan, writer of foreword.

Title: Planting letters and weaving lines : calligraphy, the Song of songs, and the Saint John's Bible / Jonathan Homrighausen ; foreword by Ewan Clayton.

Description: Collegeville, Minnesota : Liturgical Press, [2022] | Includes bibliographical references and index. | Summary: "Biblical scholar Jonathan Homrighausen shows how calligraphic art interplays visual form, textual content, and creative process"— Provided by publisher.

Identifiers: LCCN 2022014827 (print) | LCCN 2022014828 (ebook) | ISBN 9780814688168 (paperback) | ISBN 9780814688410 (epub) | ISBN 9780814688410 (pdf)

Subjects: LCSH: Calligraphy. | Creation (Literary, artistic, etc.)—Religious aspects. | Saint John's Bible. | Bible. Song of Solomon—Illustrations. | BISAC: RELIGION / Biblical Studies / Old Testament / Poetry & Wisdom Literature | ART / Subjects & Themes / Religious

Classification: LCC NK3600 .H64 2022 (print) | LCC NK3600 (ebook) | DDC 745.6/197—dc23/eng/20220607

LC record available at https://lccn.loc.gov/2022014827

LC ebook record available at https://lccn.loc.gov/2022014828

Eternal glory is his and cannot be described,
(Even) if the heavens were parchment and all the forests pens;
(And even) if all seas and gathered waters (were) ink,
(and) earth's inhabitants (were all) scribes and authors.

—from *Akdamut Milin* ("The Introduction of Words"),
an eleventh-century Jewish liturgical poem
recited at Shavuot in Ashkenazi traditions[1]

But there are also many other things that Jesus did; if every one of them were written down, I suppose that the world itself could not contain the books that would be written.

—John 21:25

Could we with ink the ocean fill,
And were the skies of parchment made;
Were every stalk on earth a quill,
And every man a scribe by trade;
To write the love of God above
Would drain the ocean dry;
Nor could the scroll contain the whole,
Though stretched from sky to sky.

—Frederick M. Lehman, *The Love of God*,
a Christian hymn written in 1917

Say: "If the sea were ink for the Words of my Lord, the sea would be exhausted before the Words of my Lord were exhausted, even if We brought the like thereof to replenish it."

—Qurʾan, *Surah al-Kahf* (18), v. 109

And if all the trees on earth were pens, and if the sea and seven more added to it [were ink], the Words of God would not be exhausted. Truly God is Mighty, Wise.

—Qurʾan, *Surat Luqmān* (31), v. 27[2]

1. Translation from Jeffrey Hoffman, "*Akdamut*: History, Folklore, and Meaning," *Jewish Quarterly Review* 99, no. 2 (2009); see also Laura S. Lieber, "*Akdamut Milin*: The Enigma and Perseverance of Tradition," *TheTorah.Com*, 17 May 2014, https://www.thetorah.com/article/akdamut-milin.

2. Translations from Seyyed Hossein Nasr and others, eds., *The Study Quran: A New Translation and Commentary* (New York: HarperOne, 2015).

CONTENTS

FOREWORD

Ewan Clayton

I come to this book both as a calligrapher, a historian of writing, and someone who has spent a few years, in his youth, happily living in a Benedictine monastery. So I naturally feel deep affinity with Jonathan Homrighausen's *Planting Letters and Weaving Lines*. This book is both a meditation and a work of scholarship. It explores images and metaphors that arise from the world of writing, specifically from Jonathan's engagement with a modern handwritten illuminated manuscript, *The Saint John's Bible*, and a study of the most poetic book of the Old Testament, the Song of Songs—the latter often read as an allegory of the relationship between our life-force and its origin, the soul and God.

Read on and you will be introduced to a refreshing vision of what writing is. By "writing" in this context we mean primarily the physical process of making marks on a page, not the arts of rhetoric and composition—though that is also to be found here in the way Jonathan explains the use of allegory and the way he weaves many images together.

I find this an enlivening vision because it addresses my entire being. All my sensory channels are opened. The strong poetic imagination of the author of the Song of Songs enthuses me, speaks to me, and I know it will draw further creativity from me. The act of writing is described here as an embodied process holding a powerful commitment to making things tangibly present.

Jonathan's original insight is that the metaphor-laden poetry of the Song of Songs and its illuminations can provide keys that unlock the meaning of the whole manuscript itself as Word (content) becoming (process) Flesh (form). It is a big claim but Jonathan delivers on it. It is given width, height, and depth by his conversion from Christianity to Judaism, meaning that he draws on sources from both traditions and reinvigorates many of them in the process. Added to this he has had the benefit of drawing on the accumulated *lectio* of the community at Saint John's and its distillation in the work of the Committee on Illumination and Text, which advised Donald Jackson and his scribal team, who then created the Bible. Crucially, also, Jonathan could draw on the reflections of Donald and the scribes themselves, who made their own living pilgrimage through all the orchestration of images, logistics, material preparations, painting, gilding, and writing the eighteen miles of script that it took to make the Bible.

Planting Letters and Weaving Lines offers us a new reading of scribal labor that differs from the aggressive images we might come across in late classical sources that speak of using pen and ink as weapons, wounding and fighting against the wiles of the devil. Here we are introduced to a labor that is kind, loving, nurturing, pastoral—even domestic. The primary metaphors suggested by a reading of the Song of Songs are those of planting and weaving, the garden, the field, beauty and relationship, and also walking, touching, gesturing.

In this book, the phrase "sensory experience is taken to be sacramental embodiment of divine presence" leapt out at me from the text. The black furrows of the lines on a page are planted with letters, seeds that will flower into a text, a "Word." The writing of text is also likened to a weaving, just as a child (another "Word") is knitted together in a mother's womb. This perspective emphasizes our relationships, embeddedness in nature, and participation in the unhurried rhythms of walking and breathing, of repetition with variation, and embraces recent anthropological readings of making and contemporary framings of what it is to be human. Writer and reader are sustained by nature and themselves nurture it; scribal activity is a process that engages the whole person.

The other perspective folded within this work is that of understandings arrived at by doing, of working with a *practice* (be it writing or reading) rather than by studying an artwork as data from the outside. What we witness here time and again are statements that arise from an inquiry into "how people perceive and relate to their surroundings in currents of space, time and movement" as well as story.[1] What Jonathan brings forward is how calligraphic work has value as an

1. Tim Ingold, "Knowing from the Inside," in *Making: Anthropology, Archaeology, Art and Architecture* (New York: Routledge, 2013), 11.

activity, what he calls a process. Yes, alongside the content and form of a text there is also a "becoming."

The calligrapher Edward Johnston (1872–1944), who is at the root of the lineage in which Donald Jackson and his scriptorium worked, pondered deeply on what it meant to write. Like Jonathan's content, form, and process, he too had a triform understanding. In his short essay "On Formal Penmanship defined by The Thing" his metaphors are drawn from flowing water, flame, and the nib of the broad-edged pen itself, but he held also that three essential qualities of writing were his guides: Sharpness, Unity, and Freedom.[2] He understood these qualities broadly: sharpness was tangibility, explicitness, material; unity was the form of the material, the nature of its complexities of togetherness; and freedom was movement, dynamic activity, spontaneously arising afresh. For him there was a connection between this triform definition and Word made Flesh. He thought of it as reflecting the dynamic defined by the early church in the Trinity as Father, Son, and Spirit.

But lest we get too conceptually preoccupied, abstracted from thinking in flesh and blood and with our senses—which is the thrust of Jonathan's appreciative text—I want to thank him for returning the calligrapher's experience and ordinary writing to center stage. As he mentions early in his text, the remarkable thing about this Bible is that it is handwritten. We may turn with enthusiasm to the magnificent illuminations but it is the fact that it is entirely written by hand that marks it out as unique in an age of mechanical reproduction. Each letter is formed in its own micro-context, adjusting to those on either side and to the quality of the ground (vellum) in which it is planted, knitting together over time into textures given character through the rhythmic but varied movements of an individual scribe's hand, heart, breath, and imagination until the book is complete. Every part of it is lived and in this way word and flesh unite in a unique creation, a tangible declaration of a love that is stronger than death.

2. Essay found in Edward Johnston, *Formal Penmanship and Other Papers*, ed. Heather Child (London: Lund Humphries, 1971).

PREFACE AND ACKNOWLEDGMENTS

The fact that I wrote this book strikes me as both inevitable and surprising. Inevitable, because I knew I wanted to write it even during the gestation of *Illuminating Justice* and the subsequent year spent writing a thesis on the Song of Songs. I intended this book to be a follow-up to the previous: a tome on intertextuality and canonical criticism in the Song of Songs illuminations of *The Saint John's Bible.* My first foray into the topic, a conference paper for the Society of Biblical Literature (SBL), resulted in an invitation to publish the paper in an edited volume—an encouraging start.[1] As with most books, including *The Saint John's Bible* itself, I thought this one would be simpler and quicker to write than it actually was. Over the next two years, the idea lay dormant as I struggled through the stress of doctoral coursework. So yes, I knew I wanted to write this book for the last four years. I have been somewhat impatient to do so, even as I thank the mentors who wisely told me to let it sit, to trust that it would remain present and take on more depth and richness.

On the other hand, the themes and questions that drove me to write *Illuminating Justice* have receded into the rearview mirror of my intellectual and spiritual journey. I converted to Judaism, ironically while teaching future pastors at Duke Divinity School. Yet *The Saint John's Bible* still drew me in. After presenting about it to many different audiences, I can still attest that people on paths far outside

1. Jonathan Homrighausen, "'I Sought Him Whom My Soul Loves': Symbol, Ornament, and Visual Exegesis of the Song of Songs in *The Saint John's Bible*," in *The Art of Biblical Interpretation: Visual Portrayals of Scriptural Narratives*, ed. Heidi J. Hornik, Ian Boxall, and Bobbi Dykema, 67–101, The Bible and Its Reception 3 (Atlanta: SBL Press, 2021).

the Christian sheepfold can be enthralled by the artistic creations of Donald Jackson and the many others who scribed and painted this Bible. One of those scribes, Izzy Pludwinski, is himself Jewish. More to the point, Judaism's rich calligraphic heritage, best known in the ritual craft of the scribes who engage in the holy work of writing Torah scrolls, provided a mirror that helped me make sense of the material "Word made Flesh" that is this Bible handwritten on animal skin. With that lens, I found ample Christian reflections from the pre-Gutenberg world showing how many monk-scribes conceived of their own physical labor copying Gospels as holy work.

And so, like many books, this tome began as one thing and ended as another. There is certainly much intertextuality and canonical exegesis here. But each chapter also uses the Song of Songs in *The Saint John's Bible* to come to a larger meditation on the fleshliness, the materiality, of sacred text, whether in reading it silently, holding its physical form, or writing its letters. If the Song of Songs is the Bible's most profound poetry of embodied desire, however Jews and Christians have made sense of its lovers' identities, then why not read its lyrics as the embodied desire for the sacred Word made Book? Here the materiality of sacred text, the forms of its carbon-black letters, the warp of its dead parchment surface, the keratin of the quills used to write it, all play as large a part in this Bible's meaning as the semantic contents of its chapters and verses.

As with all books, much is omitted. I hope you read the following chapters less as comprehensive surveys and more as meditations. The structure is not a singular built-up argument, but a series of variations on a theme. I promise something of interest here not only for lovers of *The Saint John's Bible* but also for readers of the Song of Songs and lovers of calligraphy.

A note on terminology and translations. I use the term *Old Testament* to refer to biblical books shared by Jews and Protestants (and some extra books in the Catholic and Orthodox canons) when being read in a Christian context. I do not think *Old Testament* is inherently a dirty or supersessionist word. When discussing specifically Christian exegesis, the kind of interpretation underlying this Bible's art, it is the most accurate term. When discussing Jewish exegesis, I use the term *Tanakh*, and when discussing non-confessional scholarship, I employ *Hebrew Bible*. Unless otherwise noted, I employ the NRSV translation throughout, as does *The Saint John's Bible*.

I have many people to thank. My earliest readings of the Song were sharpened in seminars with Robert Alter, Deena Aranoff, the late John

Endres, and Daniel Matt; just when I thought I knew the Song well, I learned even more from Marc Brettler and Laura Lieber. Although I never studied the Song with her in the classroom, Ellen Davis's Song commentary and encouragement in pursuing the arts alongside the Bible have proved invaluable. The feedback of the Bible and Visual Art section at the SBL annual meeting also helped, especially the invitation from Heidi Hornik to publish an earlier version of this work in an edited volume.

While writing this book, many others answered queries, suggested primary sources, and encouraged: Jenny Knust, Jill Marcantonio, Libbie Schrader, Galia Goodman, Abigail Emerson, Mary Berry, Tom Hendrickson, Ewan Clayton, George Greenia, Katie Kehoe, Lucinda Mosher, April Flowers, and Aaron Rosen, to name a few. William Hart Brown looked over the whole draft and gave superb comments. Lacey Hudspeth of the Duke Divinity School Library supplied me with many needed tomes.

Outside academia, the calligraphy community and *The Saint John's Bible* community continue to display the generous and sharing spirit I have come to know them for. Anne Kaese and Jason Paul Engel, as with *Illuminating Justice*, have shared the results of their keen knowledge of the illuminations. Michael Patella, Susan Sink, Sue Hufton, Susie Leiper, and Tim Ternes have supplied useful insights. A special thanks to Cari Ferraro, who sent me a treasure trove of calligraphy newsletters while cleaning out her studio—among which were invaluable articles by Sally Mae Joseph and Sue Hufton that I didn't even know existed!

As with the last book, I am indebted to Hans Christoffersen for championing my proposal to the press and for printing the book with color, design, and paper quality that not a few art historians will envy. I am also grateful to Stephanie Lancour, Michelle Verkuilen, and Tara Durheim (again) of Liturgical Press for helping my book move out into the world with color and crisp formatting.

Between the day I proposed this book to Liturgical Press and the day I turned it in, I wrapped up a grueling final semester of doctoral coursework, moved to a new state, agonized over several major exams, helped my mom move across the country, and started a new teaching job at the College of William & Mary. Also, a global pandemic hit. Somehow through that mess, this book came out—most likely due to the encouragement and prodding of Michael Runyon. Michael, there's nobody I'd rather be stuck at home for a year and a half with. I dedicate this book to you.

Chapter One

OPENING THE BOOK

Over the last five years, I have shown *The Saint John's Bible* to several hundred people: college students studying women in the Bible, participants at an interfaith peace conference in western North Carolina, and calligraphers focusing on the techniques of this unique manuscript. Over time, I saw an irony. While many Bibles have art, this one's unique claim to fame is not its bold, thought-provoking images (called "illuminations" in Saint John's lingo) but the fact that each one of its 1,150 pages is handwritten. Indeed, far more pages contain only text than contain text and illuminations. Yet, few viewers asked to see all those pages. Few wanted to leaf through even one of the seven volumes from start to finish.

What were they missing? I struggled to explain *why* those pages upon pages of quilled words held just as much visual interest as Donald Jackson's bright, gilded images of Jesus, or Suzanne Moore's intimate portrait of Ruth and Naomi, or Thomas Ingmire's full-page illumination trumpeting Isaiah's messianic prophecies echoing the tune of Handel's *Messiah*. I strained to explain how to look at the calligraphy in its own right.

Western calligraphy, or Roman-alphabet calligraphy, is not an art form typically given a great deal of scholarly attention.[1] My college art history survey did not touch it. Arabic and East Asian calligraphic traditions enjoy cultural prestige, a lengthy tradition of commentary, and close ties to religious rituals and sacred texts. Their Roman alphabet

1. I use the phrase "Roman-alphabet calligraphy" because contemporary lettering artists working in German, English, Spanish, French, and other languages that employ the same alphabet do draw inspiration from one another's work—and from the Latin-language manuscripts of the past two thousand years.

cousin, sadly, is too often relegated in the popular mind to "just" craft, or storefront signs, or wedding invitations. As a result, too many people who view *The Saint John's Bible* lack an ability to articulate exactly what makes its scribal art so powerful or how it affects them. We might resort to a pat definition: calligraphy, from the Greek roots, means "beautiful writing." But this bland etymology fails to convey what calligraphy does or why.

The Saint John's Bible is often described as a visual and material affirmation of the incarnation. This Bible is Word made Flesh: on animal skin, with bird feathers. But the phrase "Word made Flesh" also helps unpack calligraphic art more broadly. In this Bible, Word (content) becomes (process) Flesh (form). My premise is that the power of calligraphic art lies in its ability to form connections between content, form, and process. By *content* I mean the words, the texts, which the scribe writes. The *form* those words take can mean many things: the visual forms of the letters, the images around the words and in the margins, the material out of which the manuscript is made. The *process* is the means and modes by which the artists and scribes created the work: the journey from idea to sketches to final product, and the tools used. As painter and lettering artist Ben Shahn emphasized: "Form is not just the intention of content, it is the embodiment of content."[2] The three are inseparable.

Further, the metaphor-laden poetry of the Song of Songs, and its vivid and potent illuminations in *The Saint John's Bible*, provide the keys that unlock the meaning of this whole manuscript. Its textual and visual images and metaphors supply us with powerful lenses to explain what makes calligraphy beautiful, such as calligraphy's connections with weaving and ploughing. The Song of Songs also supplies compelling ways to construe the incarnate form of the Bible as a divine presence, a material presence that engages the Christian believer's senses much like the Eucharist and other sacraments.

The connection between content and form in *The Saint John's Bible* should be clear from one of the most famed illuminations of the project, corresponding to the text with which Jackson began writing the Bible on Ash Wednesday in 2000: "And the Word became flesh" (John 1:14).[3]

2. Ben Shahn, *The Shape of Content* (Cambridge: Harvard University Press, 1957), 53.

3. Christopher Calderhead, *Illuminating the Word: The Making of* The Saint John's Bible, 2nd ed. (Collegeville, MN: Liturgical Press, 2015), 166.

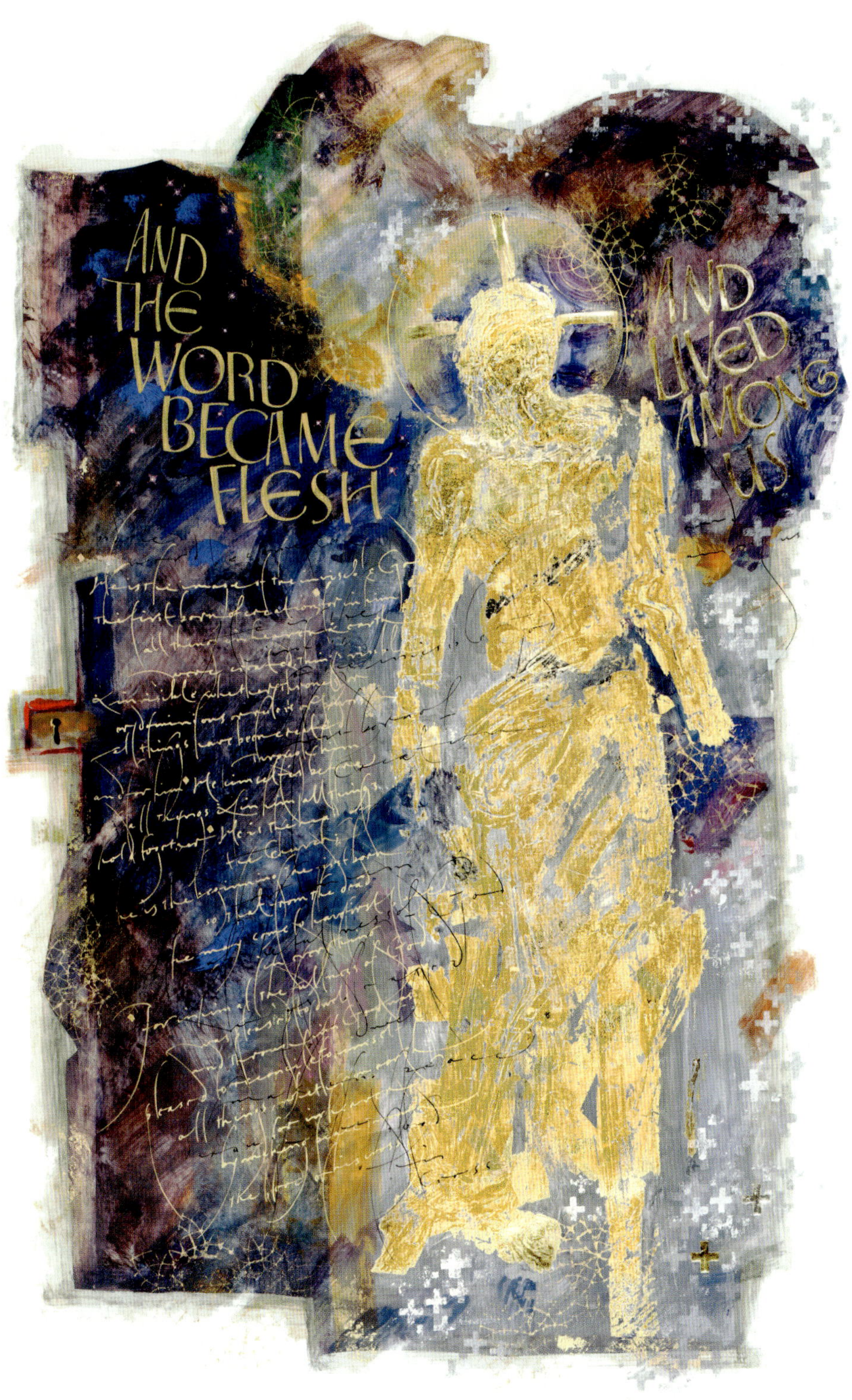
AND THE WORD BECAME FLESH
AND LIVED AMONG US

The words of John's prologue allude to Jewish concepts of personified Wisdom and the Torah (God's teaching) as a blueprint for creation. John's paradox is that Word and flesh are opposites conjoined: one immaterial and eternal, the other "denoting human existence in its fragility, transience, and mortality."[4] Jackson's illumination of John's prologue conveys this by portraying Jesus in the process of being made golden flesh, against a backdrop of astronomical imagery taken from the Hubble Space Telescope, which conveys contemporary understandings of creation.[5] Likewise, the words of this Bible are written quite literally on flesh: calfskin vellum. Its materiality reflects the incarnational theology of those who made it. This is a tactile Bible.

The Saint John's Bible reclaims the sensory and material dimensions of sacred text. In the context of Christian tradition, this Bible is not doing something new so much as retrieving something old in a new way. After all, Jesus himself in the Gospels engages Jewish Scriptures as material artifacts:

> When he came to Nazareth, where he had been brought up, he went to the synagogue on the sabbath day, as was his custom. He stood up to read, and the scroll of the prophet Isaiah was given to him. He unrolled the scroll and found the place where it was written:
> "The Spirit of the Lord is upon me,
> because he has anointed me
> to bring good news to the poor.
> He has sent me to proclaim release to the captives
> and recovery of sight to the blind,
> to let the oppressed go free,
> to proclaim the year of the Lord's favor."
> And he rolled up the scroll, gave it back to the attendant, and sat down. The eyes of all in the synagogue were fixed on him. Then he began to say to them, "Today this scripture has been fulfilled in your hearing." (Luke 4:16-21)

4. Brendan Byrne, *Life Abounding: A Reading of John's Gospel* (Collegeville, MN: Liturgical Press, 2014), 27.

5. Jackson has commented on this image in various places: Peter Halliday, ed., *Holy Writ: Modern Jewish, Christian, and Islamic Calligraphy* (Lichfield: Lichfield Cathedral, 2014), 41; Patricia Lovett, *The Art and History of Calligraphy* (London: British Library Publishing, 2017), 207; Donald Jackson, "The Dream and the Realities," *The Scribe* 75 (2002): 8.

In Luke's telling, Jesus seems familiar with how to handle the scroll: he unrolls and rolls it fluidly, he can find the passage he is reading, and he knows the rituals of public reading familiar to the synagogue of his day.[6] Matthew's Jesus mentions another material scriptural practice in a diatribe against the Pharisees:

> They do all their deeds to be seen by others; for they make their phylacteries broad and their fringes long. (23:5)

These phylacteries are known in Hebrew as *tefillin*, small leather boxes containing passages from Exodus and Deuteronomy worn by observant Jews in daily prayer. Not only are *tefillin* still used in Jewish prayer today, but they have been found at Qumran, suggesting that the tradition was current among some first-century Jews as well.[7] The import of Jesus' invective is not that phylacteries are themselves bad but that his are narrower and less showy.[8] Just as Christians hold that Jesus is Word made Flesh, so Jesus held the Sacred Scriptures to his own flesh, in holding the Isaiah scroll and possibly wrapping *tefillin* in prayer. Christians throughout history likewise engaged Scripture as a material, sensory, tangible artifact. The advent of the printing press, and later digital books, has largely erased this practice of embodying Scripture from both Christian practice and consciousness. This particular Bible reclaims it.

The Saint John's Bible's historical reclamation is also a theological one. In this Bible's incarnational theology, sensory experience is taken to be sacramental embodiment of divine presence. Michael Patella is the Benedictine monk at Saint John's Abbey and the New Testament scholar who chaired the Committee on Illumination and Text, which gave theological and exegetical guidance for *The Saint John's Bible*. He writes:

> In the Christian West, as in the Christian East, Bibles, lectionaries, and Gospels were viewed as Christ, the Word of God, present in

6. Anne F. Elvey, *The Matter of the Text: Material Engagements between Luke and the Five Senses*, Bible in the Modern World 37 (Sheffield: Sheffield Phoenix Press, 2011), 44–53.

7. Yehudah B. Cohn, *Tangled Up in Text: Tefillin and the Ancient World*, Brown Judaic Studies 351 (Providence, RI: Brown Judaic Studies, 2008).

8. Amy-Jill Levine, *The Misunderstood Jew: The Church and the Scandal of the Jewish Jesus* (San Francisco: HarperSanFrancisco, 2006), 24.

> the book. To hear the Bible read was to hear Christ. Of course, for Christians today, the same understanding is still true. The difference is that those living in the pre-modern period were more prone than we to absorb the book through senses other than hearing. Even if most of the people could not read the text, they could see the gold, lapis lazuli, knotted patterns, and images both illustrative and abstract. All these features made the Divine a present reality in their lives. Hence, the book was carried in great processions, incensed, kissed, and venerated; as with the tradition of icons in the East, the book became a window into heaven. Peer into the Gospels, and peer into the heavenly court. . . . Of course, in much contemporary liturgy and theology, there is still the appreciation for the sacramental character of the Bible and Gospel Book, but how deeply this appreciation runs or to what extent it carries over into other dimensions of life is certainly of a lesser nature.[9]

The arsenal of techniques used by medieval scribes, illuminators, and bookbinders to create enchanting biblical manuscripts will be on display in chapters to come. In the words of medieval art historian Michelle Brown writing about the Lindisfarne Gospels and other early Anglo-Saxon and Irish manuscripts, these codices function as "Word made word."[10] The words of these Sacred Scriptures were doorways into the presence of Christ. Like Bezalel and Oholiab's holy work of creating the tabernacle in Exodus, the scribal work of copying a Bible required a healthy dose of awe, of fear of the Lord. From his work with Donald Jackson and the other scribes who wrote *The Saint John's Bible*, Patella suggests that the process of writing such a Bible is just as incarnational as the product:

> The scribe taps three to four drops of water onto the stone and slowly grinds the ink stick on the scratchy surface. The black mixture, now glistening like obsidian, trickles into the reservoir. The scribe picks up the finely cut goose quill, dips it in the fresh ink, and allows that same black dye to flow from the quill onto the parchment. A letter is formed, a word is made, then a phrase, a sentence, a paragraph, a column, and a page are created. It is not too much of an exaggeration to say that the act of writing a biblical manuscript is analogous,

9. Michael Patella, "The Theology of The Saint John's Bible," *ARTS* 17, no. 1 (2005): 21.

10. Michelle P. Brown, *"In the Beginning Was the Word": Books and Faith in the Age of Bede*, Jarrow Lecture 2000 (Jarrow, UK: St. Paul's Church, 2000), 2.

in a very real way, to the Incarnation. In both cases, a metaphysical reality, as it were, takes on physical shape and form.[11]

Here the material form of the Bible embodies Scripture in a way similar to Jesus embodying the Word in John 1. The books that contained those words became, by extension, incarnational presences of Christ as well. Just as Christians ingested the Word in the Eucharist, they read the Word in the codex.

What is true on the theological and historical levels also rings true on the aesthetic level. *The Saint John's Bible* links content, form, and process through a series of interrelated metaphors and analogies that draw from the Bible but that also clarify exactly what makes calligraphy "beautiful writing."[12] A metaphor describes one thing in terms of another: "My love is a red rose." Metaphors draw on knowledge and sensory experience from one well-known domain of life (red rose) and apply them to another, less-known or less-easily-described domain of life (love). Metaphors often revel in ambiguity, especially when poets use them. "My love is a red rose," for example, could refer to the beauty of one's love: "My love's skin is warm and flush like a rose, and her beauty is as delicate as its petals." It could just as easily refer to pain: "Falling in love appears to give joy, but the moment you grasp it, the thorns bite into your fingers." In the hands of a poet, both meanings may be intended. Each chapter of this book unpacks a different metaphor for calligraphic art, such as weaving lines and planting letters. In these metaphors, the form and process of the writing are metaphorically entangled with the content of Holy Writ—in particular, the Song of Songs.

WHY THE SONG OF SONGS?

When I served as a docent for *The Saint John's Bible* Heritage Edition, viewers usually clamored toward the Gospels & Acts volume. This volume has some of the Bible's most famous full-page illuminations. The

11. Patella, "The Theology of The Saint John's Bible," 28; see also Laura Kendrick, *Animating the Letter: The Figurative Embodiment of Writing from Late Antiquity to the Renaissance* (Columbus: Ohio State University Press, 1999).

12. See also Jonathan Homrighausen, "Curator's Statement: Creating Words, Creating Worlds," *Visual Music: Calligraphy & Sacred Texts, Henry Luce III Center for the Arts & Religion*, 1 September 2021, https://www.luceartsandreligion.org/curators-statement.

frontispieces to each Gospel are a wonder: John's gilded Jesus in outer space; Mark's illumination of John the Baptist walking away from the scene of Jesus' baptism, his work done; Luke's nativity with prehistoric cave paintings and the Saint John's Abbey bell tower; and, my favorite, Matthew's full-page menorah, which highlights Jesus' Jewishness even as it nods to Islam, Buddhism, and modern scientific seekers of knowledge.

But my favorite volume was always the Wisdom Books. The Wisdom volume also contains the most densely illuminated book of the entire Bible: the Song of Songs, also known as the Song of Solomon, the Canticle of Canticles, or just "the Song" when brevity is called for. These illuminations, and the poetry of the Song of Songs they accompany, are the subject of this book.

For a Bible commissioned by monks, monks who gave a great deal of theological and exegetical guidance to the artists, great theological importance was attributed not only to *how* biblical books were illuminated but also to *how much*. Some books remain scarcely adorned for their relative lack of importance for Christian life (1–2 Chronicles) or for their relatively nonvisual content (Paul's letters). Conversely, books with intense visual content and major significance in Christian theology and spirituality were given great artistic attention. No surprise, then, that the book of Revelation enjoys lavish treatment.

But of all the books of the Bible, in terms of sheer text-to-image ratio, none elicits as much visual elaboration as the Song of Songs. This Hebrew book's eight chapters of poetry narrate the desire between two lovers, a man and a woman, in conversation with a chorus, the young women of Jerusalem. It lacks any explicit reference to God—yet in both Jewish and Christian interpretation, it is often upheld as the most vivid poetic description of God's relationship to the soul, to the church, or to Israel. The Song's highly visual imagery and sensory metaphors practically beg for the artist's attention. Consider this brief dialogue between the man and woman:

I am a rose of Sharon,
    a lily of the valleys.

As a lily among brambles,
    so is my love among maidens.

As an apple tree among the trees of the wood,
    so is my beloved among young men.
With great delight I sat in his shadow,
    and his fruit was sweet to my taste.

He brought me to the banqueting house,
    and his intention toward me was love.
Sustain me with raisins,
    refresh me with apples;
    for I am faint with love. (2:1-5)

In these verses we have many agrarian images of trees and plants. The poetry appeals to our senses: we see the flowers, we taste (and, implicitly, smell) the raisins and apples. These romantic images provide ripe fruit for the artist's imagination.

The visual illuminations of the Song of Songs in *The Saint John's Bible* also draw inspiration from the long history of Christian exegesis of the Song. While not given much weight in many churches today, in the Middle Ages, especially in the Latin Church of Western Europe, the Song of Songs loomed far heavier. It garnered more commentaries than any other book of the Old Testament—by one count, almost one hundred.[13] It was read, reread, and preached upon by famed theologians and spiritual authors from Origen to Gregory the Great, Bede to Bernard of Clairvaux, Hildegard of Bingen to Teresa of Ávila. Homilists also snuck the Song into discourses on other biblical works as well as into the whole liturgical calendar.[14] Many of these authors were formed in the tradition of monastic spirituality, of St. Benedict and the orders who followed him—such as the monks of Saint John's Abbey who created this Bible alongside Donald Jackson and his team of artists. Sadly, the Song is now largely neglected in many churches. It appears but once in the three-year Revised Common Lectionary cycle of Sunday and feast day readings used by many mainline Protestants. Christian biblical scholar David Carr has deemed this the "decanonization" of the Song: once the allegorical reading was jettisoned, often

13. E. Ann Matter, *The Voice of My Beloved: The Song of Songs in Western Medieval Christianity* (Philadelphia: University of Pennsylvania Press, 1992), 3. Current surveys of the Song's history of interpretation include Timothy Robinson, ed., *A Companion to the Song of Songs in the History of Spirituality*, Brill's Companions to the Christian Tradition 98 (Leiden: Brill, 2021); Ilana Pardes, *The Song of Songs: A Biography* (Princeton: Princeton University Press, 2019); Michael Fishbane, *Song of Songs*, JPS Bible Commentary (Philadelphia: Jewish Publication Society, 2015).

14. See, e.g., Ann W. Astell, "The Song of Songs in Aelred of Rievaulx's Liturgical Preaching," in *A Companion to the Song of Songs in the History of Spirituality*, ed. Timothy Robinson, Brill's Companions to the Christian Tradition 98 (Leiden: Brill, 2021), 157–88.

by Protestant Reformers, the Song lost its theological value and fell into neglect.[15] The monks of Saint John's Abbey, however, inherited the tradition of Bernard of Clairvaux. It is no surprise that they have given the Song such attention in *The Saint John's Bible*.

This tradition of spiritual reading does not shy away from using the Song's erotic, sexual language to describe the soul's longing for God. The bulk of this reading, both Jewish and Christian, has taken the Song as a script for the spiritual life, identifying the female lover as humanity and the male lover as God—whether they are Israel and God, the church and the Trinity, or the individual soul and Christ. This mode of reading, very generally, may be called allegory: a kind of reading in which the surface or literal meaning is untrue or incomplete, and the deep, spiritual, true meaning must be found. For allegorical readers, the Song's language of sexual desire is at best a distraction, at worst a delusion or deception. Another mode of Christian reading of the Song, similar but not identical, is typology: an interpretive mode in which later events, stories, or individuals are paralleled with earlier ones. The Gospels, for example, discern Jesus as typologically related to many events, people, and narratives in the Scriptures of Israel: Jesus is like Moses, delivering a new covenant; Jesus is like Jonah, miraculously delivered from death to life; and so forth.[16] Scholars debate exactly when allegorical and typological styles of reading the Song of Songs began. Some discern its presence in Jewish texts from before the first century; some discern it in the New Testament; but certainly, by the time of the Mishnah, a compilation of rabbinic discourses dating circa 200 CE, some Jews were reading the Song as a poem of divine-human love.[17] Early Christian exegetes such as Origen (ca. 184–ca. 253) and

15. David M. Carr, "The Song of Songs as a Microcosm of the Canonization and Decanonization Process," in *Canonization and Decanonization: Papers Presented to the International Conference of the Leiden Institute for the Study of Religions (LISOR) Held at Leiden 9–10 January 1997*, ed. A. van der Kooij and K. van der Toorn, Numen 82 (Leiden: Brill, 1998), 173–89.

16. These terms are complex, and their meanings change over time; for fuller accounts, see John J. O'Keefe and R. R. Reno, *Sanctified Vision: An Introduction to Early Christian Interpretation of the Bible* (Baltimore: Johns Hopkins University Press, 2005); Deeana Klepper, "Theories of Interpretation: The Quadriga and Its Successors," in *The New Cambridge History of the Bible: Volume 3, From 1450 to 1750*, ed. Euan Cameron, 418–38 (Cambridge: Cambridge University Press, 2016).

17. In m. Ta'anit 5:8. See Jonathan Kaplan and Aren M. Wilson-Wright, "How Song of Songs Became a Divine Love Song," *Biblical Interpretation* 26 (2018);

Hippolytus of Rome (d. 236) followed Jewish exegetes and established major Christian allegorical readings of the Song. While the precise birthday of Song of Songs allegory is not essential for our purposes, what is key is that it is quite ancient among Jews and Christians, and the art of *The Saint John's Bible* draws on some of these allegorical and typological readings throughout Christian history.

This book, then, focuses on the particular: the Song of Songs, as treated in the calligraphy and illuminations of *The Saint John's Bible*. In the particulars of these pages, I find one answer to the question of what calligraphy is and how it makes meaning and beauty. The metaphors this book explores—the page as a garden, reading and writing as holy pilgrimage, texts as woven textiles, touching the page as touching the hand of the scribe, and parchment as the skin of Christ—resonate with medieval Christian writings on the sensory, material dimensions of scribal art and bookmaking craft. They also resonate with some of today's calligraphers, whose keen understanding of their artform is too little known by most viewers of *The Saint John's Bible*. I hope these metaphors and analogies resonate with you.

THE SAINT JOHN'S BIBLE: THE BASIC STORY

I suspect most readers of this book know the basics of what *The Saint John's Bible* is. But, for those who don't, here's the on-one-foot version.[18]

The Saint John's Bible is the first major illuminated manuscript of the Catholic Bible made in five hundred years. *Manuscript* simply means that it was made by hand. *Illuminated* means that its pages are adorned with gold leaf and colorful pigment. This Bible is written using medieval techniques: bird feathers cut to form its pens, calf skins treated to become its pages. The project began in 1998 when the Benedictine monks of Saint John's Abbey in Minnesota commissioned Donald Jackson to create it. The monks wanted to celebrate the new millennium with a major project that would express their particularly Benedictine Christian values for centuries to come. It is not without reason that one of the slogans for this Bible is "America's Book of

---

Ronald Hendel, "The Life of Metaphor in Song of Songs: Poetics, Canon, and the Cultural Bible," *Biblica* 100 (2019).

18. The best telling of this story remains Calderhead, *Illuminating the Word*.

Kells."[19] This Bible was completed in 2011, and the monks hope it will still be viewed and read in 3011. This manuscript is also large: when open, roughly two feet tall by three feet wide, and employing 1,150 sheets of vellum. While the original pages reside, unbound, at Saint John's University, the project also includes the Heritage Edition, a limited-edition, full-size reproduction of the original.

Donald Jackson, born in 1938, has been one of the English-language world's foremost practitioners and evangelists of calligraphic art for decades. Jackson had wanted to create such a Bible since at least 1970. He frequently referred to the task as "a calligrapher's Sistine Chapel" for its sheer scale, creative labor, and technical demands. The monks of Saint John's resonated with Jackson's vision. Art was already part of their monastic identity and spiritual vocation. Decades prior, they had commissioned modernist architect Marcel Breuer to design much of their campus, including their distinctively poured concrete Abbey Church.

Once the contract was signed, Jackson and the monks began their collaboration. Jackson, from his scriptorium in Wales, formed a team of scribes and illuminators who wrote the text of this Bible and created its many images. Jackson himself wrote many pages of Bible text. The monks formed their own team, the Committee on Illumination and Text, comprised of art historians, medievalists, theologians, and biblical scholars, most of them monks (but not all!). The Committee decided which biblical passages would merit special treatment. They held group brainstorming sessions resulting in briefs in which they suggested textual meanings, historic Christian symbols, and theological ideas that the artists might keep in mind when they created sketches of each illumination. Jackson and the artists took these briefs, made their sketches, and began a back-and-forth with the monks for each illumination before quill or brush ever went to page.

Each illumination, then, is a group effort: the Committee, working with Jackson; and if the image was not being made by Jackson, then the artist as well. Jackson personally created the Song of Songs illuminations, with the exception of the three butterflies created by Sarah Harris.[20] However, he did not write the Song of Songs text. For clarity I refer to the Song illuminations as Jackson's images throughout this book. But the reader should keep in mind that Jackson actually

19. As far as I can tell, this epithet first came from Margaret Nelson, "America's Book of Kells," *Newsweek*, 6 March 2000, 52. The monks ran with it.

20. Calderhead, *Illuminating the Word*, 338.

worked with a large team, and the images result from their collective effort, not a lone artistic genius.

Jackson, for his part, was trained in a heritage of Roman-alphabet calligraphy that dates back both to the start of the twentieth century and to the advent of the Roman alphabet over two millennia ago. The more recent origin lies in Edward Johnston (1872–1944), an Englishman who, after abandoning his medical training due to poor health, rediscovered the heritage of writing the Roman alphabet with a broad edge pen as medieval scribes did. In hours examining medieval manuscripts, Johnston discovered that the medievals created beautiful lettering by holding the pen at a consistent angle, which generated an artful contrast of thick and thin lines. (This is different from the pointed pen calligraphic tradition in England and America, such as Spencerian letters.) Johnston, a charismatic teacher, taught his calligraphic art to decades of students at the Central School in London (now Central St. Martin's University), and in a series of books, the most famous being *Writing & Illuminating & Lettering* (1906). Irene Wellington and Mervyn Oliver, Jackson's teachers at the Central School, were direct students of Johnston.[21] Jackson credits Wellington in particular with pushing him beyond the technical, formal aspects of letterforms and into creating calligraphic art.[22]

21. Jackson's thoughts on his calligraphic training can be found in Donald Jackson, "Irene Wellington in the Context of Her Time: A Personal View," in *More than Fine Writing: Irene Wellington, Calligrapher (1904–1984)*, ed. Heather Child, 28–37 (Woodstock, NY: Overlook Press, 1987); Donald Jackson, "An Evening with Donald Jackson," Concordia University, St. Paul, 12 February 2015, https://www.youtube.com/watch?v=HRx_Vm-XNJ8; and a series of lectures Jackson gave over the internet in fall 2021, available at https://www.youtube.com/channel/UCWlngVNwWPr_CVlpD8HigFw. Also Ann Hechle, "Ann Hechle, Calligrapher: Based on an Interview at Her Home in Somerset with Bridget Wilkins, 15 November 1999," in *Making Their Mark: Art, Craft and Design at the Central School, 1896–1966*, ed. Sylvia Backemeyer, 139–44 (London: A & C Black, 2000); Hechle was a year behind Jackson in the same course, and she went on to her own successful career as a lettering artist. See also Jonathan Homrighausen, "Words Made Flesh: Incarnational, Multisensory Exegesis in Donald Jackson's Biblical Art," *Religion and the Arts* 23, no. 3 (2019): 243–46.

22. Heather Child, ed., *More than Fine Writing: Irene Wellington, Calligrapher (1904-1984)* (Woodstock, NY: Overlook Press, 1987); Ann Hechle and Ewan Clayton, *Findings: In the Calligraphic Work and Teachings of Irene Wellington, 1904–1984* (Pinner, UK: Irene Wellington Educational Trust, 2021).

Suffice it to say that while *The Saint John's Bible* may be the most famous work of contemporary Roman alphabet calligraphic art, Jackson is in fact part of a movement of those in the heritage of Johnston. He is one of many offspring of Johnston today who create calligraphy that transcends mere "beautiful writing" to become a form of self-expression as layered, complex, and aesthetically compelling as any other art form. Some of these artists are this Bible's scribes, such as Susan Hufton and Sally Mae Joseph. Some are Jackson's students, such as Thomas Ingmire. But there are others: Ann Hechle, Denis Brown, Peter Halliday, Martin Wenham, to name just a few. So far, little of this work has garnered the kind of thoughtful appreciation it deserves. In my opinion, this scholarly inattention explains the paucity of language for looking at calligraphic art, for grasping its magic. This book addresses that lack.

Rather than an academic monograph with a singular thesis tightly argued, I invite you to treat this book like a bouquet of flowers or a symphonic theme and variations. Each chapter dives into the Song's text and illuminations, unpacking and elaborating one metaphor or analogy, or two closely related ones. Each metaphor unlocks specific ways in which calligraphic art intertwines form, content, and process. The first two chapters focus on the first three pages of the Song of Songs (Song 1:1–5:1); chapters 3 and 4 focus on the fourth and fifth pages (5:2–8:5); and chapter 5 focuses on the final page (8:5-14). In this book, we consider the page as a garden and writing as plowing and planting (chapter 2), writing as walking and the eye's movement on the page as a pilgrimage (chapter 3), writing as weaving and text and textile (chapter 4), touching the page as touching the scribe's gestures and touching the Word (chapter 5), and how a "love as strong as death" lovingly creates a manuscript, a creation that also entails the death of animals just as Jesus' resurrection requires his death (chapter 6).

Chapter Two

SCRIBES TENDING THE GARDEN

In the Song of Songs, the lovers cavort in a garden, and the woman's body is also described as a garden full of sensory delights. In *The Saint John's Bible*, the page itself becomes a garden of delights: lush colors, graceful letters, the texture of fine vellum. If we view the page as a garden and the process of writing it as planting and plowing, we gain insight into the particular beauty of calligraphic art. Like a garden, every page of *The Saint John's Bible* balances human order with natural chaos. The handwritten words show their beauty in harmony, a harmony rooted in human-made variety rather than mechanical uniformity. And just as a gardener or a farmer works with natural tools and encounters the risks, surprises, and happy accidents of the natural world beyond her control, the calligrapher cannot always tame the unruliness of vellum, quills, and even her own hands.

A GARDEN LOCKED, A PAGE ENCLOSED

Among the diverse array of sensory images for love in the Song of Songs, the garden stands as one of the centers. In the narrative world of the poem, the garden is one of the key settings in which love takes place. The garden also serves as a metaphor for the sensual delight of the woman's body. In *The Saint John's Bible*, the page itself is a garden of visual delights for the viewer. This metaphor fits with the symbols on the page and their placement, and it generates insight into Jackson's calligraphic art.

In the most extensive garden metaphor in the Song of Songs, the man compares his beloved's body to a garden:

> A garden locked is my sister, my bride,
>   a garden locked, a fountain sealed.
> Your channel is an orchard of pomegranates
>   with all choicest fruits,
>   henna with nard,
> nard and saffron, calamus and cinnamon,
>   with all trees of frankincense,
> myrrh and aloes,
>   with all chief spices—
> a garden fountain, a well of living water,
>   and flowing streams from Lebanon. (4:12-15)

The man's comparison suggests many facets of her and their love: the privacy of their love, the abundance of the garden, and the multisensory pleasures of her body.[1] This garden is not a purely natural paradise, however. Its assemblage of plants is not found in nature; indeed, in antiquity, these plants and spices were rare and expensive. This is a highly cultivated pleasure garden. The lengthy list of plants, and the use of plural verbs, also suggests an aesthetic of excess, of a man overwhelmed by the delights of his beloved. The woman replies:

> Let my beloved come to his garden,
>   and eat its choicest fruits. (4:16c)

The romance is mutual. He seduces her with words, and she invites him in. He accepts:

> I come to my garden, my sister, my bride;
>   I gather my myrrh with my spice,
>   I eat my honeycomb with my honey,
>   I drink my wine with my milk.

1. See discussions in Robert Alter, *The Art of Biblical Poetry*, rev. ed. (New York: Basic Books, 2011), 231–54; Brian P. Gault, *Body as Landscape, Love as Intoxication: Conceptual Metaphors in the Song of Songs*, Ancient Israel and Its Literature 36 (Atlanta: SBL Press, 2019), 110–22; J. Cheryl Exum, *Song of Songs*, Old Testament Library (Richmond: Westminster John Knox Press, 2005), 151–83; Carey Ellen Walsh, *Exquisite Desire: Religion, the Erotic, and the Song of Songs* (Minneapolis: Fortress, 2000), 87–94.

Eat, friends, drink,
and be drunk with love. (5:1)

It goes without saying that this passage is a fairly transparent euphemism for sex. The man moves from merely contemplating the beauty of her body to entering it and losing himself in it.[2] The final phrase—"Eat, friends, drink, and be drunk with love"—raises questions, since its speaker is unclear. But whether spoken by the man or the woman, the invitation carries a double meaning. While the invite could be for the daughters of Jerusalem who serve as a kind of chorus for the woman in the Song, the "save the date" could also address the reader to find her own encounter of love.

Like the man overwhelmed by the splendor of his beloved's physical form, when we turn to the opening pages of the Song of Songs in *The Saint John's Bible*, we are immediately confronted with a dense proliferation of images.[3] As the reader moves from the final verses of Ecclesiastes to the opening of the Song, she sees already a geometric pattern scattering around the page. The viewer finds herself lost in an abundance of ornament flowing between and around the calligraphed poetic verses. This is not the standard script designed for *The Saint John's Bible* but a lighter variant used for biblical poetry.[4] The traditional title of the book among

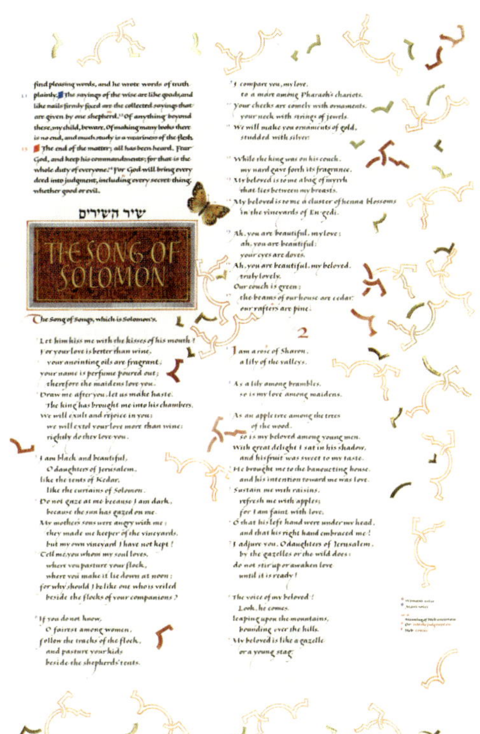
find pleasing words, and he wrote words of truth plainly. The sayings of the wise are like goads, and like nails firmly fixed are the collected sayings that are given by one shepherd. Of anything beyond these, my child, beware. Of making many books there is no end, and much study is a weariness of the flesh. The end of the matter; all has been heard. Fear God, and keep his commandments; for that is the whole duty of everyone. For God will bring every deed into judgment, including every secret thing, whether good or evil.

שיר השירים

THE SONG OF SOLOMON

The Song of Songs, which is Solomon's.

Let him kiss me with the kisses of his mouth!
For your love is better than wine,
your anointing oils are fragrant,
your name is perfume poured out;
therefore the maidens love you.
Draw me after you, let us make haste.
The king has brought me into his chambers.
We will exult and rejoice in you;
we will extol your love more than wine;
rightly do they love you.

I am black and beautiful,
O daughters of Jerusalem,
like the tents of Kedar,
like the curtains of Solomon.
Do not gaze at me because I am dark,
because the sun has gazed on me.
My mother's sons were angry with me;
they made me keeper of the vineyards,
but my own vineyard I have not kept!
Tell me, you whom my soul loves,
where you pasture your flock,
where you make it lie down at noon;
for why should I be like one who is veiled
beside the flocks of your companions?

If you do not know,
O fairest among women,
follow the tracks of the flock,
and pasture your kids
beside the shepherds' tents.

I compare you, my love,
to a mare among Pharaoh's chariots.
Your cheeks are comely with ornaments,
your neck with strings of jewels.
We will make you ornaments of gold,
studded with silver.

While the king was on his couch,
my nard gave forth its fragrance.
My beloved is to me a bag of myrrh
that lies between my breasts.
My beloved is to me a cluster of henna blossoms
in the vineyards of En-gedi.

Ah, you are beautiful, my love;
ah, you are beautiful;
your eyes are doves.
Ah, you are beautiful, my beloved,
truly lovely.
Our couch is green;
the beams of our house are cedar;
our rafters are pine.

2

I am a rose of Sharon,
a lily of the valleys.

As a lily among brambles,
so is my love among maidens.

As an apple tree among the trees
of the wood,
so is my beloved among young men.
With great delight I sat in his shadow,
and his fruit was sweet to my taste.
He brought me to the banqueting house,
and his intention toward me was love.
Sustain me with raisins,
refresh me with apples;
for I am faint with love.
O that his left hand were under my head,
and that his right hand embraced me!
I adjure you, O daughters of Jerusalem,
by the gazelles or the wild does:
do not stir up or awaken love
until it is ready!

The voice of my beloved!
Look, he comes,
leaping upon the mountains,
bounding over the hills.
My beloved is like a gazelle
or a young stag.

2. Elaine T. James, *Landscapes of the Song of Songs: Poetry and Place* (Oxford: Oxford University Press, 2017), 55–87.

3. Material in this section drawn from Michael Patella, *Word and Image: The Hermeneutics of* The Saint John's Bible (Collegeville, MN: Liturgical Press, 2013); Susan Sink, *The Art of* The Saint John's Bible*: The Complete Reader's Guide* (Collegeville, MN: Liturgical Press, 2013); Christopher Calderhead, *Illuminating the Word: The Making of The Saint John's Bible*, 2nd ed. (Collegeville, MN: Liturgical Press, 2015). I have also been given images of the drafts and sketches that Jackson sent to the Committee on Illumination and Text, in which he explains some of the symbols he employs.

4. Calderhead, *Illuminating the Word*, 299.

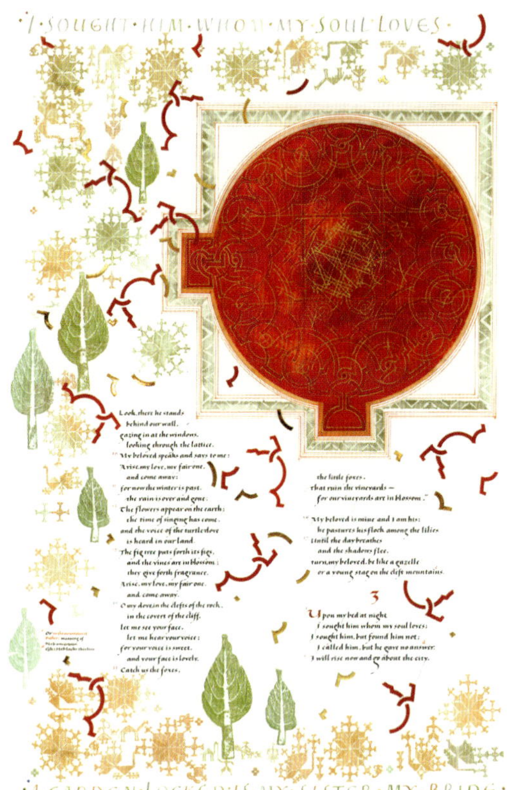
I·SOUGHT·HIM·WHOM·MY·SOUL·LOVES·
·A·GARDEN·LOCKED·IS·MY·SISTER·MY·BRIDE·

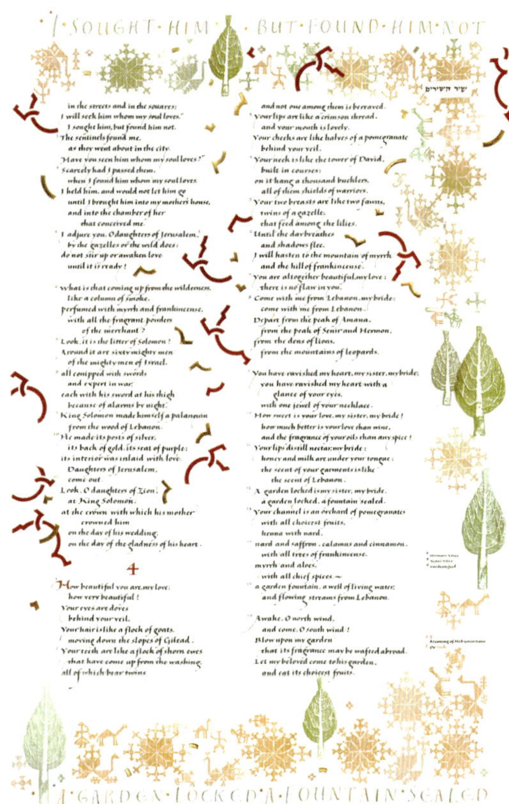
I·SOUGHT·HIM·BUT·FOUND·HIM·NOT
A·GARDEN·LOCKED·A·FOUNTAIN·SEALED

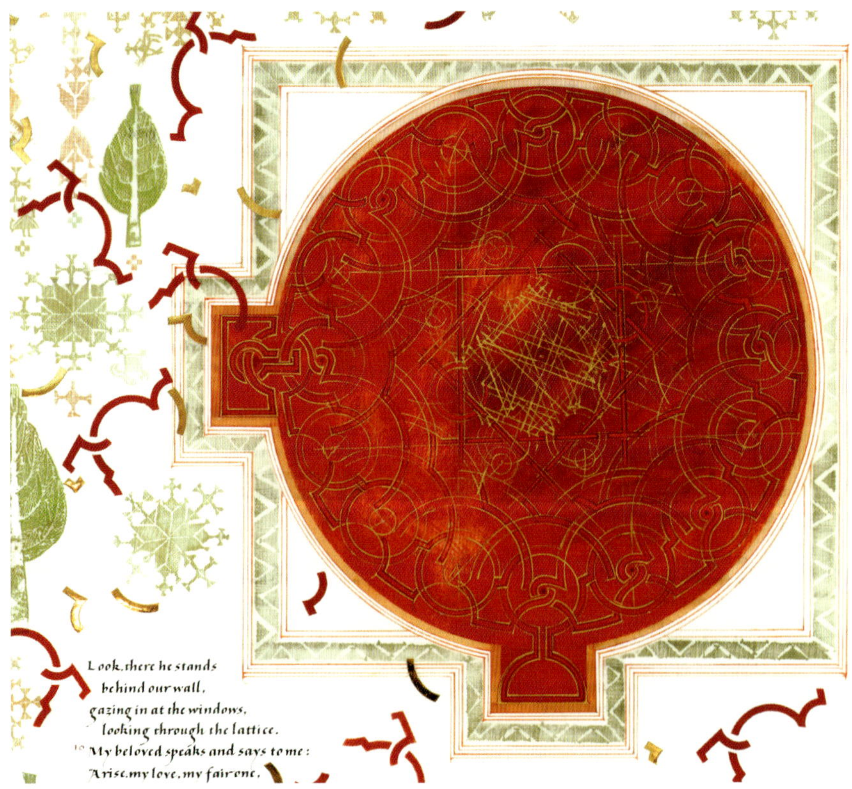
Look, there he stands
behind our wall,
gazing in at the windows,
looking through the lattice.
10 My beloved speaks and says to me:
"Arise, my love, my fair one,

Christians, "The Song of Solomon," stands against a deep red background with a subtle floral pattern, setting the color palette and the symbolism for the next several pages. As the viewer's eyes follow these patterns from left to right, these geometric fragments vary between a lighter orange to a darker red, between being fully colored-in or only outlined. Some smaller flecks are in gold, a signifier of God's presence in *The Saint John's Bible*, hinting at the full divine presence to come.[5] The geometric motif continues and intensifies on the next two-page spread. At the bottom of these pages, Jackson writes out Song 4:12:

> A garden locked is my sister, my bride,
> a garden locked, a fountain sealed.

These geometric patterns here exude more sense of presence: all of the geometric pieces are filled in, all are darker reds and browns, and they are more complete. The ornament itself mesmerizes the reader. At top left stands a scarlet circle that resembles a pomegranate with two calyxes; the circle is inside a square motif. The pomegranate encloses a series of labyrinthine geometric patterns, which are the complete versions of the fragments around this page and the page before. We might think of this as the center of the garden. These fragments float about the two pages as if blown by wind. Visually, it is unclear whether these fragments are gathering toward the garden or floating out from the garden's abundance. If they are gathering, they echo the woman's words at the top of the page: "I sought him whom my soul loves, / I sought him, but found him not" (3:1). If they are flowing out from the garden, they echo another line spoken by the woman in which her body is a garden:

> Awake, O north wind,
> and come, O south wind!
> Blow upon my garden
> that its fragrance may be wafted abroad. (4:16a)

The perceptual interplay between these possibilities further transfixes the viewer.

5. Gold and gilding are an immense part of Jackson's technique and *The Saint John's Bible*'s theology; see Jonathan Homrighausen, "Words Made Flesh: Incarnational, Multisensory Exegesis in Donald Jackson's Biblical Art," *Religion and the Arts* 23, no. 3 (2019): 130–33; Donald Jackson, "Gilding," in *The Calligrapher's Handbook*, ed. Heather Child, 177–98, 2nd ed. (New York: Taplinger, 1986).

Alongside the geometric fragments, Jackson surrounds the text on the page with marginal imagery suggesting a garden's borders. Perched atop the title of the Song of Solomon is a butterfly, elsewhere in this Bible a symbol of angelic presence (as in the illumination of Genesis 28) or of Christ's metamorphosis from human (caterpillar) to death (chrysalis) to splendid resurrection (butterfly), as in the depiction after Mark 16. While this butterfly could suggest angels or the presence of Christ, it may also suggest that this page is a luscious garden that would attract a butterfly. This stable, whole butterfly contrasts to the butterflies blown about in the beginning of Ecclesiastes, the book just before the Song of Songs in this Bible. The Ecclesiastes image reflects the poet's refrain that all life is as breath or wind. Perhaps the Song's poet has found more stability in the loving embrace of the garden. This butterfly is calm, not caught in a hurricane. It is joined by two other butterflies on the fourth and fifth pages of the Song illuminations. Two of these three butterflies are species found at Saint John's Abbey.[6]

On the second and third pages, the text is enclosed by a wall of images around the page to protect the plants growing within. These symbols are in shades of green and brown suggesting the soil and foliage of plants and trees. In terms of color, the boldest images in the margins are large leaves or trees in varied sizes and shades of green. The main motif is a light red and brown textile pattern with geometric shapes, camels, men and women, and even a large-plumed bird (a peacock?) and a weathervane. Jackson based this motif on a textile pattern for a camel girth from Rajasthan—a textile wrapped around a camel so it can draw water, plough, and pull carts in this desert region of northern India.[7] A textile in the Cooper Hewitt (on the next page), the Smithsonian's Design Museum, looks nearly identical to the one Jackson cited as his inspiration. The desert camel at the edge of the garden alludes to the significance of the well-watered garden ("a

6. Larry Haeg, ed., *The Nature of Saint John's: A Guide to the Landscape and Spirituality of Saint John's Abbey Arboretum* (Collegeville, MN: Saint John's University Press, 2015), 11.

7. Donald Jackson shared with me that this pattern was inspired by John Gillow and Nicholas Barnard, *Traditional Indian Textiles* (London: Thames & Hudson, 1993), 94–95. For more context on this textile tradition, see Vandana Bhandari, *Costume, Textiles and Jewellery of India: Traditions in Rajasthan* (London: Mercury Books, 2005), 68–69.

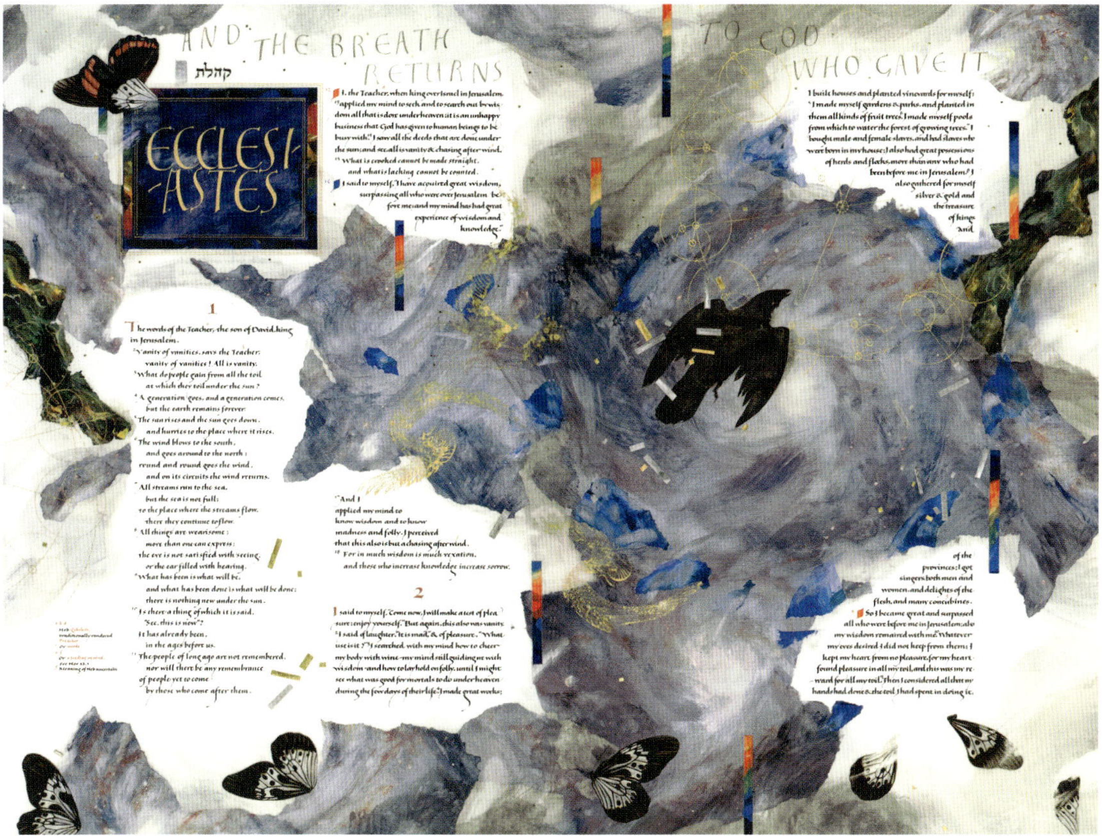

AND THE BREATH RETURNS TO GOD WHO GAVE IT

קהלת

ECCLESI-ASTES

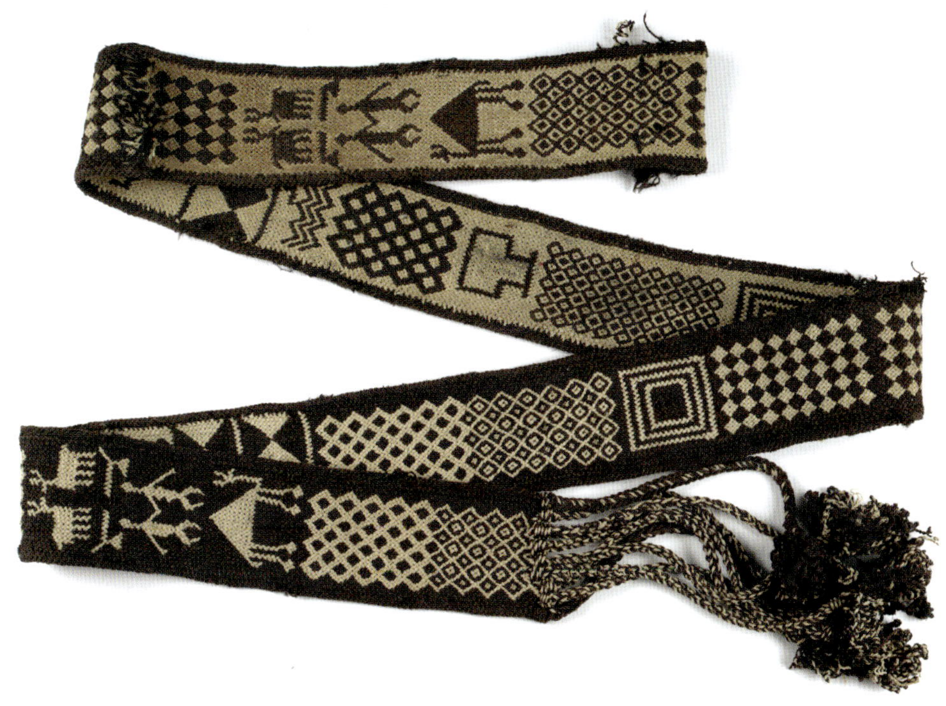

fountain sealed") in the midst of Israel's dry landscape.[8] It evokes the threats outside the garden to the lovers' bliss, and the dry landscape in contrast to the springs and channels of water in the garden. It also suggests the Israelites wandering in the desert before reaching Canaan.

By suggesting the desert outside the lovers' garden, Jackson's marginal imagery evokes the Song's allusion to the Garden of Eden in Genesis 2–3. Eden is, of course, the start of all garden imagery in the Hebrew Bible. At Eden, God's creative activity and human nourishment were easily available, ever-present, until Adam and Eve were expelled. In response, the Song has been read as an extended comment on the story of Adam and Eve and the expulsion from the Garden, a healing of the rupture between the sexes that constitutes life outside Eden (Gen 3:16).[9] Though Genesis does not report Eden being surrounded by a desert, it is not a far leap for the artist's associative mind, especially given the significance of desert in biblical Israel as a place of chaos, desolation, and threat. And while in the Song, as in Eden, creation's bounty is freely on offer, outside the garden lies agrarian toil and hardship (Gen 3:17-19).

Finally, the implied desert outside the garden underscores the abundant waters within:

> a garden fountain, a well of living water,
> and flowing streams from Lebanon. (Song 4:15)

For the calligrapher, liquid imagery immediately evokes the joy of wet ink. Unlike the rapidly drying, thick, tar-like flow of a ball-point pen, calligraphers' inks dry slowly. (Anyone who uses a fountain pen will also understand.) The wetness of the ink on the page allows the scribe to drag the ink around and to thrill in the visceral pleasure of watching ink dry. When once asked whether he would ever consider creating digital lettering art, Jackson replied that computers "are not wet enough, there is not enough paint to slop about."[10] Like a garden, calligraphy needs water to grow.

8. Jill M. Munro, *Spikenard and Saffron: The Imagery of the Song of Songs*, Journal for the Study of the Old Testament Supplement Series 203 (Sheffield: Sheffield Academic Press, 1995), 102–4.

9. Phyllis Trible, *God and the Rhetoric of Sexuality*, Overtures to Biblical Theology (Philadelphia: Fortress, 1978), 144–65; David M. Carr, *The Erotic Word: Sexuality, Spirituality, and the Bible* (New York: Oxford University Press, 2005).

10. Margot Coatts, "Donald Jackson," *Baseline* 14 (1991): 11.

On the poetic level, just as the garden in the Song of Songs is enclosed, in the structure of the eight-chapter book itself, the garden imagery comes at the center: the fourth chapter. Thus, not only is the garden a central metaphor of the Song—a root metaphor from which other floral metaphors sprout—but the main passage about the garden is enclosed by the rest of the poem. In *The Saint John's Bible*, this passage (4:12–5:1) ends the third page, emphasizing that these verses act as a midway point of the whole Song of Songs and enclosing these verses in the book's shape.

This textile motif provides a kind of stability, an architectural frame, for the stamped-on leaves of different sizes, shades, and slightly differing patterns, adding to the garden imagery in the text. Also, small crosses made up of four squares echo a motif used throughout the Gospels illuminations. Far from reflecting the Song in a wooden fashion, Jackson chooses very deliberate imagery that dialogues with the Song in interesting ways, focusing on capturing the imaginative world of the Song's garden without visually rendering every poetic image or metaphor in the text. Like a real garden, this page balances stability, formality, and architecture with the chaos, movement, and spontaneous growth of living flora and fauna inhabiting a garden.

GARDENS TEXTUAL AND MATERIAL

The material form of this manuscript brings the textual garden in the Song of Songs to life, appealing to more senses than a text alone would. Word becomes flesh—or perhaps, the word becomes dirt and flora. Indeed, the Song of Songs is both inspired by real-life gardens and has inspired such gardens. *The Saint John's Bible*'s pages continue this interplay of textual, visual, and material gardens.

Behind the textual image of the garden in the Song of Songs lies real gardens in the ancient Near East and the Hellenistic world—particularly royal gardens constructed in the palace complexes of ancient Persia.[11] In Song 4:13's "orchard of pomegranates," the word for "orchard," *pardes*, is not the typical Hebrew word for garden (*gan*)

11. Deborah Green, "'Come South Wind, Blow upon My Garden That Its Spices May Flow': Experience in the Ancient Jewish Garden," in *Sound and Scent in the Garden*, ed. D. Fairchild Ruggles, 53–76, Dumbarton Oaks Colloquium on the History of Landscape Architecture 38 (Washington, DC: Dumbarton Oaks Research Library and Collection, 2017); Othmar Keel, *The Song of Songs*, trans. Frederick J. Gaiser, Continental Commentaries (Minneapolis: Fortress, 1994), 169.

but a loanword from Persian (*pairadaeza*), which refers to an enclosed park (Neh 2:8) planted with fruit trees (Eccl 2:5).[12] These Persian royal gardens also make an appearance in Ahasuerus's palace in the book of Esther (1:5; 7:7-8). *The Saint John's Bible*'s visual treatment of the Song alludes to ancient Near Eastern gardens with a visual quotation from a carved relief depicting the gardens of Ashurbanipal, king of Assyria, in his palace at Nineveh (ca. 645 BCE). These reliefs depict the garden, built atop a small hill with an aqueduct for irrigation.[13]

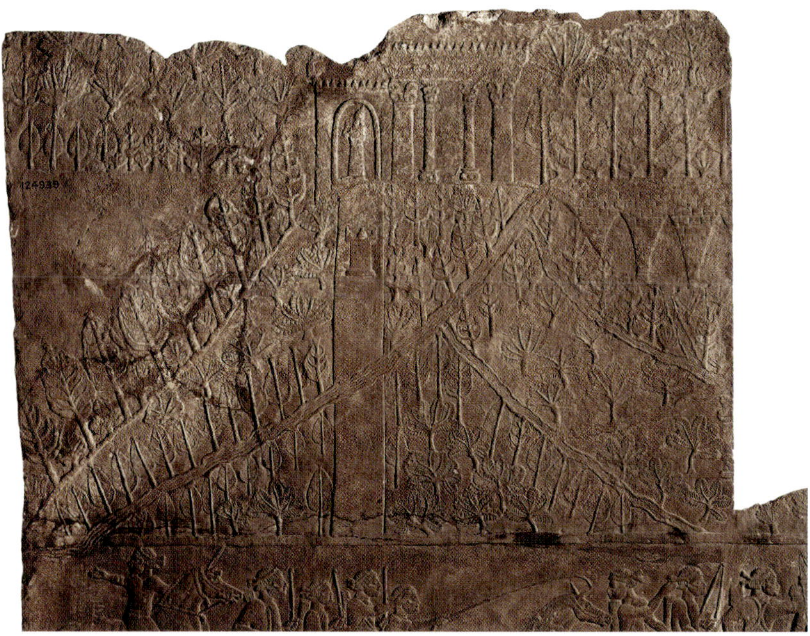

The leaves represent the trees and shrubs of the garden. They also resemble the large green leaves encircling the Song's page. Most likely, Donald Jackson alluded to this relief intentionally; elsewhere in *The Saint John's Bible* he includes visual quotations of ancient Near Eastern

12. Exum, *Song of Songs*, 177.

13. Item in British Museum Catalogue: https://www.britishmuseum.org/collection/object/W_1856-0909-36_1/. "Paradise on Earth: The Gardens of Ashurbanipal," *British Museum Blog*, 4 October 2018, https://blog.britishmuseum.org/paradise-on-earth-the-gardens-of-ashurbanipal/; Pauline Albenda, "Royal Gardens, Parks, and the Architecture Within: Assyrian Views," *Journal of the American Oriental Society* 138, no. 1 (2018).

art.[14] These trees suggest the wild fertility of Ashurbanipal's garden. This, too, fits with the Song and Jackson's imagery.

The second material backdrop to the garden in the Song of Songs is the land of Israel itself. By using metaphors drawn from the land and its produce, the Song of Songs directs its readers' attention to creation.[15] Specifically, the Song describes not *a* land but *the* land: the geological features, plants, and sites of ancient Israel. Christian exegete Ellen Davis points to lines such as "Your hair is like a flock of goats, / moving down the slopes of Gilead" (4:1c) and

> Your neck is like the tower of David,
> built in courses;
> on it hang a thousand bucklers,
> all of them shields of warriors. (4:4)

To Davis, these lines speak of the Song's "romance of the land" in addition to the divine romance and the human romance. But while the reader can affirm the particular significance of the land of Israel in the Song (as in most of the Hebrew Bible), we can also expand this care and attention to the land to the ends of the earth.

The Saint John's Bible also draws inspiration from gardens that came after the Song of Songs was written, especially the gardens found in medieval monasteries.[16] Such gardens were a central part of the monastic space, termed in Latin a *paradisum*, and provided a place to contemplate the beauty of God's creation. Gilbert of Hoyland, a twelfth-century English Cistercian, wrote in a letter to a fellow abbot:

> The site of your monastery is secluded, cultivated, irrigated, and fruitful. Your wooded valley in springtime so echoes with the sweet melodies of songsters that it could charm a dead spirit back to life, dissipate the distaste of a delicate soul, and soften the hard-heartedness of a mind devoid of devotion.[17]

14. As in, for example, *Ezekiel's Vision at the River Chebar*. See Calderhead, *Illuminating the Word*, 207.

15. Ellen F. Davis, "Romance of the Land in the Song of Songs," *Anglican Theological Review* 80, no. 4 (1998): 533–46; James, *Landscapes of the Song of Songs*.

16. Tom Turner, *Garden History: Philosophy and Design, 2000 BC–2000 AD* (London: Spon Press, 2005), chap. 5; Patella, *Word and Image*, 168.

17. Paul Meyvaert, "The Medieval Monastic Garden," in *Medieval Gardens*, ed. Elisabeth B. MacDougall, 23–54 (Washington, DC: Dumbarton Oaks, 1986), 42–43.

Gilbert alludes to the medicinal qualities of the monastic garden where healing herbs were grown alongside sustaining food. It is no wonder he appreciated the pleasures of the garden—he himself wrote forty-eight sermons on the Song of Songs! A later Benedictine, Louis of Blois (1506–1566), wrote verses to adorn the gate to his monastery garden:

> May the beauty of flowers and other creatures draw the heart to love and admire God, their creator.
> May the garden's beauty bring to mind the splendor of paradise.
> The birds sing the praise of God in heaven so that man may learn to praise Him in his heart.[18]

Louis suggests the physical garden as a reenactment of Eden and a hint of paradise. These medieval monks saw the sensual pleasures of the garden as a window into the wonder of God who created the natural world that humans tend. These physical gardens were allegories for spiritual splendor.

For the erotic love poetry of the Song, the garden is an apt description for the sensory delights of the woman's body, as well as an ideal setting for lovemaking. In the Near Eastern world from which the Song of Songs emerges, imperial gardens convey luxury, royalty, and the human ability to form and shape nature into a particular aesthetic. For medieval monks who read the Song as a love poem between the church and God, the garden served as a symbol of paradise, not yet fully present but hinted at in God's sacramental presence in creation. For the calligrapher fashioning the words of the Bible into Word made Flesh, fashioning the page into a garden suggests the sensory possibilities of manuscript art, of making Word into Flesh. The sensory pages of this Bible suggest the sensory gardens and landscapes that inspired and were inspired by the Song.

LETTERS AS SEEDS, FRUIT, AND FLOWERS

If the page is a garden, then the letters are flowers—flowers that sprout from seeds. In both word and image, *The Saint John's Bible* suggests that words are seeds that grow into fruit-bearing trees and budding flowers, the harmonized and ordered chaos of a garden.

18. Meyvaert, "The Medieval Monastic Garden," 46.

In artist Aidan Hart's illumination of the parable of the sower and the seed in Mark, the words visually become seeds falling onto the disciples. As Jesus tells it:

> "Listen! A sower went out to sow. And as he sowed, some seed fell on the path, and the birds came and ate it up. Other seed fell on rocky ground, where it did not have much soil, and it sprang up quickly, since it had no depth of soil. And when the sun rose, it was scorched; and since it had no root, it withered away. Other seed fell among thorns, and the thorns grew up and choked it, and it yielded no grain. Other seed fell into good soil and brought forth grain, growing up and increasing and yielding thirty and sixty and a hundredfold." And he said, "Let anyone with ears to hear listen!" (4:3-9)

As Jesus explains the parable in both Mark (4:3-20) and its parallels in Matthew (13:3-23) and Luke (8:4-15), the seeds are "the word of God" (Luke 8:11), "the word of the kingdom" (Matt 13:19). The soils signify people with different levels of receptiveness to teaching.[19] In *The Saint John's Bible*, Hart renders the sower as Christ. The image draws on Hart's training as a Greek Orthodox iconographer, but with an obvious change: Jesus wears blue jeans, like a modern farm worker. The sower scatters his seeds, but oddly, they do not land on any of the four types of dirt under his feet. The seeds scatter beyond the borders of the image and into the text, landing on the names of the twelve apostles being appointed in Mark 3:13-19: Simon Peter, James son of Zebedee, and John the brother of James. The interplay of word and image suggests that the "good soil" is the apostles. No seed comes near the name of Judas.

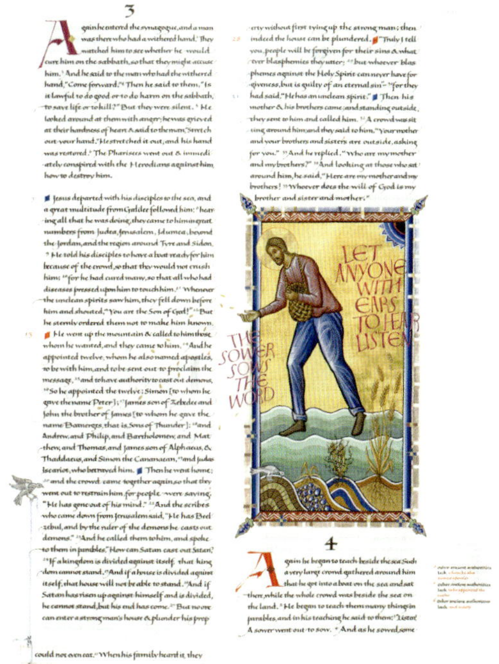

19. Useful commentary can be found in Klyne R. Snodgrass, *Stories with Intent: A Comprehensive Guide to the Parables of Jesus* (Grand Rapids: Eerdmans, 2018), chap. 4.

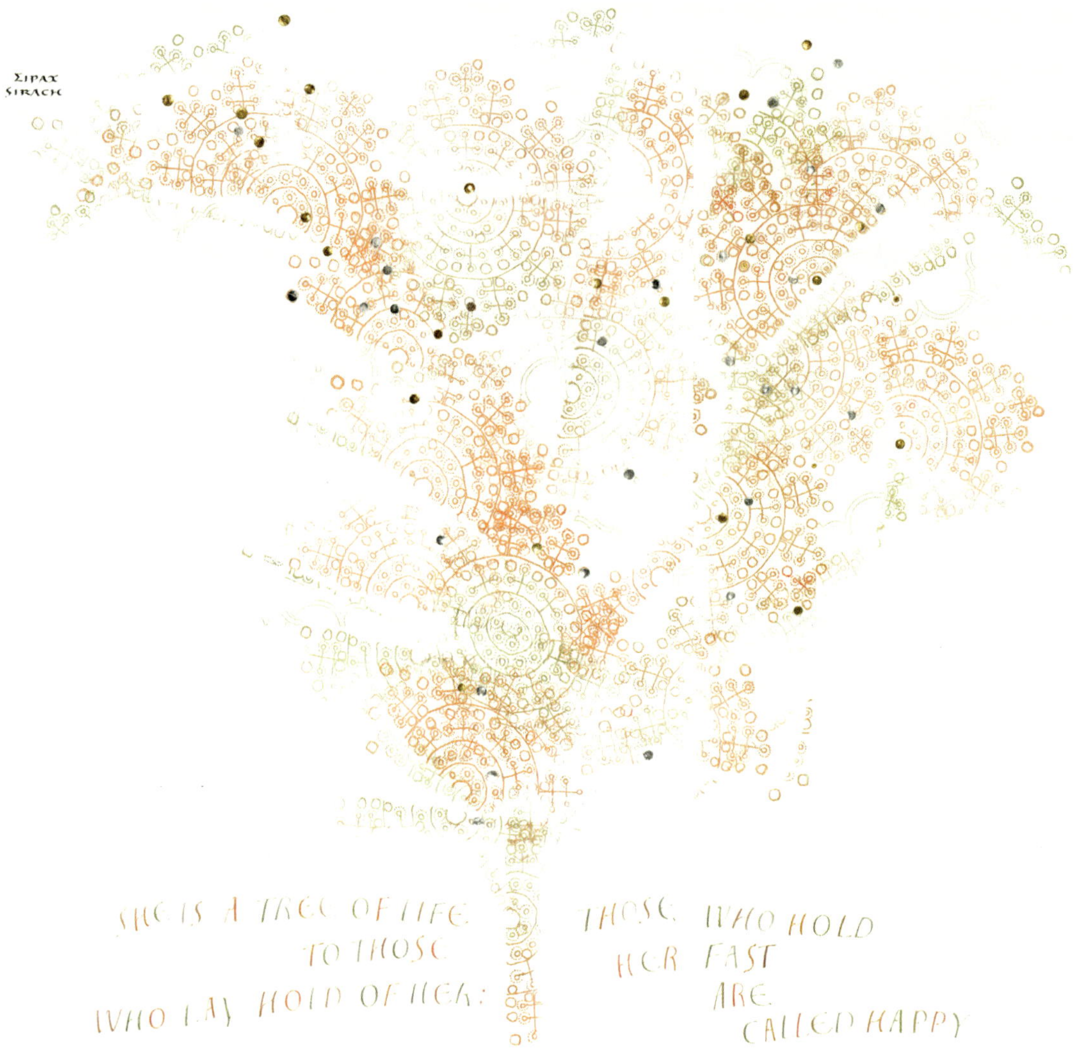

Just as Jesus elsewhere tells of tiny seeds that grow into a mustard tree (Mark 4:30-32), so in this Bible's art, the small golden seeds in Mark grow into a tree that bears golden fruit in the Song's garden. In an illumination at the end of Sirach, the seeds have become fruit on the Tree of Life, identified in Sirach 51 with Wisdom itself.[20] A verse below the tree invites the reader to grasp it:

20. Jonathan Homrighausen, *Illuminating Justice: The Ethical Imagination of* The Saint John's Bible (Collegeville, MN: Liturgical Press, 2018), 68–75.

She is a tree of life to those who lay hold of her;
those who hold her fast are called happy. (Prov 3:18)

In the Old Testament, the tree of life is both a tree in Eden and an epithet for Wisdom, a force both personified and eroticized in ancient Jewish literature (for example, Sirach 24).[21] Jewish tradition would later describe the Torah as a tree of life. In this illumination, the tree's fruits are golden and silver-hued, a motif that in *The Saint John's Bible* suggests feminine and masculine images of God, with the silver also suggesting the image of Wisdom as a mirror of God (Wisdom 7:26). This tree also contains faint outlines of the geometric motifs from the Song of Songs illuminations. I imagine this tree growing in the garden of the Song, sprouting from the golden seeds of divine wisdom. If one loves Wisdom with the devotion of the Song's lovers, the fruit of that wisdom will be as sweet as the fruit of the Tree of Life in Eden. Both the Sirach illumination and Hart's rendition of the sower suggest that the metaphor of a page as a garden resonates more deeply throughout this Bible's illuminations.

The seeded words then grow into flowers, ranged in carefully cultivated rows—lines of writing. At first, describing these calligraphed letters as flowers seems surprising. In a garden we expect color: blossoms in red, white, yellow, and blue, vegetation in vivid hues of green. But in the letters of the Song of Songs, scribed by Sally Mae Joseph, we see only the dark black of the carbon ink used for the whole of *The Saint John's Bible*.[22] Yet the Song affirms that black can be beautiful too. In verses often treasured among African and African-American readers, the woman of the Song proclaims:

I am black and beautiful,
O daughters of Jerusalem,
like the tents of Kedar,
like the curtains of Solomon.
Do not gaze at me because I am dark,
because the sun has gazed on me.
My mother's sons were angry with me;
they made me keeper of the vineyards,
but my own vineyard I have not kept! (1:5-6)

21. Peter Schäfer, *Mirror of His Beauty: Feminine Images of God from the Bible to the Early Kabbalah* (Princeton: Princeton University Press, 2004), 31–32.
22. Sink, *The Art of* The Saint John's Bible, 372.

Here the female lover, the main speaker of the Song, addresses the young women of Jerusalem. The term rendered here as "black" could refer either to naturally dark skin or to skin darkened by exposure to sunlight. Contemporary Black readers have seen in these verses a protest echoed in the modern slogan "Black is beautiful" and the reclamation of Afrocentric beauty standards in skin color and hairstyles.[23] These lines remind us that at times, beauty can arise in places where one's culture does not direct us to notice it.

On the pages of *The Saint John's Bible*, I imagine these words of self-affirmation spoken by the letters themselves. If Black is beautiful, then so are these black letters. One way to see the beauty of the black letters on the page: turn it upside down, so you can focus on the shapes and lines of the letters without being distracted by the part of your brain focused on decoding their semantic content. See, for example, the delicate descenders on letters such as *g* and *y*, especially at the bottoms of each column where there is more room to flourish. See the exuberant bottoms of the *f*, as in "of which bear twins" (Song 4:2). See the playful flourishes at the ends of the lines, where the final stroke of *e*, *l*, and *d* are dragged up, bouncing for our attention. Also note the lovely curves, not only in the descender of the *f* but also those

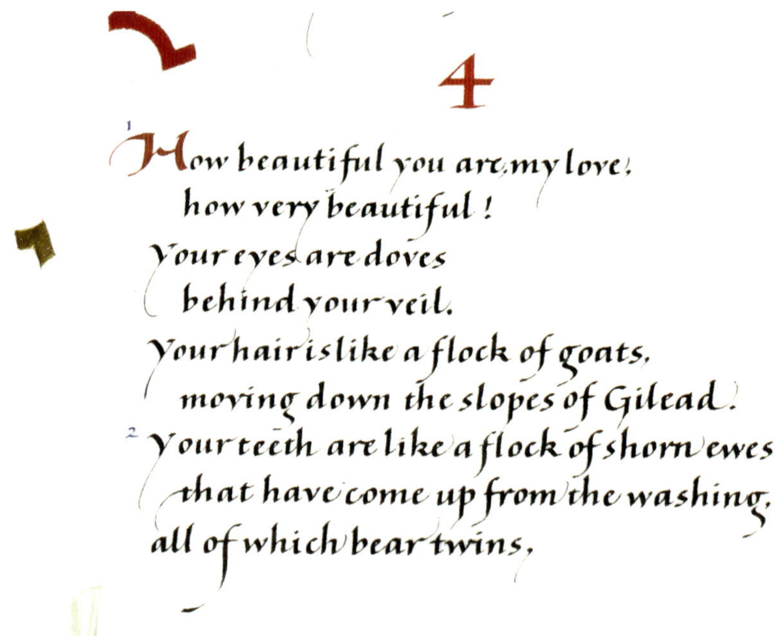
4

1 How beautiful you are, my love,
how very beautiful!
Your eyes are doves
behind your veil.
Your hair is like a flock of goats,
moving down the slopes of Gilead.
2 Your teeth are like a flock of shorn ewes
that have come up from the washing,
all of which bear twins,

23. Renita J. Weems, *What Matters Most: Ten Lessons in Living Passionately from the Song of Solomon* (New York: Warner, 2004), 32–35.

of the majuscule *G* in "Gilead" and the letters *a*, *o*, and *g*. These curves recall the man in the Song praising his lover's curves:

> Your rounded thighs are like jewels,
> the work of a master hand. (7:1)

These letters are indeed the work of a master hand. The forms of the letters seduce our eyes, just as the sounds of the Song's Hebrew poetry seduce even if their meaning is often opaque.[24] Even the opening line gives us lovely assonance in the original Hebrew: *shir hashirim asher lishlomo* (1:1).

Like grapes growing on a trellis, each line of writing has visual structure and order. A great deal of planning went into the landscape architecture of the page. Jackson drew inspiration from a similarly large medieval English manuscript, the twelfth-century Winchester Bible.[25] Jackson wanted an architecture for each page of this Bible that would hold it together visually and enable that structure to hold even on pages with a great deal of artistic embellishment. You may note that this Bible does not have paragraph breaks in prose sections; instead, small diamond shapes show where the New Revised Standard Version translators broke paragraphs.[26] The lack of paragraph breaks is just one design choice that keeps the structure of the columns intact. Not only does this structure hold for each page, but it does so also across many pages. As calligrapher and book artist Nancy Leavitt explains:

> Composing page layouts for a book is like planning a well-designed garden. You want to be welcomed into the space, to be enveloped by the garden with vistas unfolding as you move through, and to be allowed to linger without getting stranded. Each new vista should offer a new scene, but with enough similarities so that you know you are in the same space and story.[27]

24. Walsh, *Exquisite Desire*, 290–91; Ellen F. Davis, "Reading the Song Iconographically," in *Scrolls of Love: Ruth and the Song of Songs*, ed. Peter S. Hawkins and Lesleigh Cushing Stahlberg, 172–84 (New York: Fordham University Press, 2006), 184.

25. Calderhead, *Illuminating the Word*, 89–95; Claire Donovan, *The Winchester Bible* (Toronto: University of Toronto Press, 1993).

26. This had to be negotiated with the NRSV licensing committee; Calderhead, *Illuminating the Word*, 99.

27. Christopher Calderhead and others, "The Poetics of Space," *Letter Arts Review* 32, no. 3 (2018): 18.

In *The Saint John's Bible*, the sturdy, stable trellises allow creativity to bloom. In the Latin language familiar to medievals, the word *pagina* refers to a page of writing as well as a row of vines joined together. Here the baseline of the letters is the trellis, and each letter is a part of the vine, perhaps a cluster of grapes.[28] Even the practice of calling a manuscript page a *leaf* dates back to early medieval times and is found in Bede.[29] The blocks of writing maintain order, yet stray vines and branches, flourishes, give each line visual uniqueness and life. The architecture of each page is solid enough to unify the many, many different visual styles of art in this illuminated Bible.

Finally, one major aesthetic pleasure of any garden is that no two plants are the same. You can plant a row of roses, yet each one will grow in different directions, and each bloom will have its own variations. The gardener plants many seeds, of many diverse kinds—yet often in a way such that the different plants will look good next to one another. In short, the aesthetic of a garden, of nature curated, is not uniformity in which every item is the same. The beauty lies in the ideal combination of variety with harmony. This aesthetic fits calligraphy too. Form and content intertwine.

The scribes who wrote this masterwork are all skilled in precision and detail; their training includes an entire vocabulary to dissect letters. So, for example, to write the letter *b* in any script, the scribe looks at the relationship between the *b* and other letters, in particular the *o*, whose shape is roughly found in the bowl of the *b*. She studies the relationship between the nib width and the height of the letter, which can vary to give letters with different feels: short and chunky, tall and elegant. She studies the ratio between the bowl of the *b* and the part that ascends above the line. This geometric vocabulary enables a scribe to dissect any script, and to replicate it uniformly enough for both legibility and pleasing visual consistency.

Yet the human touch—variation—remains. In *The Saint John's Bible*, no two letters are identical. Look, for example, at the row of majuscule Ys in 4:1-2. The first one descends downward and turns to the right; the second stays relatively straight and ends slightly thicker; the third extends down further and finishes in a very fine line. And yet

28. Pliny, *Natural History*, 17.169, translated in Ivan Illich, *In the Vineyard of the Text: A Commentary to Hugh's* Didascalicon (Chicago: University of Chicago Press, 1996), 57.

29. *Oxford English Dictionary*, s.v. "leaf," 8:753.

each is clearly the same species, the same proportions—with minor variants. This is the human touch in calligraphy, its warmth and organic quality, rather than the cold, perfect uniformity of most printed and digital words we encounter. Compared to the visual quality of these calligraphed flowers, most type looks like Astroturf.

Not only does each letter of the alphabet—each species of plant in the garden—harmonize due to the human touch, so does each letter of the alphabet harmonize with the others—in our metaphor, each different species of plant in the garden. In many Roman alphabet scripts, for example, the *o* provides the blueprint for other letters. So, the *p*, *b*, *d*, *e*, *q*, *g*, and even *s* all contain the shape of the *o* within them. This consistency in proportions and shapes across many different letters within a script gives the letters their visual harmony.

The aesthetic of harmony-with-variants also resonates with the medieval theological tradition that Jackson alludes to in his choice of imagery. The Venerable Bede (673–735), an early medieval Anglo-Saxon monk, comments on Song 4:12: "Now the church is a garden because she brings forth diverse buds of spiritual works, which are subsequently enumerated under the names of various spices."[30] Here Bede draws on Paul's language of the church as body of Christ with various limbs that work together (1 Cor 12). Other authors compare the church's diverse gifts to the many seeds in a pomegranate, like the pomegranate in Jackson's illuminations. Jerome writes:

> For there is nothing more beautiful than this fruit; in its redness it signifies the modesty of the church, in the range of its seeds the grades and members of the whole body distributed through the various offices.[31]

Just as the garden is unity with diversity, just as the pomegranate is multiplicity within the unity of one fruit, so the church is visually multiplicity-with-unity. So is the human body. So is the page. As humans we seem to be attracted to this aesthetic in many forms. As

30. Bede, *On the Song of Songs and Selected Writings*, trans. and ed. Arthur Holder, Classics of Western Spirituality (New York/Mahwah: Paulist Press, 2011), 130.

31. Jerome, *Commentary on Zechariah*, 3.12, translated in George Hardin Brown, "Patristic Pomegranates, from Ambrose and Apponius to Bede," in *Latin Learning and English Lore: Studies in Anglo-Saxon Literature for Michael Lapidge*, ed. Katherine O'Brien O'Keeffe and Andy Orchard, vol. 1, 132–49 (Toronto: University of Toronto Press, 2005), 135.

calligrapher and historian of lettering Ewan Clayton writes of the script in the tenth-century Ramsey Psalter:

> [The scribe] uses forms of letters that resonate with a practiced spirit of community; they echo each other's proportions harmoniously, rather than jar with self-conscious individualism. These letters possess as Benedictine an architecture as any early English abbey.[32]

The letters' aesthetic reflects the monastic, Christian value of harmony. They thrive together, no letter jostling for attention from the others. Their beauty lies in their collective effort.

In this aesthetic, variations between letters are not imperfections. And even the letters that are not perfect, that the scribe is frustrated with, end up being a perfect imperfection:

> You are altogether beautiful, my love;
> there is no flaw in you. (Song 4:7)

As Donald Jackson stressed to every one of his scribes: "Perfection is not an option."[33] Nor is it necessarily desirable. It would remove the human touch.

The letters on this page, then, protest that they are black and beautiful. They invite us to look *at* them, to see each one as distinct, as harmonious in their diversity. Their beauty makes them better seeds and makes the viewer more fertile soil for the Word. And just as the woman of the Song yearns to care for her body better, so each letter scribed on this page is given its own care, attention, and love. There is a reason each page took several hours to write.

WRITING AS PLOWING, TENDING, AND WORKING WITH NATURE

So far, we have focused on connections between writing and gardening at the level of form and content: the page is a garden. But a related metaphor also intertwines agrarian labor with the process of

32. Ewan Clayton, *The Golden Thread: A History of Writing* (Berkeley: Counterpoint, 2014), 62.

33. Calderhead, *Illuminating the Word*, 47–49.

writing lines of letters. Writing is plowing and planting.[34] The connection between writing and plowing resonates with the scribe's physical labor and use of natural tools.

The link between writing and plowing dates back at least two millennia. It arises from eras when far more people worked the land than knew how to write, and when those who did write were much less removed from agrarian activity than the modern city-dweller. Perhaps the first Christian author to employ this metaphor, the Roman Christian poet Prudentius (ca. 348 CE), uses it in his telling of the martyrdom of Cassius of Imola. According to legend, Cassius, a teacher who practiced strict discipline, was martyred by his own students for refusing to sacrifice to the Roman gods. Prudentius narrates how the pupils stabbed their teacher with their pens:

> Others dart at him pens made of iron, sharp-pointed and cruel,
> One end of which they write ploughed furrows in wax,
> And the other to blot out the letters engraved on its surface
> And make the land bright and smooth again.[35]

Later, Isidore of Seville (ca. 560–636), whose *Etymologies* served as a kind of encyclopedia of knowledge in the medieval West, explains the etymology of the word *verse*:

> A verse (*versus*, also meaning "furrow") is commonly so called because the ancients would write in the same way that land is plowed: they would first draw their stylus from left to right, and then "turn back" (*convertere*) the verses on the line below, and then back again to the right—whence still today country people call furrows *versus*.[36]

34. For surveys, see Stephen A. Barney, "The Plowshare of the Tongue: The Progress of a Symbol from the Bible to 'Piers Plowman,'" *Mediaeval Studies* 35 (1973): 261–93; Ernst Robert Curtius, *European Literature and the Latin Middle Ages*, trans. Willard R. Trask, Bollingen 36 (1953; Princeton: Princeton University Press, 2013), 313–14; Julia Bolton Holloway, *The Pilgrim and the Book: A Study of Dante, Langland, and Chaucer*, rev. ed. (New York: Peter Land, 1992), 197–98.

35. Prudentius, *The Martyrs' Crowns*, 9.51-54; translation adapted from Prudentius, *The Poems of Prudentius*, trans. M. Clement Eagan, Fathers of the Church 43 (Washington, DC: Catholic University of America Press, 1962), 186.

36. Isidore of Seville, *Etymologies*, 6.15, translated in Isidore of Seville, *The Etymologies of Isidore of Seville*, trans. Stephen A. Barney and others (New York: Cambridge University Press, 2010), 142.

Isidore describes here a much older tradition from the first millennium BCE: *boustrophedon* ("ox-turning") Greek inscriptions. In these inscriptions, the line of writing changes from right to left, to left to right, and back again—like an ox plowing a field.[37] Perhaps today we would call this lawn-mower writing. Here the page is an empty field, each line a neat row, and the pen pressing down on the page is like the plow breaking through dirt to plant seeds, to lay letters.

Like plowing, writing is hard physical work. While we know far less than we wish about medieval scribes, at times they leave notes at the end of copying a manuscript. These notes, called colophons, often tell us their name, the date they finished, and perhaps how they felt about their labor. Eleventh-century French monk Rodulfus, upon finishing a copy of Jerome's commentary on the Psalms, prays:

> When I write a book, St. Vedast looks down
> From highest heaven, and notes how many letters I depict,
> With my pen, by how many furrows the page is ploughed,
> By how many sharp points the folio is punctured here and here
> And then, looking with favour on my work and my labour, he says:
> "As many letters, as many furrows, as many points as there are
> In this book, so many sins I now forgive you."[38]

For Rodulfus, writing is not a hobby but hard physical labor and penance. Similarly, Susan Hufton, one of the scribes on *The Saint John's Bible*, recounts:

> I can write for between 30 and 60 minutes at a time without a break. Then I stop, and stretch my eye muscles by focusing out of the window, and rest them by putting the palms of my hands over my eyes for a few minutes. I often get up and walk around too. Keeping up that level of concentration is difficult for any longer than an hour, and that is usually too long.[39]

37. Rudolf Wachter, "Inscriptions," in *A Companion to the Ancient Greek Language*, ed. Egbert J. Bakker, 47–61 (Malden, MA: Wiley-Blackwell, 2010), 50–53; Stephen Colvin, *A Brief History of Ancient Greek* (Hoboken, NJ: Wiley Blackwell, 2014), 83–84.

38. Elizabeth Sears, "The Afterlife of Scribes: Swicher's Prayer in the Prüfening Isidore," in *Pen in Hand: Medieval Scribal Portraits, Colophons and Tools*, ed. Michael Gullick, 75–96 (London: Red Gull Press, 2006), 87.

39. Susan Hufton, "Getting It Right: The Making of the St John's Bible," *Alphabet* 27, no. 2 (2002): 29.

Though the scribe sits indoors, and though she is hardly handling heavy metal equipment, the physical strain on shoulders, arm, eyes, and brain is real.

Like a farmer, the calligrapher must work with natural tools and know them intimately to best use them. Both farm and garden elude the neat divide between nature and culture. Gardens are nature, but tended by human hands, with human technology. The gardener fashions her work into something desirable to human ends: fresh fruits and vegetables, visual splendor, olfactory delight. Those who garden avidly—including my spouse, Michael—tell me that one of its joys comes from the garden being both wild nature and human culture, both the wild's ability to surprise us and the expected joys of our goal-oriented labor. The gardener plants his flowers at the right time; he knows which soil will nourish the seeds most. In my own backyard, when nighttime brings freezing temperatures, Michael knows which potted plants must come inside and which must be covered outside. He knows how much to prune the tomatoes to grow the largest fruit. And yet, surprises come: seeds that were thought dead sprout in the compost pile. A family of birds decides to nest atop a light fixture next to our shed door. As biblical scholar Elaine James notes, "the garden's order is permeable, it is always circumscribed by wildness."[40] Gardener and farmer alike hope this wildness brings serendipitous joy rather than leaf-eating insects or a wasp's nest.

The calligrapher, too, finds her work circumscribed by wildness. Partly this wildness comes from the tools. Donald Jackson was trained in a generation of scribes who learned the medieval techniques thoroughly: writing with quills and reeds, mixing their own inks and pigments, arduously preparing vellum rather than just buying paper. Though they cost more money and take more time and skill, *The Saint John's Bible* employs these techniques because they still give the best results. Jackson explains that quills, for example, can produce more subtle shapes and forms than metal-nibbed pens:

> Most people start the practice of calligraphy by using a steel pen; at first it seems to answer all needs but after practice and careful study the sense of touch and an awareness of subtle form develop and there is more readiness to appreciate the value of tools which helped to create the forms of the Roman alphabet still used and adapted in the designs of today. The quill pen is capable of forming

40. James, *Landscapes of the Song of Songs*, 65.

> a particular but many-shaded repertoire of marks, and through the medium of ink, enables us to transmit fluently and sensitively onto a page images in the mind's eye.[41]

Jackson's labor involves understanding of how to cultivate nature that any farmer would recognize: which species of birds give the best quills; how turkey, swan, and goose quills differ in strengths and weaknesses; which part of the wing gives the best feathers; how to cut the quills and make them last. Like any harvest, a gathering of quills varies in quality. Sally Mae Joseph, one of the scribes on the Bible, recalls an occasion when she and Jackson surveyed one hundred quills. Only fifteen of the hundred were high enough quality for scribing.[42] Fellow scribe Angela Swan recalls the thrill of another quill: "My fourth quill was a little beauty. I wrote twenty-four pages with it. . . . It kept its edge; it never split; it never misbehaved."[43]

The quills are less predictable, less tame, than steel-nibbed pens. Rabbi Shira Gluck, reflecting on her experience training as a scribe and writing a Hebrew scroll of the Song of Songs, comments on learning how to write with a quill:

> In learning to write samekh [one of the letters of the Hebrew alphabet], I became most keenly aware of the role that physics/mechanics plays in this style of writing. Writing with a ballpoint pen offers the writer nearly complete control over the instrument. Writing with a feather quill does not offer complete control. On the contrary, one can only write with a limited set of motions—the ink must be pulled laterally in one direction and the quill can only deliver ink when held at certain angles.[44]

Elsewhere, Gluck remarks that "learning to be a scribe is really a series of tactile experiences."[45] Using a tool with more sensitivity requires more skill. But this tool gives more satisfaction—the difference between fresh backyard fruit and canned produce. As Jackson beams:

41. Donald Jackson, "Preparation of Quills and Reeds," in *The Calligrapher's Handbook*, ed. Heather Child, 15–36, 2nd ed. (New York: Taplinger, 1986), 20.

42. Sally Mae Joseph, "The Studio Manager," *The Scribe* 75 (2002): 30.

43. Calderhead, *Illuminating the Word*, 78.

44. Shira H. Gluck, "Uchtavtam 'and You Shall Write': An Integrative Study and Practice of Safrut STa"M" (Rabbinic thesis, Hebrew Union College–Jewish Institute of Religion, 2019), 7.

45. Gluck, "Uchtavtam 'and You Shall Write,'" 38.

> [The quill] can go from fine to absolute impact of an explosion on the page. It needs to be nurtured; it needs to be kept sharp—it sometimes isn't sharp but that doesn't matter because the form of the letters flows from your hands. It's made of the same substance as your fingernail, it's a part of you, it becomes part of you just as a violinist plays wonderful sounds out of a—basically, a cigar box, you know, with a string tight across it. It's sympathetic, it's warm and it takes to ink.[46]

Unlike a metal nib, which is made of cold, hard matter, the quill is made of the same matter as the fingernails of the hand holding it. Jackson again: "It's an extension of my fingers, almost like a phonograph needle, but the music it plays comes from inside me."[47] To extend Jackson's record player metaphor, the quill acts as a kind of oscillograph of our inner self.

Wildness, surprise, and unpredictability also arise from the vellum—the animal skins on which *The Saint John's Bible* was written. Early in the project, Jackson and his patrons at Saint John's Abbey struggled to find a vellum supplier who could deliver both the quality and the quantity required.[48] The vellum had to fit the right specifications. A trip to Jerusalem's parchment suppliers, who sell to Jewish scribes writing Torah scrolls and other sacred texts, proved fruitless. The skins were high quality but not prepared in the right way for Jackson's Bible: they could only be scribed on one side and could not take gold and pigments well. Even when they found the right supplier, every skin had its own quirks, since each comes from a once-living creature:

> When using vellum, the calligrapher needs to know the material intimately with all its strengths and weaknesses. As the scribe writes, he or she becomes involved closely with the surface, aware of its every shift in thickness and texture. The pen glides across rough areas and smooth. It reacts differently on either side of the skin. Every skin is unique, individual.[49]

46. Donald Jackson, "Earning and Luck" (lecture, The Society for Calligraphy, 4 September 2021), https://youtu.be/3uHRDpjkdms.

47. William Plummer and Margaret Nelson, "Holy Writ," *People*, 14 June 1999, 98.

48. Calderhead, *Illuminating the Word*, 53–65.

49. Calderhead, *Illuminating the Word*, 56.

Just as different species of bird give quills of different qualities, different sheets of vellum and even different sections of each sheet serve different purposes. Since the vellum has a translucent quality, a thinner sheet would not serve well for a densely colored illumination. Anthropologist Tim Ingold contrasts medieval scribes writing on vellum with modern printing on paper: the scribes must follow the surface of the vellum as they write, while the printer can stamp the same uniform text on hundreds of sheets of uniform machine-made paper.[50] Similarly, a farmer cannot materialize perfect soil from nothing; they must work with the oddities and limits of the soil they are planted on.

In the daily practice of the writing studio, the scribe must take into account even more factors than just sensitive quills and unique sheets of vellum. The scribe's ability to produce their best work also depends on how these two interact with each other and with a host of other factors: the ink, the day's humidity, even the scribe's own body. Susan Hufton recalls this being a source of frustration as she wrote:

> All I can say from the experience of writing day after day, month after month, is that sometimes there are changes going on, that do not seem to be controllable, but that do affect the quality of the writing.[51]

The medieval scribe is more like the farmer who knows their soil intimately and knows how to plant in it. Like a farmer or a gardener, the scribe works with natural tools, tools with far more quirks and variables than machine-made steel nibs and paper. Not only is the page visually like a garden, but its creation is like farming a field.

The garden, then, is not only where lovemaking happens in the Song of Songs, and not only a metaphor for the sensory pleasures of the woman's body in the Song. The garden is also the page of text, and writing the furrowed lines of this Bible is also much like plowing and planting. These metaphors unpack the form and process of calligraphic art and the way those relate to the Song's garden metaphors and garden setting. In the next chapter, let us walk to, from, and around that garden.

50. Tim Ingold, *Lines: A Brief History* (London: Routledge, 2007).

51. Susan Hufton, "Day-by-Day: The Writing of the St John's Bible," *Alphabet* 28, no. 1 (2002): 22.

Chapter Three

PILGRIMS WALKING THE PATH

At one point in his sermons on the Song of Songs, Bernard of Clairvaux apologizes for his slow progress through the book. (After eighty-six sermons preaching through the Song in order, Bernard did not make it past 3:1.) He would like to preach faster, to make more progress, but cannot stop himself from slowing down and savoring Scripture:

> I actually thought that one sermon would suffice, and that passing quickly through that shadowy wood where allegories lurk unseen, we should arrive, after perhaps one day's journey, on the open plain of moral truths. We did not succeed. . . . Looking into the distance a man can see the tops of trees and the mountain peaks; but his eye cannot range over the great glens beneath them, nor pierce the pathless thickets.[1]

Bernard compares the process of reading (and preaching that reading) to a journey that seemed short but turned out to be long. The journey was delayed, at least in part, by dense forests. In this forest of allegory, Bernard suggests, the walker does not spritely sprint through in a line. This is not the latest detective novel that one reads through, rapidly, for the plot. This is slow language. Your eye and your mind meander

1. Bernard of Clairvaux, *Sermon on the Song of Songs* 16.1; translation in Bernard of Clairvaux, *On the Song of Songs 1*, trans. Kilian Walsh, Cistercian Fathers 4 (Kalamazoo, MI: Cistercian Publications, 1971), 114–15.

around the page, rereading, going back and forth. While Bernard seems apologetic, his pace does not quicken. He enjoys the journey.

Like Bernard, who reads the Song of Songs slowly, we are in no hurry as we take in the illuminated pages of the Song in *The Saint John's Bible*. Like Bernard, our eye makes its journey around the page, undertaking its pilgrimage to its Holy of Holies. Writing, too, is a journey, a long walk in which every pen's stroke is a step. Both walking and writing engage the body's rhythms, its heartbeat and breath. And like so many pilgrims, the scribes of *The Saint John's Bible* travelled and grew together.

THE SONG'S TEMPLE AND THE HOLY OF HOLIES

The Song of Songs famously makes no explicit reference to God, the temple, the covenant, or other theological foci of the Hebrew Bible. Yet many of the Song's repeated images and metaphors allude to these themes. The Song's "you whom my soul loves" (1:7) and "the one whom my soul loves" (3:1-4), for example, seem odd: why not just say "the one I love"? Ellen Davis discerns here a veiled allusion to the Shema, a passage in Deuteronomy that Jews treat as a central creed of faith and daily prayer:

> Hear, O Israel: The LORD is our God, the LORD alone. You shall love the LORD your God with all your heart, and with all your soul, and with all your might. (6:4-5)

The words rendered into English as "love" (*ahavah*) and "soul" (*nefesh*, better translated "life-force") are the same in the Song's refrain and the Shema.[2] Further, much of the Song alludes to the textual descriptions of the sights and sacrifices of Solomon's temple.[3] The lovers speak of myrrh and frankincense (3:6, 4:6, 4:13-14, 5:1, 5:5), used in

2. Ellen F. Davis, *Proverbs, Ecclesiastes, and the Song of Songs*, Westminster Bible Companion (Louisville, KY: Westminster John Knox Press, 2000), 255.

3. See Edmée Kingsmill, *The Song of Songs and the Eros of God: A Study in Biblical Intertextuality*, Oxford Theological Monographs (Oxford: Oxford University Press, 2009), 155–78; Ellen F. Davis, "Reading the Song Iconographically," in *Scrolls of Love: Ruth and the Song of Songs*, ed. Peter S. Hawkins and Lesleigh Cushing Stahlberg, 172–84 (New York: Fordham University Press, 2006); Davis, *Proverbs, Ecclesiastes, and the Song of Songs*, 267–72.

temple worship (Exod 30:23). The man compares his beloved's cheeks to halves of a pomegranate (4:3; 6:7), a key decoration in priestly garments (Exod 28:33-34) and temple architecture (2 Kgs 25:17). *The Saint John's Bible* picks up on this Song-temple connection and expands it in the illuminations. This visual and textual connection between the Song of Songs and the temple opens the door for the sensory language of love in the Song to be employed for the sensory experience of worshipping God. The book of the Word itself opens a portal of prayer, a doorway to the divine.

The square motif in the Song illuminations parallels other temple images in *The Saint John's Bible*—which suggest, among other things, pilgrim journeys to the temple in ancient Israel. It first appears in Jackson's illumination of the description of Solomon building the precisely ordered first temple and the king's ceremony opening the temple (1 Kings 8:1-66). The purple hues of this illumination suggest

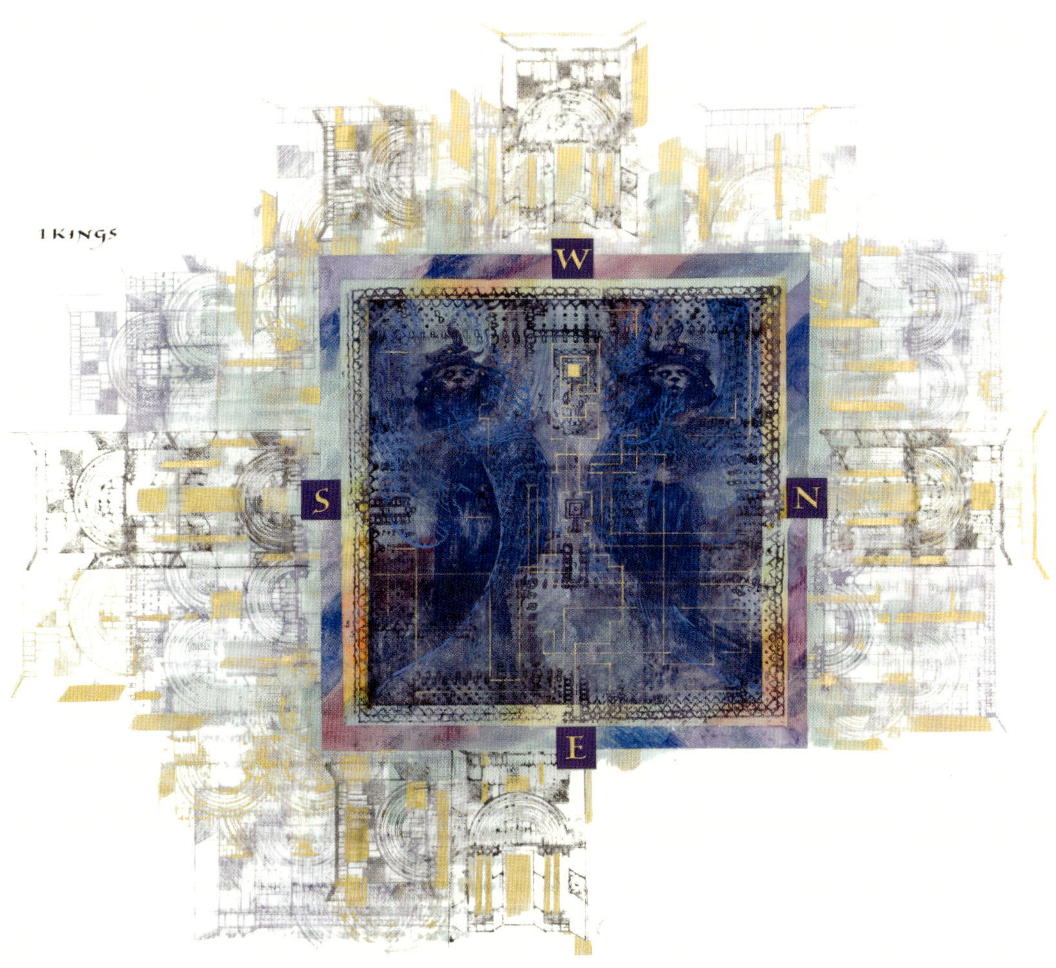

Solomonic royalty. Jackson borrows the architectural blueprint of this temple from a seventeenth-century Dutch engraving of Solomon's temple; such temple diagrams are common in early printed Bibles.[4] Surrounding the blueprint of the temple in Jerusalem, Jackson adds images of the double-arched doorway at the south façade of the Cathedral of Santiago de Compostela.[5] Susan Sink suggests that the doorway could

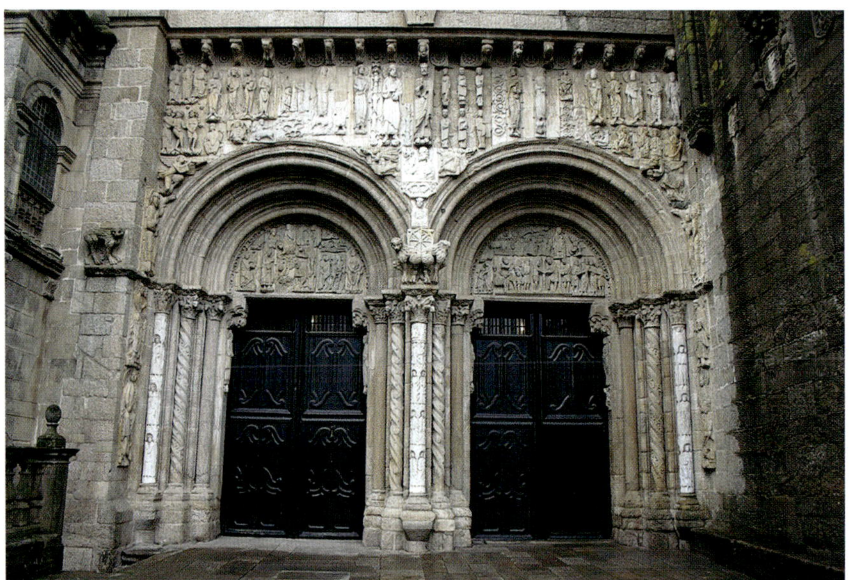

signify "sacred spaces built by humans and passageways to greater knowledge and insight into God. We approach God through those doors."[6] One recalls Jesus' "I am the gate for the sheep" (John 10:7), illuminated by Thomas Ingmire in the *I Am Sayings Anthology* in *The Saint John's Bible*. While Jews and Christians still make pilgrimage to Jerusalem to this day, another major pilgrimage route among Christians is the Santiago de Compostela, culminating in the Cathedral of

4. James Clifton and Walter S. Melion, eds., *Scripture for the Eyes: Bible Illustration in Netherlandish Prints of the Sixteenth Century* (New York: Museum of Biblical Art, 2009), 37–41, 109–10.

5. This double-arched doorway appears frequently in *The Saint John's Bible*. A special thanks to Susan Sink for helping me identify this motif. An image of the stamp itself can be seen in Christopher Calderhead, *Illuminating the Word: The Making of* The Saint John's Bible, 2nd ed. (Collegeville, MN: Liturgical Press, 2015), 148.

6. Personal correspondence, May 28, 2017.

Santiago de Compostela in Galicia. Likewise, ancient Israelite pilgrims traveled into Jerusalem three times a year for religious festivals (Exod 23:14-19; 34:22-23; Deut 16:16). Here the image of the temple, in a kind of architectural blueprint design, suggests the theme of pilgrimage.[7] It connects the journey to sacred space in ancient Israel with those walking the Camino to this day.

Jackson's choice of temple imagery also links *The Saint John's Bible* to a long heritage of Christian Bibles that liken the presence of the Word made Book to the presence of Christ. After the temple's destruction in 70 CE, the Jewish people—both those who followed Jesus and those who did not—faced a theological challenge. The temple was the major locus of divine-human communication, a necessary site for rituals such as animal sacrifices. What would replace it? Those Jews who would later coalesce into the rabbinic movement (the ancestor of modern Judaism) replaced temple with Torah, sacrifice with study. For Christ-following Jews, however, the destruction of the temple was proof that Jesus himself was the new temple, the Word made temple:

> Jesus answered them, "Destroy this temple, and in three days I will raise it up." The Jews then said, "This temple has been under construction for forty-six years, and will you raise it up in three days?" But he was speaking of the temple of his body. (John 2:19-21)[8]

Indeed, both traditions would come to use the imagery of the temple in their manuscripts to suggest divine presence. One such diagram is found in Codex Amiatinus, a massive Bible made at Wearmouth-Jarrow (Bede's monastery) in Northumbria in the early eighth century.[9]

7. The square temple motif can also be found in illuminations to Isaiah 6:1-13, Ezekiel 40–48, Nehemiah, and Revelation 21:2–22:5.

8. See Craig R. Koester, *Symbolism in the Fourth Gospel: Meaning, Mystery, Community* (Minneapolis: Fortress, 2003), 86–89.

9. Florence, Biblioteca Medicea Laurenziana, MS Amiatino 1, fols. 2v-3r. Comments drawn from Jennifer O'Reilly, "The Library of Scripture: Views from Vivarium and Wearmouth-Jarrow," in *Early Medieval Text and Image 2: The Codex Amiatinus, the Book of Kells and Anglo-Saxon Art*, ed. Carol A. Farr and Elizabeth Mullins, 3–40, Variorum Collected Studies (New York: Routledge, 2019); Conor O'Brien, "Tabernacle, Temple or Something in Between? Architectural Representation in Codex Amiatinus, Fols II v –III," *Leeds Studies in English* 48 (2018): 7–20; Christopher de Hamel, *Meetings with Remarkable Manuscripts* (London: Penguin, 2016), 54–95.

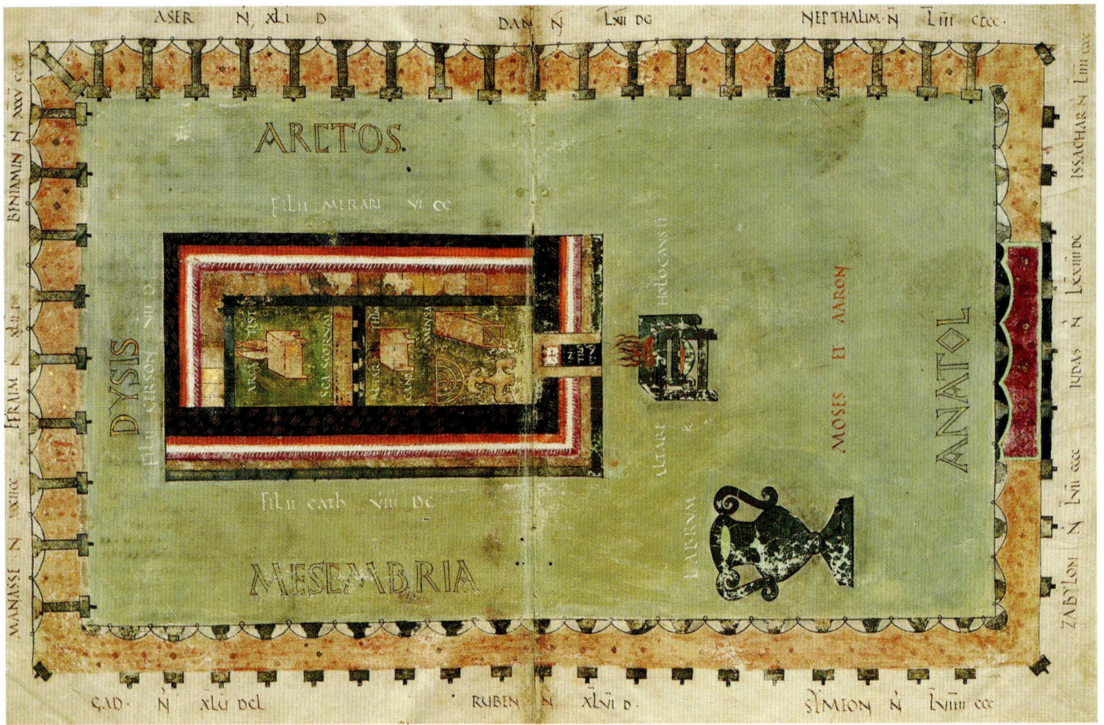

This diagram of the tabernacle appears in the beginning of this pandect Bible—a manuscript of the entire Christian canon, an expensive and laborious task fairly uncommon among medieval Christians. It suggests that the reader of this massive Bible was entering sacred space. The diagram also suggests that the tabernacle prefigures both Church and monastery. In the Gospel of John, Jesus proclaims that he is the path: "I am the way, and the truth and the life" (John 14:6). The book itself, the physical divine word, is a pathway into communication with God.

Anyone who has shown *The Saint John's Bible* can attest that it becomes a portal of prayer for all kinds of audiences. Donald Jackson tells the story of when two pages from the *Gospels and Acts* volume were first unveiled at Saint John's Abbey Church:

> When Holy Week was over a celebration of the Book took place in the Abbey Church. . . . I had kept the page opening with the Death of Christ and the Road to Emmaus illustrations strictly under wraps until the last moment. This double page spread was carried by Mabel [Jackson's wife] and myself and placed flat on the altar. After the pages were read by the Abbot, they were lifted and placed on a lectern facing the congregation of over a thousand people (something

> like my original dream as I now realise). They all seemed to hold their breath as the lights hit the gilded pages and for that moment we were as one, the dream became a reality.[10]

At this point, early in the project, there were still critics who felt that this Bible was a lavish expenditure, a waste of money better spent on other things. Moments like these silenced such voices. At the project's end, Donald and Mabel Jackson again processed down Saint John's Abbey Church carrying pages from this Bible—this time Revelation. As the pages rested on the altar at the center of the congregation, the gilded and scribed vellum again became a portal to prayer in the liturgy.[11] The final pages with the great "Amen" were placed on the altar, where Abbot John Klassen burnished some of the pages' gold as the congregation looked on.

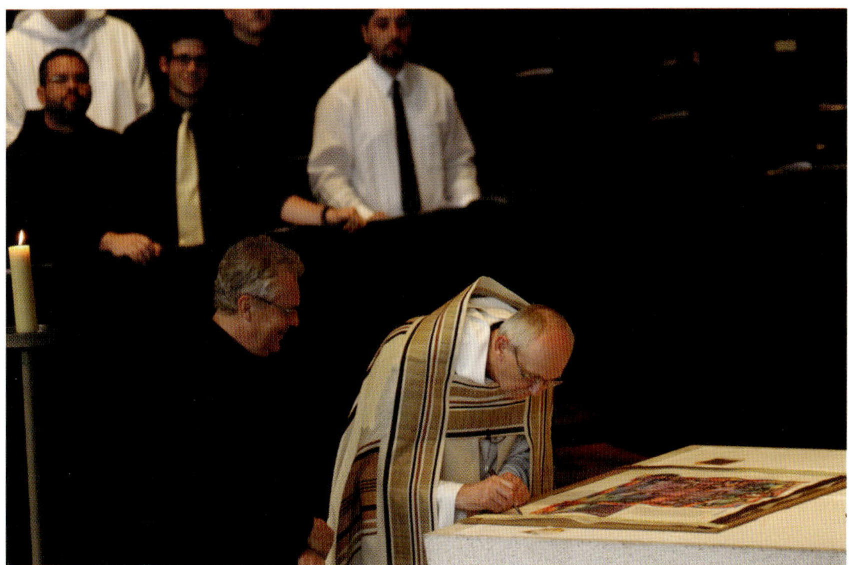

Similarly, Jason Paul Engel, a lay oblate at Saint John's Abbey who spent years on the road showing this Bible to diverse groups (not just churches!) and preaching from it, gives one unique interpretation of an enigmatic symbol in the very first page of this Bible—Genesis 1. Jackson

10. Donald Jackson, "The Dream and the Realities," *The Scribe* 75 (2002): 8.

11. The Saint John's Bible, "AMEN—The Saint John's Bible," 22 November 2011, https://www.youtube.com/watch?v=SY0onA4WAb0; Calderhead, *Illuminating the Word*, 261.

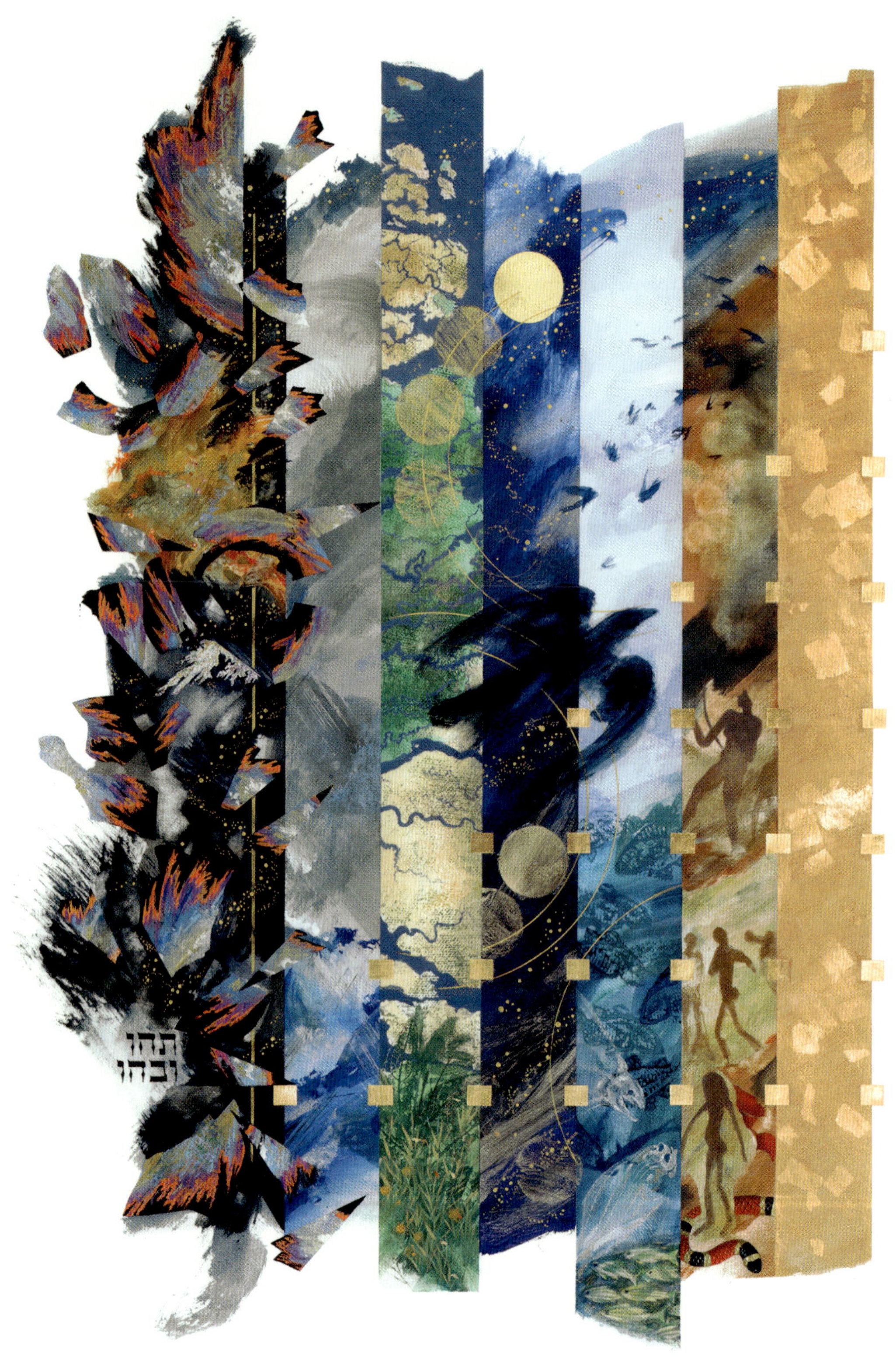
תהו
ובהו

divides his illumination into seven columns, one for each of the seven days of creation. Viewers often ask about the black bird in the center. Some see it as a raven, as in the raven Noah sent out (Gen 8:8-12) or the raven who saved St. Benedict from death by poison.[12] Engel suggests another possible take: this is not a black bird, but the shadow of a dove over the page. In Christian art, the dove represents the Holy Spirit, which is present, as Jesus preaches, "where two or three are gathered in my name" (Matt 18:20). Each page of *The Saint John's Bible* is large: a foot and a half wide, two feet tall. So, when Engel shows this Bible on the road, each volume is more than large enough for two or three people, even four, to gather around it. If all seven volumes are in the room, the crowd can be even larger. The physical artifact, the material Bible, opens this portal to God through prayer and study. Such prayer and study are not lone enterprises but communal activities. This Bible makes people gather and brings about the Holy Spirit.

THE EYE'S PILGRIMAGE TO THE HOLY OF HOLIES AND THE LETTERS AND WORDS

Not only does this Bible represent a portal to prayer, it also invites the viewer on a mental pilgrimage to the ancient temple, represented in the Song as the square motif in the garden that is the page. At the center of the temple is the Holy of Holies—in these illuminations, the circle with geometric patterns, patterns that draw in the viewer's eye. The viewer's gaze moves around the page in a pilgrimage of the eye, to and from the temple, evoking the medieval practice of the labyrinth as a device for both meditation and mental pilgrimage. Finally, both the geometric patterns in the Song illuminations and the practice of the labyrinth suggest a crucial way in which the forms of these letters act upon the viewer. These calligraphed letters require more focus to be read, and their lovely forms invite us to stop and behold them. All three invite the beholder to slow down, to contemplate.

Just as ancient Israelite pilgrims travelled to the temple and back home every year, so, in viewing the pages of this Bible, the viewer's eye finds itself drawn by the geometric patterns into the temple and out again, around the page, in all directions. Jackson explains: "I

12. Jonathan Homrighausen, *Illuminating Justice: The Ethical Imagination of* The Saint John's Bible (Collegeville, MN: Liturgical Press, 2018), 81.

thought of this garden motif as being like a magnet surrounded by iron shavings."[13] As one medievalist explains the tabernacle image in Codex Amiatinus: "The varying perspectives cause the 'mind's eye' to move about, not as an observer looking or even pacing from a fixed distance, but in the manner of one walking about the building in his or her mind."[14] This pilgrimage of the eye, our embodied gaze moving around the page, can also function as a kind of pilgrimage to the ancient, long-destroyed temple.

If the square motif represents the temple, then the circular pomegranate within represents its most sacred precinct: the Holy of Holies. Here, the viewer's eye beholds a dense thicket of geometry that draws on a long medieval heritage of geometric patterns in Jewish, Christian, and Islamic manuscript art.[15] These geometric patterns are more than mere joyful beautification. They entrap the eye, slow the viewer's mind down, and facilitate the mental absorption key for the slow practice of monastic reading, or *lectio divina*. One such medieval predecessor is the Lindisfarne Gospels, a manuscript of the Gospels in Latin created in England in the 710s; it contains one such page of geometric pattern that creates an ocular absorption in its viewers. This carpet page, so called because it resembles a rug, also echoes metalwork patterns from the same period. It combines carpet motifs with an image of a cross.[16] It has been suggested that pages like this could have been shown for the whole congregation in the monastery's liturgy.[17] Several features of this page grab the viewer's attention, even those who are far away. Though we might expect the cross to be the foreground and the patterns to be background, the latter's bold contrasts in color make them stand out.

13. Calderhead, *Illuminating the Word*, 234.

14. Carruthers, *Craft of Thought*, 237.

15. Calderhead, *Illuminating the Word*, 234.

16. British Library, Cotton Nero D.IV. fol. 2v. See discussion in Michelle P. Brown, *The Lindisfarne Gospels: Society, Spirituality and the Scribe* (London: British Library, 2003), 305–8, 312–25. Carpet pages are also found in five of the seven volumes of *The Saint John's Bible*. Each volume's carpet page(s) use motifs found throughout that volume's illuminations; see Calderhead, *Illuminating the Word*, 169–72; Susan Sink, *The Art of* The Saint John's Bible*: The Complete Reader's Guide* (Collegeville, MN: Liturgical Press, 2013), 33–34.

17. Carol Farr, "The Lindisfarne Gospels and the Performative Voice of Gospel Manuscripts," in *The Lindisfarne Gospels: New Perspectives*, ed. Richard Gameson, 153–56, Library of the Written Word 57 (Leiden: Brill, 2017).

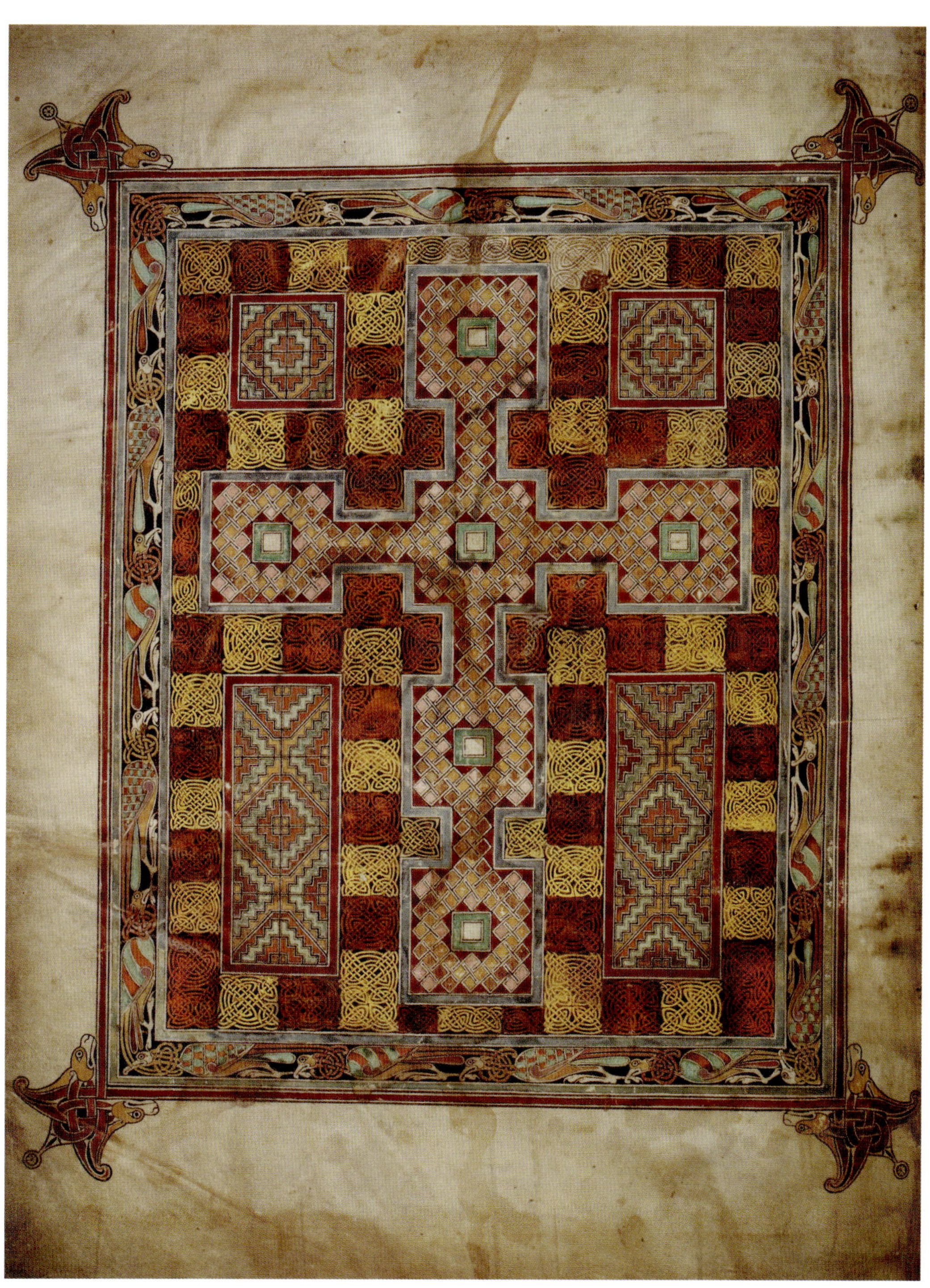

The viewer's perception is caught in a kind of indecision over how to view the page: What is foreground, and what is background? Both those who make this sacred geometry and those who view it find themselves absorbed in "sacred vertigo" as their eyes follow these geometric patterns and their mind fills them in.[18] Such geometric patterns also produced in some viewers a sense that the art was itself divinely created. Gerald of Wales, a priest who chronicled his travels to Ireland in the twelfth century, described seeing a manuscript with similar patterns:

> Look more keenly at it, and you will penetrate to the very shrine of art. You will make out intricacies, so delicate and subtle, with colours so fresh and vivid, that you might say that all this was the work of an angel, and not of a man.[19]

The sense of divinely inspired art, or even divinely created art, would naturally extend to the words of the manuscript as well. Michelle Brown explains that such densely ornamented insular Gospel manuscripts were not just containers for textual information but "vehicles of *contemplatio*."[20] She terms these carpet pages "painted labyrinths" and compares them to prayer mats, used at the time in Christian communities and known also in mosques to this day, which likewise orient the supplicant spatially and spiritually.

18. Benjamin C. Tilghman, "Pattern, Process, and the Creation of Meaning in the Lindisfarne Gospels," *West 86th: A Journal of Decorative Arts, Design History, and Material Culture* 24 (2017); Emmanuelle Pirotte, "Hidden Order, Order Revealed: New Light on Carpet Pages," in *Pattern and Purpose in Insular Art: Proceedings of the Fourth International Conference on Insular Art Held at the National Museum and Gallery, Cardiff 3-6 September 1998*, ed. Mark Redknap and others, 203–8 (Oxford: Oxbow Books, 2002). The "sacred vertigo" line was suggested by George Greenia in conversation.

19. Gerald of Wales, quoted and translated in William J. Diebold, *Word and Image: An Introduction to Early Medieval Art* (Boulder, CO: Westview Press, 1999), 24. It is often thought that he was describing the Book of Kells, but we cannot know.

20. Michelle P. Brown, "Images to Be Read and Words to Be Seen: The Iconic Role of the Early Medieval Book," in *Iconic Books and Texts*, ed. James W. Watts, 93–118 (Bristol, CT: Equinox, 2013), 102; Brown, *The Lindisfarne Gospels*, 324–25. In a 1988 interview Jackson stated that the Book of Kells is one of his favorite artistic sources on which to draw. Marion Muller, "The Scribe Who Renounced the Pen," *Upper & Lower Case: The International Journal of Typographics* 15, no. 4 (1988): 28.

The eye's journey to the Holy of Holies suggests that this page may function as a kind of mental pilgrimage to the long-gone ancient temple. While pilgrimage typically involves distant travel, medieval and contemporary pilgrimage practices include spiritual journeys that emulate physical peregrinations but do not require long travels.[21] These "imagined pilgrimages" in medieval times were often undertaken by cloistered monks and nuns who still yearned to travel to Jerusalem.[22] Some material remains of medieval imagined pilgrimage appear in manuscripts, especially those with images of maps following paths to the Holy Land. The labyrinths that appear in many Gothic cathedrals have also been suggested as possible imagined pilgrimages—most famously those in the Chartres Cathedral, completed in the 1200s.[23]

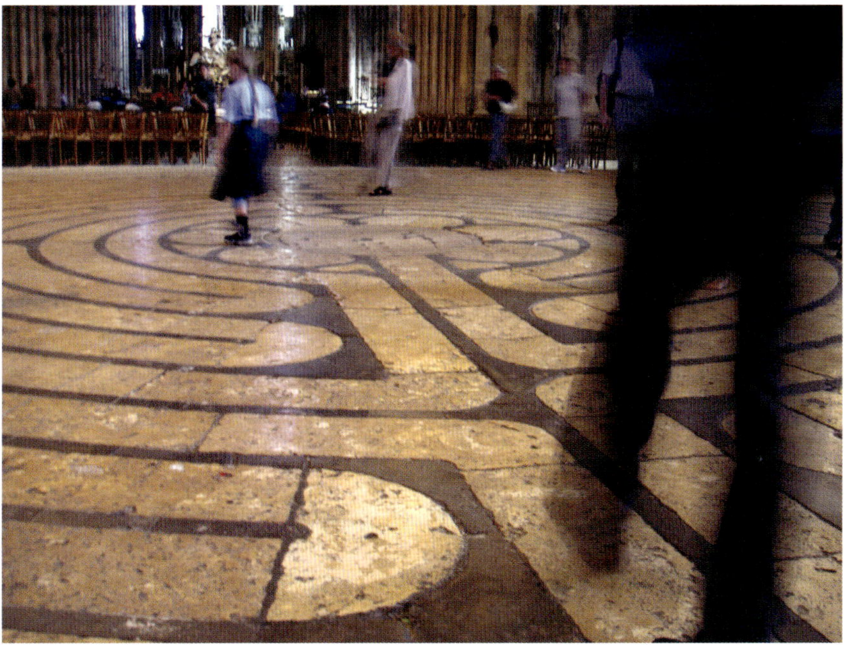

21. A useful summary of how religious studies scholars define (and debate) pilgrimage can be found in George Greenia, "What Is Pilgrimage?," *International Journal of Religious Tourism and Pilgrimage* 6, no. 2 (2018).

22. Daniel Kevin Connolly, "Imagined Pilgrimage in Gothic Art: Maps, Manuscripts and Labyrinths" (PhD diss., University of Chicago, 1998).

23. Lauren Artress, *Walking a Sacred Path: Rediscovering the Labyrinth as a Spiritual Practice*, rev. ed. (New York: Riverhead Books, 2006); Kathryn Barush, "Labyrinths as an Embodied Pilgrimage Experience: An Ignatian Case Study," in *Material Christianity: Western Religion and the Agency of Things*, ed. Christopher

The labyrinth could serve as a pilgrimage by proxy to the center of the world—for many medieval Christians, Jerusalem. Labyrinths have enjoyed a revival, as in the two at the Episcopal Grace Cathedral in San Francisco. As a didactic tool, the slow, meditative walk of the labyrinth conveys crucial truths about life's metaphorical journey. While traversing the "hypnotic vision of the pavement receding beneath [his] alternating steps," the pilgrim finds that his goal remains elusive.[24] In many labyrinths, the path edges just to the center, only to turn back to the outside of the circle. Spiritual growth remains nonlinear, indirect; we are not always clear how far along we are in the journey. At times the center, spatially and spiritually, seems within grasp—only to vanish. Throughout, the narrow path requires our full focus to stay within the bounds. Once we arrive, we spend just as much time leaving the center, returning back to mundane life—only to reenter the labyrinth and seek the center again.

The ocular absorption and the continual seeking-and-finding suggested by the labyrinth and the Lindisfarne Gospels also shed light on the eye's movement around these two pages of *The Saint John's Bible*—how the letters make us slow down and contemplate the text. In these pages of *The Saint John's Bible*, the pilgrimage is undertaken not with the feet, nor with the rhythms of walking. Rather, the rhythm lies in the eye. Like the ancient Israelite pilgrim who goes to the temple and then back home, and like the medieval labyrinth-walker, the viewer of these illuminations finds their eye going out and coming in, roaming around the page, into and out of the pomegranate Holy of Holies.

So too with the lovers of the Song. Like the pilgrim seeking the center of the labyrinth, edging closer to it only to find herself back on the circle's periphery, the lovers of the Song of Songs engage in a continual dance of "desire and fulfillment, seeking and finding," which is "repetitive, ongoing, and never-ending."[25] Chapters 3–5 of the Song exemplify this well. Song 4:1–5:1, as partially discussed in the previous chapter, represents the closest the lovers get to one another; many

---

Ocker and Susanna Elm, 197–222 (Cham, Switzerland: Springer, 2020); Daniel K. Connolly, "At the Center of the World: The Labyrinth Pavement at Chartres Cathedral," in *Art and Architecture of Late Medieval Pilgrimage in Northern Europe and the British Isles*, ed. Sarah Blick and Rita Tekippe, 285–314, Studies in Medieval and Reformation Traditions 104 (Leiden: Brill, 2004).

24. Connolly, "At the Center of the World," 310.

25. J. Cheryl Exum, *Song of Songs*, Old Testament Library (Richmond: Westminster John Knox Press, 2005), 134.

see it as a kind of sexual climax. But both before and after the lovers' idyllic meeting in the garden, we find scenes of the woman seeking her beloved. After the first time she finds him, she warns the daughters of Jerusalem of the dangers of love:

> I adjure you, O daughters of Jerusalem,
>   by the gazelles or the wild does:
> do not stir up or awaken love
>   until it is ready! (3:5)

In other words: love can be painful. Be careful when you let your feelings stir up, and with whom. If the beloved disappears, it will hurt. Even more vividly, immediately after the ecstasy of Song 5:1's "Eat, friends, drink, and be drunk with love," the woman tells a very different story:

> I slept, but my heart was awake.
> Listen! my beloved is knocking.
> "Open to me, my sister, my love,
>   my dove, my perfect one;
> for my head is wet with dew,
>   my locks with the drops of the night."
> I had put off my garment;
>   how could I put it on again?
> I had bathed my feet;
>   how could I soil them?
> My beloved thrust his hand into the opening,
>   and my inmost being yearned for him.
> I arose to open to my beloved,
>   and my hands dripped with myrrh,
> my fingers with liquid myrrh,
>   upon the handles of the bolt.
> I opened to my beloved,
>   but my beloved had turned and was gone.
> My soul failed me when he spoke.
> I sought him, but did not find him;
>   I called him, but he gave no answer.
> Making their rounds in the city
>   the sentinels found me;
> they beat me, they wounded me,
>   they took away my mantle,
>   those sentinels of the walls.

I adjure you, O daughters of Jerusalem,
    if you find my beloved,
tell him this:
    I am faint with love. (5:2-8)

The man's absence hurts even more here. Not only did he immediately disappear after calling to her, but she is beaten and stripped in her search for him. Love involves risk, and sometimes pain. In theological readings of the Song, these tales of the beloved's absence become spiritual reflections on the elusiveness of God—most famously in John of the Cross's *Spiritual Canticle*.

Finally, even the shapes of these letters create the same kind of meditative absorption that both the Chartres labyrinth and the Lindisfarne Gospels' carpet pages generate in their beholders. The script for this Bible is not as easily read as a typeface designed for legibility. Donald Jackson intended it that way. These letters require a second look. They force us to slow down. Turning back to these verses, note the little subtleties that make this script different from most of the typeface English we see: the trills ending each *r*, the ligatures connecting letters in words such as *the* and *all*, the way in which descending parts of letters such as *y*, *f*, and *g* reach down into the space of the letters below. These factors supply the script with nuance and delicate beauty but also force us to look more closely to read it—not a great deal more closely, as this is still quite legible, but a slight effect. In reading more slowly, we read more closely.

4

1 How beautiful you are, my love,
    how very beautiful!
Your eyes are doves
    behind your veil.
Your hair is like a flock of goats,
    moving down the slopes of Gilead.
2 Your teeth are like a flock of shorn ewes
    that have come up from the washing,
all of which bear twins,

Whether the eye is following the geometry in the Song's illuminations, the twists and turns of a labyrinth, or the dance of calligraphed letters, the effect is to induce meditation. The movement of the eye absorbs and slows the mind. Then the viewer can turn to *lectio divina*, the slow prayerful reading with which Benedictine monastic tradition engages Scripture. In *lectio*, the reader slowly ponders (*ruminatio*) the text, allowing it to begin a conversation with God in prayer. Reading the sacred text surpasses a mere means to information—monastic reading always has the end goal of deeper prayer and love for God.[26] Reading becomes a site of open-ended spiritual formation, focusing on experiencing and internalizing (often memorizing) the text rather than theorizing about it. Further, in *lectio divina* readers become active participants in the text, bringing their own free associations to the Bible drawn from other biblical texts, from the world around them, from their own experience. For example, Bernard of Clairvaux's sermons on the Song of Songs are not a technical *commentary* on the text but an evocation of both his and his monastic community's personal engagements with it.[27] Likewise, the committee that gave Jackson theological guidance did their own *lectio* on each text before sending him their suggestions.[28] The symbols on these pages are tantalizingly ambiguous, open-ended enough to provoke a similar kind of meditation on the visual illumination in the mind's eye of the viewer.

This kind of ocular absorption is also found in the Song of Songs itself. Multiple times the man speaks of being conquered or taken in by the sight of his beloved's beauty:

> You have ravished my heart, my sister, my bride,
> you have ravished my heart with a glance of your eyes,
> with one jewel of your necklace. (4:9)

26. Jean Leclercq, *The Love of Learning and The Desire for God: A Study of Monastic Culture*, trans. Catherine Mizrahi (New York: Fordham University Press, 1982), 71–88. A great example of *lectio divina* inspired by *The Saint John's Bible* can be found in Matthew A. Rothaus Moser, "Should Bibles Be Beautiful? How Beauty Teaches Us to Pray," in *The Saint John's Bible and Its Tradition: Illuminating Beauty in the Twenty-First Century*, ed. Jack R. Baker, Jeffrey Bilbro, and Daniel Train, 43–58 (Eugene, OR: Pickwick Publications, 2018).

27. Duncan Robertson, *Lectio Divina: The Medieval Experience of Reading*, Cistercian Studies 238 (Collegeville, MN: Liturgical Press, 2011), 156–203.

28. Patella, *Word and Image*, 12–13, 23–24; Calderhead, *Illuminating the Word*, 110–13.

Turn away your eyes from me,
    for they overwhelm me! (6:5a)

Her beauty entrances him. He knows he is defeated, and it unsettles him. As he tells it, he has no agency in the matter. He does not choose to be entranced by her, but her very appearance does it to him.[29] In the words of one modern commentator: "He's a goner."[30] As a result, he declares:

Your head crowns you like Carmel,
    and your flowing locks are like purple;
    a king is held captive in the tresses. (7:5)

Just as the man is taken in by the visage of his lover, so our eye is taken in by the dense thicket of geometric pattern. Both captivities are more than welcomed. The eye's sojourn in the Song's visual Holy of Holies suggests the proper way to read and meditate. And like the exegete who finds new meanings of the Song every time she reads and interprets it, so the eye has many possible paths to wander this page.

WRITING AND WALKING

The viewer's eye walks around the page. So does the scribe's hand, which traverses line after line of text. Painter Paul Klee famously quipped that "a line is a dot that went for a walk." Calligraphers often echo Klee's adage, including Jackson:

> The German artist Paul Klee said, "Drawing is like taking a line for a walk." Imagine dipping a goose-pen quill into ink and taking it on a journey letter by letter, gliding from hairline stroke to fat black, word by word, from beginning to the end of every chapter and verse in the Bible.[31]

29. Exum, *Song of Songs*, 15–17, 170–72, 219–20.

30. Walsh, *Exquisite Desire*, 69.

31. Donald Jackson, "The Scribe Speaks: Making the St John's Bible," in *The Lion Companion to Christian Art*, ed. Michelle P. Brown, 410–14 (Oxford: Lion, 2008), 410.

In this case, the journey was eighteen miles of script.[32] Viewing the art of making letters as a walking journey opens the door for many connections between the act of writing and the pace of walking.

Even the terms used by calligraphers evoke an ancient connection between writing and walking. In calligraphy and paleography (the study of scripts), the term *ductus* refers to the shape and order of strokes comprising a given letter.[33] When writing with the broad-edge nib, as the scribes of this Bible did, each letter is not just one mark. The *w*, for example, would be four: one for each line. The Latin word *ductus* refers to a line, a path, or the act of leading; hence the Roman aqueducts, or "water paths." But it also refers to the shapes of letters, as in the first-century Roman rhetorician Quintilian, who describes the way in which "children follow the outlines of letters [*litterarum ductus*] so as to become accustomed to writing."[34] In medieval Latin rhetoric, *ductus* also came to refer to the author's pathway through the words and concepts of their book, the mental paths on which they lead their readers.[35] As Tim Ingold writes, "if handwriting is like walking, then the line of print (joining evenly spaced letters) is like the record of gait analysis (joining equidistant plots)."[36] In short, the word *ductus* contains within it three senses of a path: the path of water being led, the path of the mind through a writer's words, and the path of the quill leading ink on the page. Although *The Saint John's Bible* is written with quill on vellum, for scribes who work with metal nibs on paper the aqueduct image is even more convincing: metal nibs actually create small canyons in the page as they push down, streams in which the ink flows and sits—like an aqueduct.

Just as the Camino pilgrim paces his steps over hundreds of miles, so the scribe finds a rhythm of writing, a rhythm tied to the body. In both cases, the rhythm is slow but steady, step by step. In a fascinating

32. Anne Kaese, "Ink, Quill, and Goal," *Transpositions*, 30 November 2018, http://www.transpositions.co.uk/ink-quill-and-goal/.

33. Rosemary Sassoon, *The Art and Science of Handwriting* (Oxford: Intellect Ltd., 2001), 39.

34. Quintilian, *Institutes of Oratory*, 10.2.2; translation in Quintilian, *The Orator's Education*: *Books 9–10*, ed. and trans. Donald A. Russell, vol. 4, Loeb Classical Library 127 (Cambridge: Harvard University Press, 2002). See also Pliny, *Natural History*, 8.6; Quintilian, *Institutes of Oratory*, 1.1.25.

35. Carruthers, *Craft of Thought*, 77–81.

36. Tim Ingold, *Lines: A Brief History* (London: Routledge, 2007), 96.

book about walking, Rebecca Solnit writes that "the rhythm of walking generates a kind of rhythm of thinking"; both, she says, move at about three miles per hour.[37] For pilgrims on months-long walking journeys, like those on the road to Santiago de Compostela, the rhythms direct the pace of each step, the pace of each day, and the communal pace of bodies en route together:

> Pilgrimage is inherently a body-centered enterprise, the physical gesture writ large and choreographed on a finite terrain that emulates the cosmos. This is a chance to stride under the stars, to echo solar or lunar patterns, to trace the invisible geometries of grace on highways of faith. . . . This communal choreography of the pilgrim band imposes rhythms that engage the whole organic structure of the traveler, that demand nutrition and rest, and which help achieve the desired goal of enacting the sacred while reaching toward it.[38]

The pilgrim's rhythms are tied to his body's pace, its heartbeat and breath. Similarly, the scribe's rhythm is *slow*. Hufton reports that she could only write about a half page a day.[39] Her words suggest the pilgrim's need to take his journey one step at a time. As one pilgrim on the Camino put it, "In the experience of walking, each step is a thought."[40] This energy, this corporeal rhythm, manifests in the visual rhythm of ink marks. As Jackson explains: "Even the 'perfection' of a skilled hand contains the breath and heartbeat of its imperfect maker."[41] For Donald Jackson, the goal of "enacting the sacred," of making this Bible, is reached through the body's labor of writing each letter. Look at the letters and words in *The Saint John's Bible*: What is the pace of the script's visual rhythm? What is the rhythm of its scribe's heartbeat and breath?

Second, like a walking journey, every line of calligraphy in *The Saint John's Bible* began and ended at a definite point—yet surprises always

37. Rebecca Solnit, *Wanderlust: A History of Walking* (New York: Penguin Books, 2001), 5.

38. Greenia, "What Is Pilgrimage?," 12.

39. Hufton, "Getting It Right," 29.

40. Nancy Louise Frey, *Pilgrim Stories: On and Off the Road to Santiago, Journeys along an Ancient Way in Modern Spain* (Berkeley: University of California Press, 1998), 72.

41. Quoted in Patricia Lovett, *The Art and History of Calligraphy* (London: British Library Publishing, 2017), 207.

awaited in the journey from A to Z. Computer layouts enabled Jackson and his team of scribes to plan exactly where each book, chapter, and line of text would begin and end, a necessity since the columns of writing were justified both left and right.[42] Yet the journey of making this hand-produced Bible brought many surprises. For the scribes, getting from the start to finish of each preplanned line involves a great deal of tension: tension in knowing that for each line of writing, one must fit the designated letters, words, and spaces in, and must do so evenly to prevent smushed, narrow, ugly letters at the end of the line. On a much broader scale, one struggle with this Bible project was the unpleasant surprise of how long the journey really would last: the project took thirteen years, more than twice the six years the monks at Saint John's planned at the start.[43] Another unhappy accident: the "scriptos" (typos in script) and accidental omissions that required more work to fix.[44] Other surprises were more welcome. One scribe, Susan Hufton, found the words she was writing more meaningful than she realized they would be:

> As I have written out the text, time and time again I have found myself writing passages that uncannily relate to the state of the world and modern situations, Old Testament passages that have been enacted for real on the television news later in the day. Both what I have been writing and the enormous implications of work as a team have taught me a lot about the human condition and about being in a community.[45]

One example of the resonance between the text and the world came on the first anniversary of the terrorist attacks on September 11, 2001. As Hufton wrote text from 1 Samuel, she was struck by an insight, recorded in her scribal journal:

42. Calderhead, *Illuminating the Word*, 47–49; Jackson, "Dream and the Realities."

43. The optimistic six-year estimate can be found in early publicity for the project, such as Margaret Nelson, "America's Book of Kells," *Newsweek*, 6 March 2000, 52.

44. Susan Hufton, "Getting It Right: The Making of the St John's Bible," *Alphabet* 27, no. 2 (2002): 27–29.

45. Susan Hufton, "The Calligraphers: Susan Hufton," *The Scribe* 75 (2002): 43.

> 11 September 2002
>
> *Very mindful of what I was doing and writing a year ago today.* On that day, as the news about the attacks on the World Trade Center came through, I was working on Deuteronomy chapter 7, verse 5 says 'break down their altars, smash their pillars, hew down their sacred poles'. I went cold when I realized what I had copied. *Today I am writing about Saul being commanded to obliterate his enemies, and it strikes me that this particular Old Testament theme, that I have come across time and time again in writing out the Bible, still has a dreadful resonance today.*[46]

In writing out the words of the whole Bible, including the passages and even whole books that churches usually ignore, Hufton found new resonances and meanings between the Bible and the world around her. Likewise, pilgrims on the Camino report that after their first pilgrimage, the Camino shifts from being a "big space in the mind's eye," a series of romanticized and anecdotal images and abstractions, to being a first-hand journey "filled and marked with personal experiences."[47] As Solnit writes, "Part of what makes roads, trails, and paths so unique as built structures is that they cannot be perceived as a whole all at once by a sedentary onlooker. They unfold in time as one travels along them, just as a story does as one listens or reads."[48] For Hufton, the terrain of the Bible transformed from a map on a wall to a terrain she knew intimately from writing hundreds of pages from it over several years.

SCRIBES AND PILGRIMS

Like the eye making pilgrimage to the temple image, the scribes of this Bible walk like pilgrims. They traverse the space of thousands of lines and the distance of years. Both pilgrim and scribe make marks for others to follow. Calligrapher and long-distance hiker Galia Goodman compares her work creating ketubot, Jewish wedding contracts, to the blazes left on the Appalachian Trail—itself a naturalist's pilgrimage. In trail lingo, a blaze is a painted white marker on a tree that signals

46. Susan Hufton, "Day-by-Day: The Writing of the St John's Bible," *Alphabet* 28, no. 1 (2002): 24.

47. Frey, *Pilgrim Stories*, 74–75.

48. Solnit, *Wanderlust*, 72.

the path. She describes the panic that sets in when the next blaze cannot be found:

> I turn around, and for another quarter hour I pore over my maps, check my compass headings, and try to puzzle out exactly why I can't find the trail on a mountain top that has more foot traffic than anywhere I have been in six days. I do not know why I finally pushed through a thicket at the edge of the clearing on the very edge of the summit, but whatever called me (perhaps the Angel who rests there?) produced the small miracle I needed. About two hundred feet away was the White Blaze. Trail found.[49]

Once she found the elusive marker, she left her own mark: a large duct tape X to save the next hiker from the same panic. Similarly, her calligraphed ritual documents and certificates mark the journey of life: getting married, retiring, becoming a bar or bat mitzvah. Letters serve as blazes for each other too. In the script of *The Saint John's Bible*, as in most calligraphy, each letter marks how the next is to be written and shaped. Sally Mae Joseph, one of the scribes, put it: "All the designing and layout have already been done. Our only thought of design is how each letter relates to the one that has come before and the one that follows after."[50] Joseph refers here to the connections between letters, the ligatures, as in the *th* of *the*. In a demonstration of this Bible's script, Jackson shows how every letter must adjust to those around it for visual harmony. In *Egypt*, for example, the scribe must move the *y* slightly to the right to prevent its descender from colliding with the bottom bowl of the *g*.[51] Letters leave marks for others to follow, whether those others are the following letters or the reader seeking divine guidance.

But the writing of *The Saint John's Bible* was not just a solitary walk; it was a pilgrimage, with a large group of pilgrims all walking together as scribes in the Scriptorium. Scholars of pilgrimage often

49. Quoted from a talk Goodman gave at a gallery opening. A special thanks to Goodman for sharing this with me, and for her suggestion of Solnit's *Wanderlust*. A similar parallel is made in Judith Joseph, "Calligraphy as a Long Walk," *Preachy*, 22 March 2021, https://justpreachy.com/calligraphy-as-a-long-walk/.

50. Sally Mae Joseph, "About Writing, About Life," *Alphabet* 29, no. 1 (2003): 28.

51. Donald Jackson, "The Saint John's Bible: A Lifetime's Dream" (lecture, St. Mary's University, November 18, 2021).

refer to the *communitas* of pilgrimage, the development of bonds among pilgrims travelling together, a bond created by each person's removal from their usual social sphere, from home and community.[52] Just as pilgrims support one another to accomplish the physically arduous journey of walking hundreds of miles, so those who worked on this Bible frequently spoke of the community it created—particularly the scribes who worked on it full-time from 2000 to 2005.[53] One of them, Brian Simpson, recounted, "Working as a team . . . we have to become an orchestra. There is no room for solos here."[54] Several recalled that the sense of group responsibility and individual accountability pushed them to give the project their best.[55] Jackson recalls the shared rhythm and sharp focus when scribes were all working in the same room: "You heard breathing, or the creaking of a chair."[56]

Perhaps the best marker of the scribes' growth as a group can be seen in the development of the script used in the Bible. While Jackson developed the script, the scribes to whom he taught it were adamant that they were not mere copyists of his visual style:

> Donald developed a good, clear, script entirely appropriate for its purpose. But understandably it was his design, and each of us writes in an individual way. So what has happened is that the script has evolved, absorbing elements from all our writing, while remaining true to Donald's original intention.[57]

52. Victor Turner and Edith Turner, *Image and Pilgrimage in Christian Culture* (New York: Columbia University Press, 1978).

53. Jane Grayer, "The Saint John's Bible - Jane Grayer," interview by Saint John's Bible, 21 August 2013, https://www.youtube.com/watch?v=Qn05j5qEy4g; Izzy Pludwinski, "The Saint John's Bible - Izzy Pludwinski," interview by Saint John's Bible, 21 August 2013, https://www.youtube.com/watch?v=ExyyDX_uH4U; Suzanne Moore, "The Saint John's Bible - Suzanne Moore," interview by Saint John's Bible, 21 August 2013, https://www.youtube.com/watch?v=h1FCz-Bdog4. Though this Bible took thirteen years, much of that was painting illuminations and creating the Heritage Edition; Jackson and his team completed the actual writing of the text much sooner.

54. Per Ola and Emily D'Aulaire, "Inscribing the Word: At a Scriptorium in Wales, Calligraphers Are Applying Medieval Arts to Create the 21st-Century Saint John's Bible," *Smithsonian*, 1 December 2000, 86.

55. Hufton, "Day-by-Day," 21.

56. Calderhead, *Illuminating the Word*, 167.

57. Susan Hufton, "Behind the Scenes: The Making of the St John's Bible," *Alphabet* 27, no. 1 (2001): 20.

Jackson concurs with the scribes when he speaks of the challenge in "encouraging others [the scribes] to trust their instincts and not to just stop at mere analysis or imitation of the copy script."[58] In an echo of the aesthetic described in the previous chapter—the aesthetic of harmony rather than uniformity—each scribe's hand continued to remain distinct. Jackson reduced the visibility of these differences by planning each two-page spread to be written by the same scribe. However, in the last volume of the Bible, one two-page spread was planned to showcase all six scribes' work: 1 Corinthians 9–11. A close look at this page reveals the subtly different scripts, a kind of theme-and-variations. At bottom right each scribe inserts a monogram of their initials: Sally Mae Joseph, Angela Swan, Susan Hufton, Brian Simpson, Susan Leiper, and Donald Jackson. These pages were chosen to echo the theme of unity suggested by Paul's retelling of the Last Supper in 1 Corinthians 11:23-26.[59] Ironically, Jackson made a mistake here: a forgotten line that was inserted at bottom.

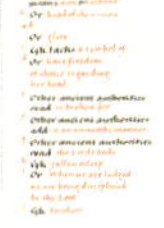

58. Jackson, "The Dream and the Realities," 6.

59. Sink, *The Art of* The Saint John's Bible, 296–97.

Visually, just as each of these letters displays a dance of thick and thin, so the *ductus* through life has its thick places and thin places.[60] The same goes for the process of creating this Bible, with all its joys and unpleasant surprises. In the Psalms, life's path also has its narrow places and wide places:

> Out of narrow straits I called on the LORD;
> the LORD answered me and set me in a broad place. (118:5)
>
> You gave me room when I was in narrow straits. (4:1b)[61]

Such images recur through the Psalms: when the psalmist is in trouble, he is in the pit; when secure, he is in a broad place, if not in the temple (Ps 23:6). Many psalms are prayers of one in a thin, narrow place, feeling constrained and trapped, praying to God to be delivered to a wide place of freedom and joy. In other psalms, the speaker thanks God for delivering him to a thick place. Likewise, in the Song of Songs, the beloved's absence makes his return all the more thrilling. In journeys of life and romance as in the shapes of letters, both thick and thin are part of the whole. Having both thicks and thins in letters creates contrast and visual delight.

This chapter's parallel metaphors of walking and going on pilgrimage, of pacing the labyrinth and meditating on letterforms, further unpack how *The Saint John's Bible* interweaves form, process, and content to powerful effect. Both the pilgrimage of the hand and the pilgrimage of the eye suggest many other kinds of journeys: journeys to God, sometimes from God; journeys to make meaning with Scripture, and roadblocks in which we are stuck in difficult passages. The geometric patterns of these pages, I suggest, point to the way we are to read and ponder these words. This kind of reading is not absorbing information but traveling with the scribe, following the journey of her hand and heart across the page and in the words. These patterns, especially the patterns and textures created in blocks of letters and words, are the subject of the next chapter.

60. I borrow this analogy from Laura Norton, "Calligraphy with Laura Norton," 17 September 2017, in *The Holden Village Podcast*, https://soundcloud.com/the-holden-village-podcast/calligraphy-with-laura-norton.

61. Examples from William P. Brown, *Seeing the Psalms: A Theology of Metaphor* (Louisville, KY: Westminster John Knox Press, 2002), 45. I have modified the NRSV translation to better show the aspects of the Hebrew I would like to draw out.

Chapter Four

MARY WEAVING THE WORD

In the second double-page spread of the Song of Songs, the garden theme continues. While the previous pages were a garden of geometry and camel girth, this garden is lilies and lace. The Song's illuminations suggest a connection to Mary, mother of Jesus, who weaves and conceives Jesus in her womb—just as, in *The Saint John's Bible*'s imagery, women knit families and weave words of wisdom. This Marian imagery suggests a pair of calligraphic metaphors: writing is weaving, and a written text has visual texture like a textile. And just as clothes can reveal and conceal a body, so a calligrapher's choice of form can at times reveal, other times conceal, the written words and their meaning.

THE SONG OF SONGS AND MARY THE WEAVER

Turning the page, we encounter a variety of colors and symbols that resonate with the Song of Songs, most obviously large purple and red flowers. Jackson created these flowers by first covering the columns of text, then boldly splattering the paint on the page and gently tipping the page vertically so the pigment could run down the margins, creating the plants' stems. The lilies could have spilled onto the letters and ruined hours of scribal work. Jackson's risk echoes the risk and vulnerability the female beloved of the Song feels while being in love, a love that leads her to seek her beloved even in the dangers of the night. Jackson remarks that to him, the brash blooms represent masculinity and the delicate stems femininity—a gender balance reflected in the

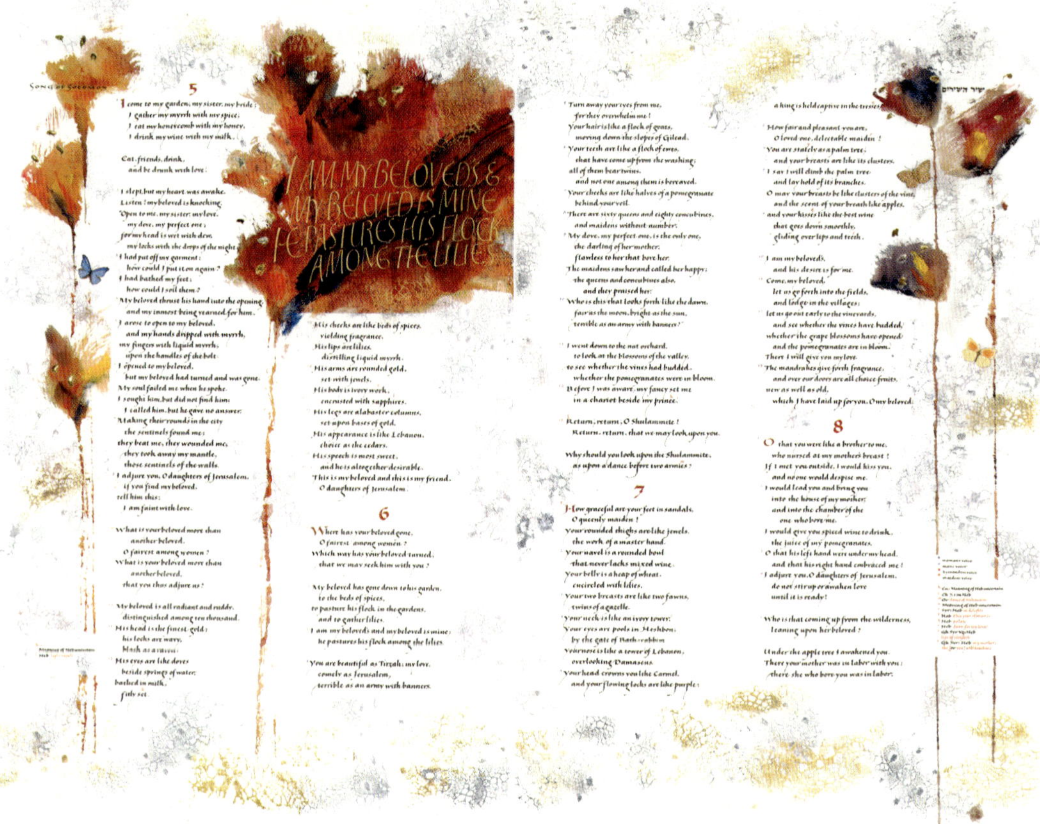

Song, often considered a gender-egalitarian book relative to the rest of the Hebrew Bible.[1] The flowers are most likely lilies, drawing on the woman's words of the text treatment on the left-hand page:

> I am my beloved's and my beloved is mine;
> he pastures his flock among the lilies. (6:3)

Alluding back to the metaphor of the page being a garden, here not only is the male lover pasturing among the lilies, but our eyes wander the lilies as we look around the page, taking in its visual delights. The lilies are also flecked with small bits of gold, perhaps an allusion to the golden seeds of the Word in the *Sower and Seed* illumination in Mark. In the margins around the columns of text and the red and purple lilies, Jackson inserts

1. Christopher Calderhead, *Illuminating the Word: The Making of* The Saint John's Bible, 2nd ed. (Collegeville, MN: Liturgical Press, 2015), 234.

purple and gold patterns of lace from an intimate garment: the hem of a woman's nightgown, dipped in watercolor.[2] Finally, small butterflies in the margins echo the butterfly at the start of the Song of Songs pages.

Jackson's use of lace connects the Song's enthused cries of love to the bonds Jesus shares with his mother Mary and Mary Magdalene. These women disciples remain present at the cross as Jesus dies in all four Gospels (Matt 27:55-56 // Mark 15:40-41 // Luke 23:49 // John 19:25). In *The Saint John's Bible*, the sole crucifixion illumination comes at the end of Luke. Around the borders of this image,

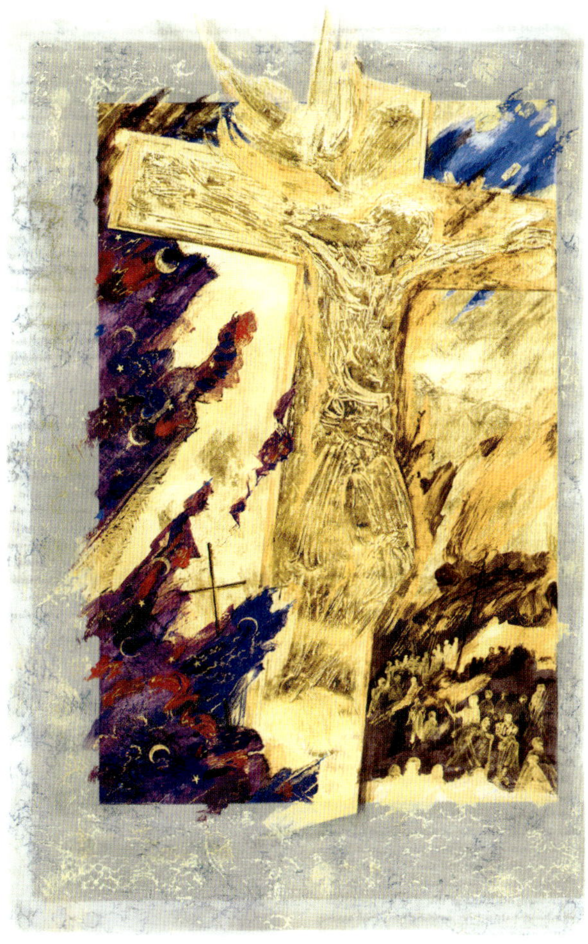

2. Calderhead, *Illuminating the Word*, 234; George Greenia, "The Bigger the Book: On Oversize Medieval Manuscripts," *Revue Belge de Philologie et d'Histoire* 8, no. 3 (2005): 740.

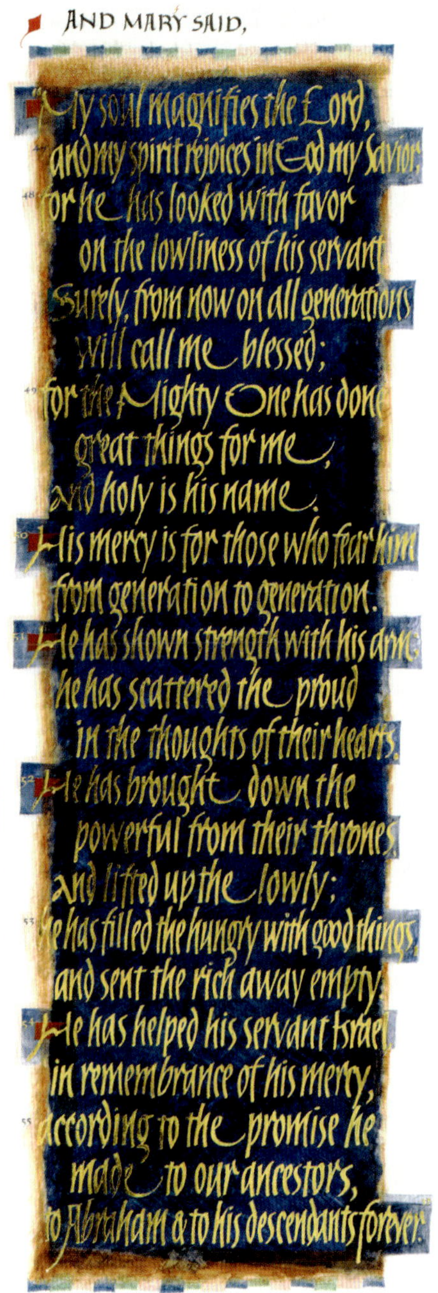

Jackson employs a lace pattern similar if not identical to those in the Song, in the same purple and gold pigments. The palette of purple and gold also appears in the text treatment for the Magnificat in Luke (1:46-55). In Jackson's illuminations, purple and gold are Mary's palette. By connecting the Song with the crucifixion, Jackson links the Song's deeply emotive language to the depths of sorrow and love that these women felt toward Jesus as he took his final breaths. We can imagine similar cries of pain felt by the Song's woman when her beloved is absent (Song 3:1-4, 5:2-8).

In visually connecting the Song to Mary, *The Saint John's Bible* follows a well-worn exegetical path. Since medieval Christian allegorical exegetes did not read the Song with the sexual emphasis that modern readers do, it was not even a far stretch to see the woman of the Song as Mary, lamenting her dead son. Medieval Christians used the Song's language for Marian devotion—in commentary, liturgy, and art—to narrate Mary's desire for Jesus' presence at her Assumption, to voice her sorrow as her son died in front of her, to express her love for her son, to describe her perpetually virginal womb as a *hortus conclusus* (sealed garden), a "garden locked, a fountain sealed" (Song 4:12).[3] Allegorically, Mary also repre-

3. E. Ann Matter, *The Voice of My Beloved: The Song of Songs in Western Medieval Christianity* (Philadelphia: University of Pennsylvania Press, 1992), 151–70; William Flynn, "*In Persona Mariae*: Singing the Song of Songs as a Passion Commentary," in *Perspectives on the Passion: Encountering the Bible through the Arts*, ed. Christine Joynes and Nancy Macky, 106–21, The Library

sents the church, which Christians hold to be Christ's bride. Many medieval Latin manuscripts of the Song contain this reading of the Song's man and woman as Jesus and Mary, who are painted in miniature inside the large "O" that begins the Latin of "Let him kiss me with the kisses of his mouth!" (Song 1:2).[4] These diverse connections between the Song and Mary suggest just how flexible and portable the Song's poetically expressed desire is.

The textile connection between the Song and Mary also suggests a longstanding tradition of Mary as a weaver, a tradition that sheds light on the calligraphy in this Bible. In this tradition, Mary is a weaver and worker of thread, an association spun from the Latin pun between *filum* (thread) and *filium* (son).[5] (We might think of the English words *tissue* or *sinew*.) Though the canonical Gospels do not depict Mary weaving, two Gospels that are noncanonical but key for Christian devotion do: the second-century Infancy Gospel of James and the early medieval Pseudo-Gospel of Matthew. In both, Mary weaves

---

of New Testament Studies (London: Bloomsbury T&T Clark, 2008); Marilyn Aronberg Lavin and Irving Lavin, *The Liturgy of Love: Images from the Song of Songs in the Art of Cimabue, Michelangelo, and Rembrandt*, Franklin D. Murphy Lectures 14 (Lawrence: Spencer Museum of Art, University of Kansas, 2001); Christina Bucher, "The Song of Songs and the 'Enclosed Garden' in Paintings and Illustrations of the Virgin Mary," in *Between the Text and the Canvas: The Bible and Art in Dialogue*, ed. J. Cheryl Exum, 96–116, Bible in the Modern World 13 (Sheffield: Sheffield Phoenix Press, 2007); Brian E. Daley, "The 'Closed Garden' and the 'Sealed Fountain': Song of Songs 4:12 in the Late Medieval Iconography of Mary," in *Medieval Gardens*, ed. Elisabeth B. MacDougall, 254–78 (Washington, DC: Dumbarton Oaks Research Library, 1986). For primary sources in translation, see Honorius Augustodunensis, *The Seal of Blessed Mary*, trans. Amelia Carr, Peregrina Translations 18 (Toronto: Peregrina Publishing, 1991); Alan of Lille, "A Concise Explanation of the Song of Songs in Praise of the Virgin Mary," in *Eros and Allegory: Medieval Exegesis of the Song of Songs*, ed. Denys Turner, 291–309, Cistercian Studies 156 (Kalamazoo, MI: Cistercian Publications, 1995).

4. Ruth Bartal, "Medieval Images of 'Sacred Love': Jewish and Christian Perceptions," *Assaph: Studies in Art History* 2 (1996); Judith Glatzer Wechsler, "A Change in the Iconography of the Song of Songs in 12th and 13th Century Latin Bibles," in *Texts and Responses: Studies Presented to Nahum N. Glatzer on the Occasion of His Seventieth Birthday by His Students*, ed. Michael A. Fishbane and Paul R. Flohr, 73–93 (Leiden: Brill, 1975).

5. John Scheid and Jesper Svenbro, *The Craft of Zeus: Myths of Weaving and Fabric*, trans. Carol Volk (Cambridge: Harvard University Press, 2001), 157–63.

the purple curtain for the temple before she conceives her son.[6] One German artwork, painted with oil on wood panel circa 1400, makes the metaphor even clearer by depicting Mary spinning a garment. The golden thread passes directly in front of the golden child in her womb. She knits his flesh and bone in her womb, clothing Jesus in flesh.[7] Since the temple, in Christian typology, represents the body of Jesus (John 2:19-21), Mary's spinning the thread suggests her conceiving the baby inside her. As the psalmist writes:

> For it was you who formed my inward parts;
> you knit me together in my mother's womb. (139:13)

Mary as weaver and conceiver appears in textual sources such as the fifth-century Greek homilist Proclus, who praises her body as the

> [w]orkshop in which the unity of divine and human nature was fashioned . . . within her is the awesome loom of the divine economy, on which the robe of union was ineffably woven. The loom worker was the Holy Spirit, assisted by the overshadowing power from on high. The wool was the ancient fleece of Adam. The interlocking warp thread was the pure flesh of the virgin. The weaver's shuttle was moved by the limitless grace of the divine artisan who entered

6. Gospel of Pseudo-Matthew 8–9; Infancy Gospel of James 10–12. For many examples both textual and visual, see Elizabeth Coatsworth, "Cloth-Making and the Virgin Mary in Anglo-Saxon Literature and Art," in *Medieval Art: Recent Perspectives; A Memorial Tribute to C.R. Dodwell*, ed. Gale R. Owen-Crocker and Timothy Graham (Manchester: Manchester University Press, 1998), 8–25; Gail McMurray Gibson, *The Theater of Devotion: East Anglian Drama and Society in the Late Middle Ages* (Chicago: University of Chicago Press, 1989), 155–66; Maria Evangelatou, "The Purple Thread of the Flesh: The Theological Connotations of a Narrative Iconographic Element in Byzantine Images of the Annunciation," in *Icon and Word: The Power of Images in Byzantium; Studies Presented to Robin Cormack*, ed. Antony Eastmond and Liz James, 269–85 (Aldershot, UK: Ashgate, 2003).

7. Berlin, Staatliche Museen, Gemäldegalerie, Upper Rhine, ca. 1400. See discussion of this image in Gibson, *The Theater of Devotion*, 164. See also See Coatsworth, "Cloth-Making and the Virgin Mary in Anglo-Saxon Literature and Art."

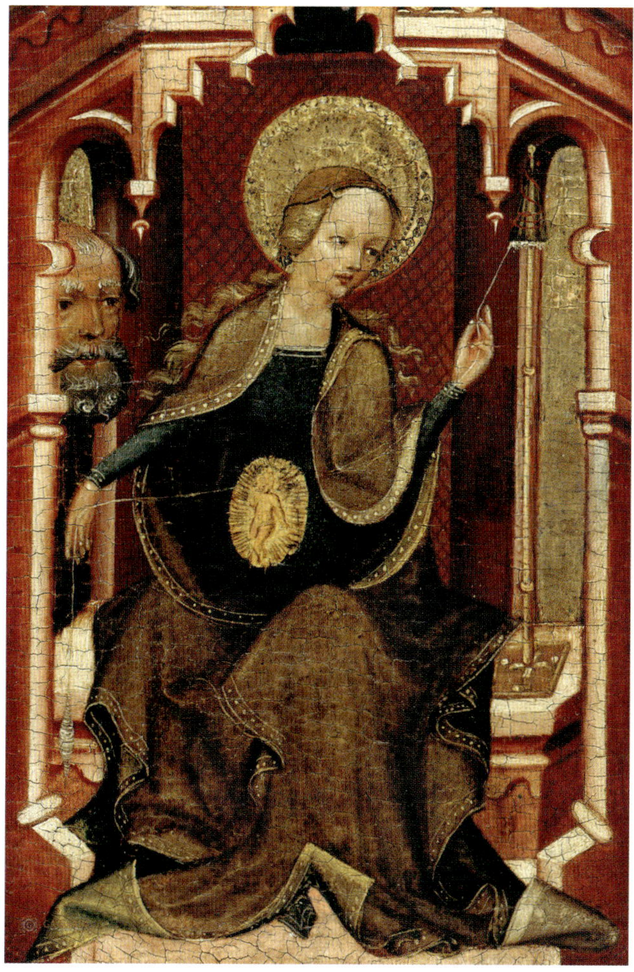

> through her sense of hearing. Therefore, do not sunder the robe of the divine economy which was woven from above.[8]

Proclus's image of Mary as weaver also patches on the Pauline typology of Christ as the new Adam: Adam and Eve clothed themselves to cover their nudity in shame, but believers clothe themselves in Christ via baptism (Gal 3:27). Just as skin and quill become the instruments of the scribe writing the Word of God, so ordinary loom and thread

8. Quote from Nicholas P. Constas, "Weaving the Body of God: Proclus of Constantinople, the Theotokos, and the Loom of the Flesh," *Journal of Early Christian Studies* 3, no. 2 (1995): 182.

17 THE WOMEN OF THE
NEIGHBORHOOD
GAVE HIM A NAME,
SAYING, "A SON HAS
BEEN BORN TO NAOMI."
THEY NAMED HIM
OBED; HE BECAME THE
FATHER OF JESSE, THE
FATHER OF DAVID.
18 NOW THESE ARE THE
DESCENDANTS OF PEREZ:
PEREZ BECAME THE FA-
THER OF HEZRON, 19 HEZ-
RON OF RAM, RAM OF
AMMINADAB, 20 AMMIN-
ADAB OF NAHSHON,
NAHSHON OF SALMON,
21 SALMON OF BOAZ, BOAZ
OF OBED, 22 OBED OF JESSE,
AND JESSE OF DAVID.

become "incarnations of that theological mystery that defied Joseph's human understanding."[9] Like the agrarian activities of plowing and planting, weaving and sewing were common tasks in premodern societies when hands made garments. It only makes sense that weaving and its processes became intertwined with many other kinds of human activity.

The image of Mary as a weaver casts a new light on the many images of textiles throughout *The Saint John's Bible*, suggesting the metaphorical links between weaving and bearing children, and between weaving and teaching wisdom.[10] The image of the genealogy at the end of Ruth connects weaving and creating a family. In *The Saint John's Bible*, images of menorahs suggest not only the presence and continuity of Judaism but Jesus' family tree as illuminated in the frontispiece to Matthew.[11] The menorah at the end of Ruth appears because Ruth is one of the surprises in Jesus' genealogy (Matt 1:5): both because she is a woman, and women are generally not mentioned in the genealogy, and because she is not a born Israelite but a Gentile (a Moabite, no less) who becomes part of Israel. (In Judaism she is often seen as the prototypical convert.) But the fabric-like quality of the diamonds of the Ruth menorah and the letters of the Ruth genealogy suggest

9. Gibson, *The Theater of Devotion*, 164.

10. Jonathan Homrighausen, *Illuminating Justice: The Ethical Imagination of* The Saint John's Bible (Collegeville, MN: Liturgical Press, 2018), 73–75.

11. Homrighausen, *Illuminating Justice*, 17–30.

another image: Ruth knitting together a family tree, a tree that Mary would continue to knit as she knits together a child in her womb. Jackson explains that such textile patterns, which occur throughout this Bible's illuminations, represent "an endless urge to unite" as the fibers go in all directions.[12] Here the fibers unite a family.

Another image in *The Saint John's Bible* connects weaving and teaching words of wisdom. Artist and scribe Hazel Dolby created the illumination for Proverbs 31:10-22. This tapestry incorporates imagery from the Proverbs poem. This woman, like Mary, wears purple:

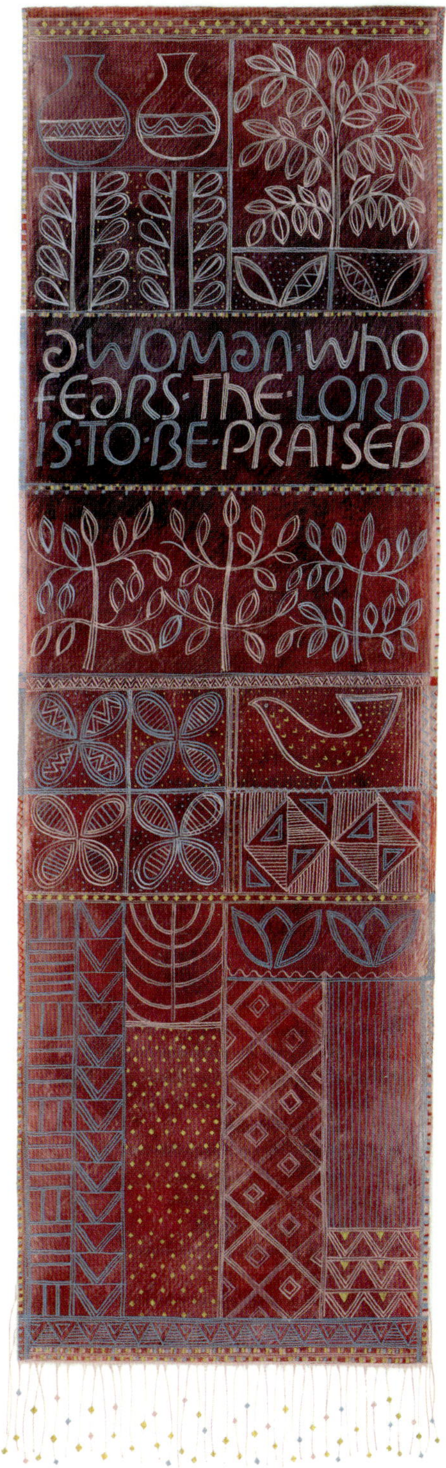

> She makes herself coverings;
> her clothing is fine linen and purple. (31:22)

The purple clothing explains the light purple (even magenta or maroon) of the tapestry. Proverbs 31:22 hints at the historical reality that in ancient Israel, women likely were those who weaved, which partly explains the association between textile patterns and women in Jackson's illuminations throughout this Bible.[13] The purple also suggests royalty; after all, Mary does bear the King of Kings. And just as women bear children to weave a family tree, so in Proverbs 31 the woman's words of wisdom unite

12. Donald Jackson, personal communication, January 22, 2019.

13. Homrighausen, *Illuminating Justice*, 45–76.

and guide her family and community. The image of Mary as weaver further suggests the link between writing and weaving, between the texture of a block of lettering and the texture of a textile.

WEAVING AND WRITING

Like a woven garment, a line of writing has its own texture. Once we see calligraphy as weaving together shapes and letters into a harmonious pattern with a visual rhythm, we see that not only do individual words and letters have their own beauty, but their form, their arrangement in a block of text on the page does as well. As Donald Jackson says, the calligrapher writing letters "stitch[es] them together."[14]

Weaving has long served as a metaphor for composing song and text, one that dates back in the West at least 2,500 years. As with *ductus*, the metaphor also lives on in English via Latin etymology: the English "text," "textile," and "texture," stemming from the Latin *textus*, *texere*, *textura*, and *textualis*. Though the earliest Greek associations of weaving and language, found in Homer and Plato, focus on the poet's ability to weave song and the orator's ability to weave speech, later Latin authors would connect the act of weaving with the composition of written text.[15] In all of these cases, the metaphor refers primarily to the craft of joining words together syntactically, not to the material, physical labor of writing—although papyrus, one of the main writing surfaces used by the Romans, is composed from strips of plants hammered flat and woven together.[16] For our purposes, a more useful medieval source is the name given to a family of Roman-alphabet scripts used by professional scribes from the twelfth century to the dawn of print. While many today would call these scripts Gothic

14. Donald Jackson, "The Saint John's Bible: A Lifetime's Dream" (lecture, St. Mary's University, 18 November 2021).

15. Scheid and Svenbro, *The Craft of Zeus*, 111–55; Arthur C. Danto, "Weaving as Metaphor and Model for Political Thought," in *The Textile Reader*, ed. Jessica Hemmings (New York: Berg Publishers, 2012), 205–9; Maren Clegg Hyer, "Text, Textile, Context: Aldhelm and Wordweaving as Metaphor in Old English," in *Textiles, Text, Intertext: Essays in Honour of Gale R. Owen-Crocker*, ed. Maren Clegg Hyer, 121–38 (Woodbridge, Suffolk: Boydell & Brewer, 2016).

16. Adam Bülow-Jacobsen, "Writing Materials in the Ancient World," in *The Oxford Handbook of Papyrology*, ed. Roger S. Bagnall, 3–29 (New York: Oxford University Press, 2009).

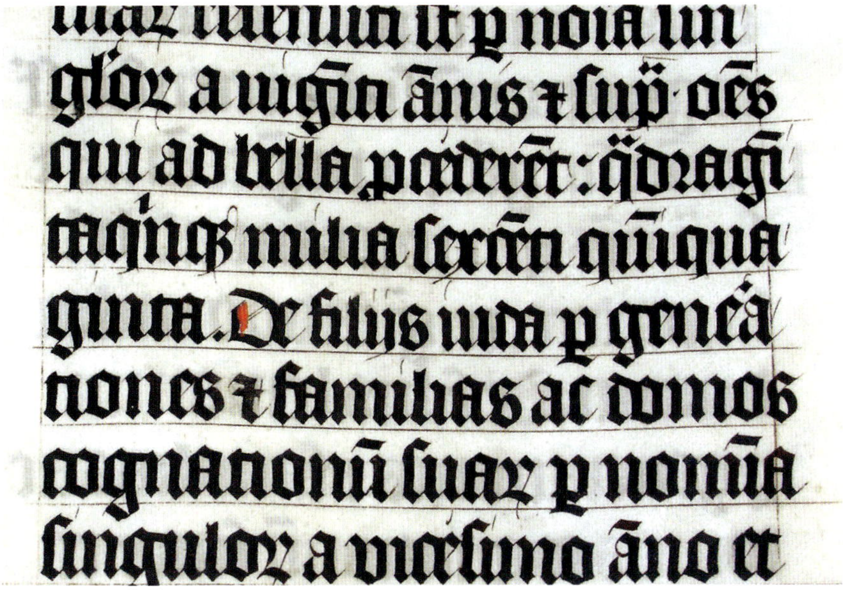

or Blackletter, another common nomenclature, even among the medievals, was *textualis* or *textura*, so-called because the densely packed script took on a texture like that of woven fabric.[17] It can be seen in this fifteenth-century example from England. Paleographer and calligrapher Stan Knight writes: "The characteristic lateral compression, heavy weight and angularity are here pushed to their limits, giving the appearance of interlacing—hence the name 'textura.'"[18] Here the metaphor of language as weaving moves from the syntactic connection of words to make meaningful sentences, to the visual stitching of lines, letters, and words to make a block of text with an entrancing and rhythmic pattern. This visual connection between woven fabrics and woven words in turn sheds light on the form of calligraphic art.

First, the weaver does not start from scratch; she has thread already at hand, threads that she must interlace to create the textile desired.

17. Albert Derolez, "The Nomenclature of Gothic Scripts," in *The Oxford Handbook of Latin Palaeography*, ed. Frank T. Coulson and Robert Gary Babcock, 301–20 (New York: Oxford University Press, 2020); Albert Derolez, *The Palaeography of Gothic Manuscript Books: From the Twelfth to the Early Sixteenth Century* (Cambridge: Cambridge University Press, 2003); Tim Ingold, *Lines: A Brief History* (London: Routledge, 2007), 71–73.

18. Stan Knight, *Historical Scripts: A Handbook for Calligraphers* (New York: Taplinger, 1986), D4.

Similarly, the calligrapher does not begin her art from scratch. She works with the shapes of the Roman letters, a tradition dating back millennia. The lineage of calligraphy from which Donald Jackson derives, the tradition of Edward Johnston, especially emphasizes the calligrapher's learning the history of Latin scripts as a wellspring for current creativity. Calligraphers often call their art "disciplined freedom": it is only through the discipline of learning this past that the scribe can truly embrace the freedom of creating the letters of the future.[19] Though Jackson created the script for *The Saint John's Bible*, the principles by which he created it draw from his education in letterforms from Roman antiquity to the present.[20] He analyzed historical manuscripts such as the eleventh-century Cnut Charter as he developed the script.

Second, just as the weaver can juxtapose contrasting threads, or interweaves warp and weft—and fashion them into a broader pattern in which they are harmonized—so the scribe can weave letters with a great deal of contrast into a harmonious fabric. Take the text accompanying the Ruth genealogy above. Like the medieval *textualis* scripts, these squat letters display great contrast between the hairline thins and the fat red thicks—even at times in the same letter, as in the *A* in which the left vertical is thin and the right is thick. Weaving together these starkly contrasting elements creates a more visually appealing whole than if the letters were all uniformly thick. Just as textiles represent "an endless urge to unite," this basic drive to "interconnectivity" shows itself in this Bible's desire to knit together different cultures, religions, and eras in Christian tradition, ancient, medieval, and modern.[21]

Third, like weavers, calligraphers create textures—the texture of a block of individual stitches, or letters.[22] While calligraphy classes

19. The phrase "disciplined freedom" comes from Raymond DaBoll (1892–1982), who coined it for a 1948 poster on calligraphy; see image in Carl Rohrs, "Raymond F. DaBoll," *Alphabet* 47, no. 2 (2021): 28. See also Sheila Waters, "Calligraphy in the Pursuit of Excellence" (lecture, Washington Calligraphers Guild, 6 August 1988), https://www.calligraphersguild.org/Resources/SheilaLecture1998/; Lloyd J. Reynolds, "Comments on Disciplined Freedom," in *Straight Impressions* (Woolwich, ME: TBW Books, 1979), 26–28.

20. Calderhead, *Illuminating the Word*, 74, 294–98; Donald Jackson, "Facing the Demons" (lecture, The Society for Calligraphy, 25 September 2021), https://youtu.be/Xk_5Xo09p_k.

21. Donald Jackson, personal communication, January 22, 2019.

22. See, e.g., Nicolete Gray, *Lettering as Drawing* (New York: Taplinger, 1982), 151–69; Christopher Calderhead and others, "The Poetics of Space," *Letter Arts Review* 32, no. 3 (2018); Victoria Mitchell, "Textiles, Text, and Techne," in *The*

often begin by learning letters one by one, the real magic arises when the letters are combined to make a whole, a block of writing with its own visual rhythm. A page of perfectly written letters with sloppy, inconsistent spacing between letters, words, and lines is, indeed, less appealing than a page of imperfect lettering with good spacing and a well-wrought texture. At times individual letters can be fudged a little for the visual harmony of the whole. And yet, at the same time, the pattern of the whole can only be as good as the sum of its parts:

> Knitting is given texture by the constant repetition of stiches, and different areas of texture can be made to contrast with one another. But just as a dropped stitch can ruin the texture of knitting, so a misshapen or badly formed letter can ruin the texture of a piece of lettering. Whichever alphabet is used, the creation of texture through the constant repetition of shape, form and movement is the basis of the calligrapher's art.[23]

These repeated shapes include the way in which the shape of the *o* is repeated in other letters such as *b*, *c*, and *d* in many Roman-alphabet scripts. This repetition is rhythmic, both for those creating patterns and for the eyes of those viewing them.

Jackson considered the text-textile metaphor for the design of the twin columns of writing that comprise the visual structure of all 1,150 pages of this Bible. Calderhead explains:

> Donald began to think more and more about the relationship between the texture of writing on the page and textiles. "This is another thread, so to speak, running through the Bible," he said. The texture of the column was meant to be like a subtly woven fabric. The viewer was meant to see the overall shape of the column as a large unit made up of the subtle variation of dense writing and clean

Textile Reader, ed. Jessica Hemmings (New York: Berg Publishers, 2012), 5–13. See also Marina Soria, "Weaving Words, Weaving Dreams," *International Exhibition of Calligraphy*, 19 September 2011, http://calligraphy-expo.com/en/about/news/weaving-words-weaving-dreams-by-marina-soria; Christopher Calderhead and others, "Text & Textile," *Letter Arts Review* 35, no. 2 (2021): 37–44.

23. Diana Hoare, ed., *Advanced Calligraphy Techniques* (Secaucus, NJ: Chartwell Books, 1989), 8.

> interlinear spaces; he didn't want the components to disappear but instead to sit on the page together, rather like a herringbone weave.[24]

Like the textura writing of medieval Gothic manuscripts, Jackson's blocks of writing balance order and playfulness, structure and spontaneity. This balance is shown on one of the many, many pages of pure writing in this Bible, in this case a page from Joshua:

יהושע

not let them see the land that he had sworn to their
ancestors to give us, a land flowing with milk and
honey." So it was their children, whom he raised up
in their place, that Joshua circumcised; for they were
uncircumcised, because they had not been circum
8 cised on the way. When the circumcising of all the
nation was done, they remained in their places in
the camp until they were healed. [9] The LORD said
to Joshua, "Today I have rolled away from you the
disgrace of Egypt." And so that place is called Gilgal
10 to this day. While the Israelites were camped in
Gilgal they kept the passover in the evening on the
fourteenth day of the month in the plains of Jericho.
[11] On the day after the passover, on that very day,
they ate the produce of the land, unleavened cakes
and parched grain. [12] The manna ceased on the day
they ate the produce of the land, and the Israelites
no longer had manna; they ate the crops of the land
13 of Canaan that year. Once when Joshua was by Jer
icho, he looked up and saw a man standing before
him with a drawn sword in his hand. Joshua went
to him and said to him, "Are you one of us, or one
of our adversaries?" [14] He replied, "Neither; but as
commander of the army of the LORD I have now
come." And Joshua fell on his face to the earth and
worshiped, and he said to him, "What do you com
mand your servant, my lord?" [15] The commander
of the army of the LORD said to Joshua, "Remove
the sandals from your feet, for the place where you
stand is holy." And Joshua did so.

6

Now Jericho was shut up inside and out
because of the Israelites; no one came
out and no one went in. [2] The LORD said
to Joshua, "See, I have handed Jericho over to you,
along with its king and soldiers. [3] You shall march
around the city, all the warriors circling the city once.
Thus you shall do for six days, [4] with seven priests
bearing seven trumpets of rams' horns before the
ark. On the seventh day you shall march around the
city seven times, the priests blowing the trumpets.
[5] When they make a long blast with the ram's horn,
as soon as you hear the sound of the trumpet, then
all the people shall shout with a great shout; and the
wall of the city will fall down flat, and all the people
shall charge straight ahead." [6] So Joshua son of Nun
summoned the priests and said to them, "Take up
the ark of the covenant, and have seven priests carry
seven trumpets of rams' horns in front of the ark
of the LORD." [7] To the people he said, "Go forward
& march around the city; have the armed men pass on
8 before the ark of the LORD." As Joshua had com
manded the people, the seven priests carrying the
seven trumpets of rams' horns before the LORD went
forward, blowing the trumpets, with the ark of the
covenant of the LORD following them. [9] And the
armed men went before the priests who blew the
trumpets; the rear guard came after the ark, while
the trumpets blew continually. [10] To the people Josh
ua gave this command: "You shall not shout or let
your voice be heard, nor shall you utter a word until
the day I tell you to shout. Then you shall shout." [11] So
the ark of the LORD went around the city, circling
it once; and they came into the camp, and spent the
12 night in the camp. Then Joshua rose early in the
morning, & the priests took up the ark of the LORD.
[13] The seven priests carrying the seven trumpets of
rams' horns before the ark of the LORD passed on,
blowing the trumpets continually. The armed men
went before them, and the rear guard came after
the ark of the LORD, while the trumpets blew con
tinually. [14] On the second day they marched around
the city once and then returned to the camp. They
15 did this for six days. On the seventh day they rose
early, at dawn, and marched around the city in the
same manner seven times. It was only on that day
that they marched around the city seven times. [16] And
at the seventh time, when the priests had blown the
trumpets, Joshua said to the people, "Shout! For the
LORD has given you the city. [17] The city and all that
is in it shall be devoted to the LORD for destruction.
Only Rahab the prostitute and all who are with her
in her house shall live because she hid the messen
gers we sent. [18] As for you, keep away from the things
devoted to destruction, so as not to covet and take
any of the devoted things & make the camp of Israel
an object for destruction, bringing trouble upon it.
[19] But all silver and gold, and vessels of bronze and
iron, are sacred to the LORD; they shall go into the
treasury of the LORD." [20] So the people shouted, and
the trumpets were blown. As soon as the people heard
the sound of the trumpets, they raised a great shout;
and the wall fell down flat; so the people charged
straight ahead into the city and captured it. [21] Then
they devoted to destruction by the edge of the sword
all in the city, both men and women, young and old,
22 oxen, sheep, and donkeys. Joshua said to the two
men who had spied out the land, "Go into the pros
titute's house, and bring the woman out of it and
all who belong to her, as you swore to her." [23] So the
young men who had been spies went in & brought
Rahab out, along with her father, her mother, her
brothers, and all who belonged to her—they brought
all her kindred out—and set them outside the camp
of Israel. [24] They burned down the city, and every
thing in it; only the silver and gold, and the vessels

[9] Related to Heb *galal* to roll
[4] Gk: Heb *devote to destruction.* Compare 7.21

WHOM · YOU · WILL · SERVE ·

We can see the rhythm of the pattern as we look up and down the page, the rhythm of white space and black space between the lines. We can

24. Calderhead, *Illuminating the Word*, 98. Calderhead discusses the prose Bible script in more depth on pp. 294–98.

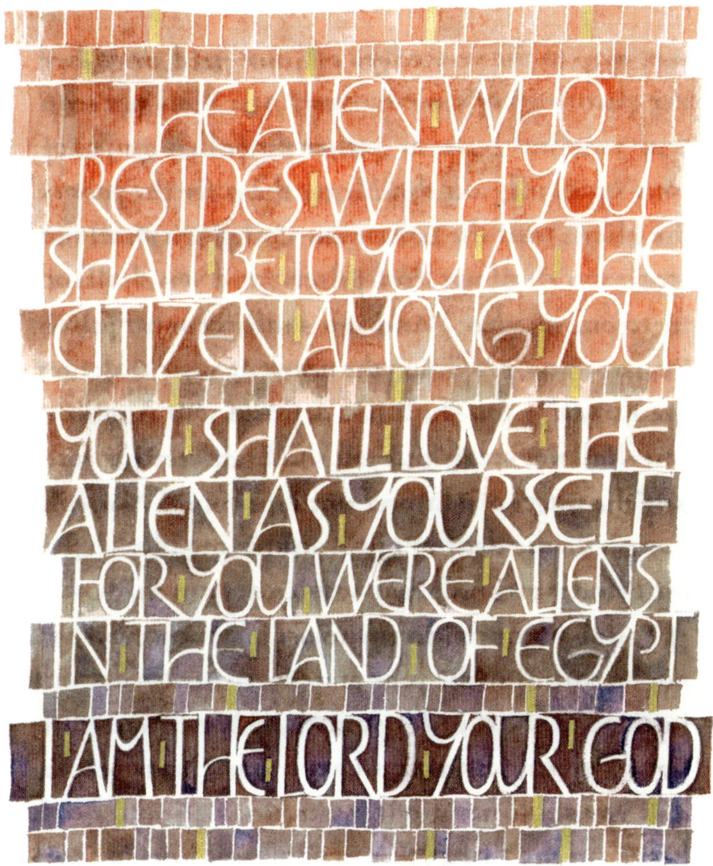

also see rhythm in the horizontal spacing between words and letters. In both cases, each line is slightly different because the letters are different.

The metaphor of writing as weaving, text, and texture also helps us better appreciate the text treatments running throughout this Bible, each with a different expressive script. In Sally Mae Joseph's special treatment of the injunction to care for the foreigner in Leviticus 19:34, she creates a dense texture by literally weaving letters together. Joseph not only creates harmony between letters but touches them to one another: "THE" in the first line and three letters of "GOD" in the last. The letters are also closely knit horizontally. Rather than employing extra spacing between words to demarcate them from one another, Joseph employs gold bars to separate words, allowing her to push them closer together to generate a more consistently tight rhythm. She generates more visual rhythm by alternating bolded and non-bolded

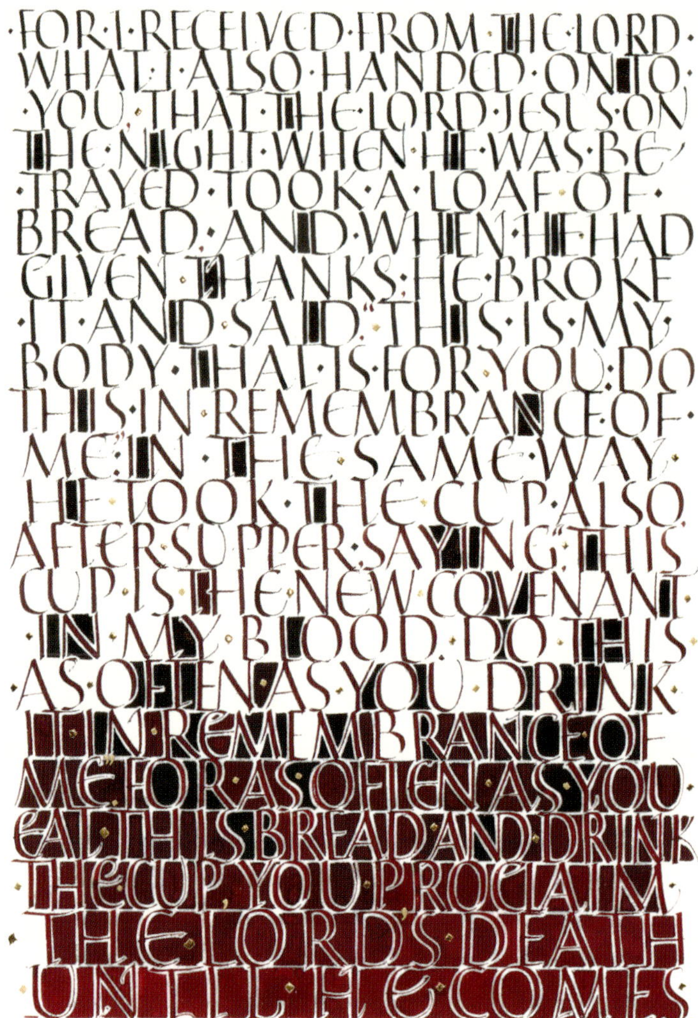

lines of lettering, using bold lines to emphasize the most crucial parts of the message: "I AM THE LORD YOUR GOD."

Thomas Ingmire's special text treatment for 1 Corinthians 11:23-26, a passage about the institution of the Lord's Supper, creates a different kind of visual rhythm as letters from each line touch the letters above and below them. Ingmire fills the bottom with wine red and justifies both left and right edges of the block of text, to create the effect of a glass of wine.[25] Under a magnifying glass, one might quibble with individual letters. The *R* in "LORD" at the end of the first line, for example, looks to me slightly cramped relative to the *D* and the *O*. (You are welcome to disagree.) But the line as a whole is right-justified with the two below. Our eye notices that harmony before it starts picking apart individual letters. Ingmire correctly chose to sacrifice a solitary perfect letter to preserve the texture of the whole block of text. Since each line touches the letters above and below it, our eye moves less left-to-right and more up-and-down, like wine pouring down into a cup. These are just two examples. Texture is crucial in many other text treatments in this Bible and in other works of calligraphy.

TEXTILES, REVEALING AND CONCEALING

Calligraphed words resemble clothes in another crucial way: both reveal and conceal. Most of the time, we do not look *at* the visual shapes of letters and words. *The Saint John's Bible* reminds us of this fact through its demand on us to look at its calligraphy. But usually we look not *at* written words but *through* them, using them as a visual means to an end: understanding the meanings of the words and sentences written. In the Song of Songs as in much of the world's erotic poetry, clothing is both looked at and looked through. The man admires his youthful lover's clothes, even as he imagines what is underneath them, what they artfully conceal. Likewise, several of the text treatments in *The Saint John's Bible* playfully conceal the meanings of the letters behind highly expressive and stylized forms. The calligraphers partially hide the letters' shapes to express some aspect of the words' meaning, or to slow the reader's attention.

In the Song, as in the Hebrew Bible more broadly, textiles are both admired for their own beauty and for what they artfully conceal. Like the lovely textiles in *The Saint John's Bible*'s illuminations, the Hebrew Bible supplies examples of textiles and clothes that are a sight to behold. We might think of Joseph's lavish tunic (Gen 37:3), the fine curtains and hangings in Ahasuerus's palace (Esth 1:6), or the curtain in Solomon's temple (2 Chr 3:14). The woman of the Song supplies another:

25. Sink, *The Art of* The Saint John's Bible, 298.

> I am black and beautiful,
> O daughters of Jerusalem,
> like the tents of Kedar,
> like the curtains of Solomon. (1:5)

Here it is not what is in the tent, or behind the curtains, that entices the eyes—it is the cloth itself. Other times, the male lover of the Song desires to look through his beloved's garments:

> How beautiful you are, my love,
> how very beautiful!
> Your eyes are doves
> behind your veil. (4:1)
>
> Your lips are like a crimson thread,
> and your mouth is lovely.
> Your cheeks are like halves of a pomegranate
> behind your veil. (4:3)

In these verses, the veil both reveals and conceals. It supplies a hint of what is missing, and lets the man's imagination run wild, keeping a part of her appearance erotically unknown.[26] Even when he praises her clothing, he is speaking euphemistically of her nude body. When he declares that "the scent of your garments is like the scent of Lebanon" (4:11), he is likely speaking of the scent of her perfumed body in the garments, not the garments themselves. Further, the nightgown lace pattern used in the Song illuminations, unlike a densely woven tapestry, reveals a great deal of what is behind it through its large holes. Yet still it conceals. Similarly, the reader of the Song of Songs never really knows what either lover looks like. Their appearance is, ironically, veiled in metaphors: "We never really 'see' the lovers."[27] They are both revealed and concealed.

In *The Saint John's Bible*, calligraphic designs by both Donald Jackson and Thomas Ingmire conceal letters' forms to express their meaning in various ways. In his illumination of the suffering servant

26. J. Cheryl Exum, *Song of Songs*, Old Testament Library (Richmond: Westminster John Knox Press, 2005), 161–62; Meik Gerhards, "Clothing and Nudity in the Song of Songs," in *Clothing and Nudity in the Hebrew Bible*, ed. Christoph Berner and others, 557–86 (London: T&T Clark, 2019).

27. Ellen F. Davis, *Proverbs, Ecclesiastes, and the Song of Songs*, WC (Louisville, KY: Westminster John Knox Press, 2000), 265.

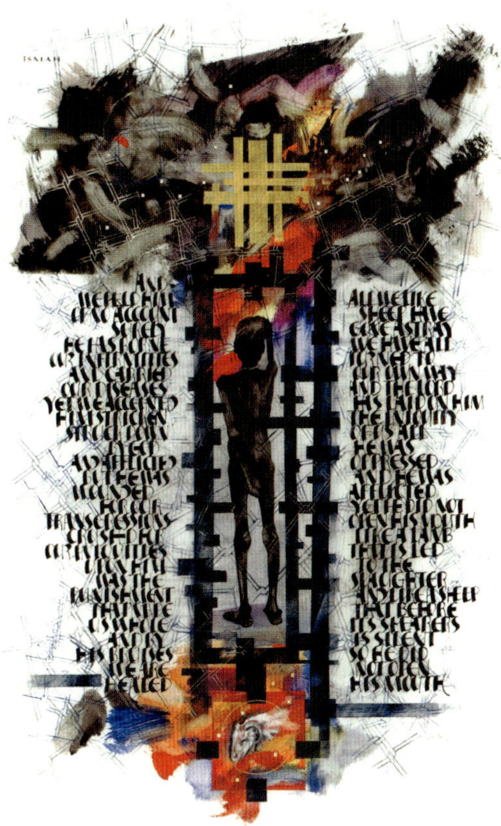

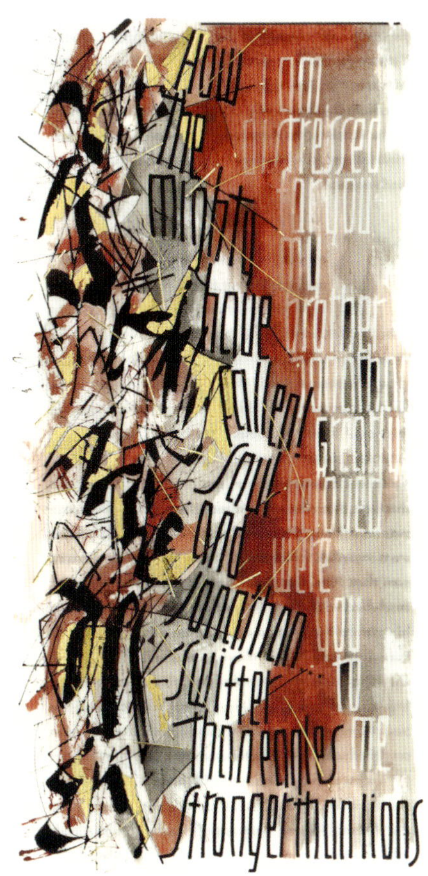

in Isaiah 52–53, Jackson incorporates images of modern-day oppression: the chain-link fence at the Guantanamo Bay detention facility, the Gate of No Return through which people were forced onto ships bound for North America in the transatlantic slave trade, a modern starving child. Flanking the child, Jackson writes lines from Isaiah's poem, beginning "and we held him of no account" (53:3). The letters are densely packed together, and their thicks and thins contrast wildly, making them hard to read as their message is hard to stomach. Michael Patella writes that "the black, block lettering forms an imprisoning wall."[28] By making these letters harder to decode, Jackson forces us to look more closely to read them and, thus, to look more closely at the world around us. Who might today's suffering servants be?

28. Michael Patella, *Word and Image: The Hermeneutics of* The Saint John's Bible (Collegeville, MN: Liturgical Press, 2013), 205.

The calligrapher can also conceal the letterforms to convey the words' emotional tone. Thomas Ingmire is especially known for breaking letters down into abstract patterns and lines that suggest another aspect of the words or that communicate emotions for which words do not suffice.[29] Sometimes the emotion is pain, as in his illumination of David's lament at Jonathan's death (2 Sam 1:1-27). At the left, Ingmire writes David's grief: "How the mighty have fallen!" (1:19b). It is only because of the more legible version in the center that we even detect actual letters in the riot of black and gold at left. This visual treatment of a grief-stricken cry suggests that David's pain is beyond words. It deconstructs into a jagged primal scream on the page. By contrast, Ingmire's treatment of two verses from Isaiah conveys the prophet's consoling message of hope:

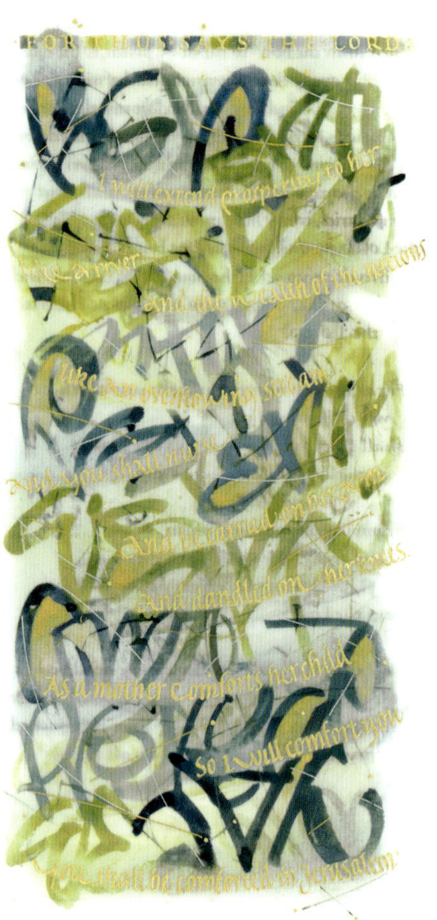

For thus says the Lord:
I will extend prosperity to her like a river,
  and the wealth of the nations like an overflowing stream;
and you shall nurse and be carried on her arm,
  and dandled on her knees.
As a mother comforts her child,
  so I will comfort you;
  you shall be comforted in Jerusalem. (66:12-13)

Again, Ingmire pairs legible lettering with what seems at first to be only abstract pattern or playful mark-making. At closer look, letters start to appear. Behind the "like" of "like an overflowing stream" is the *P* beginning "prosperity." Beneath the legible "and dandled on her knees" we can make out "comfort" and below that, "prosperity" and

29. Michael Gullick, *Words of Risk: The Art of Thomas Ingmire* (Norman, OK: Calligraphy Review Editions, 1989); Thomas Ingmire, ed., *Codici 1: Volume One, 2003* (San Francisco: Scriptorium Saint Francis, 2003); Thomas Ingmire, *Codici 2: Calligraphic Visual Communication Research* (San Francisco: Scriptorium Saint Francis, 2021).

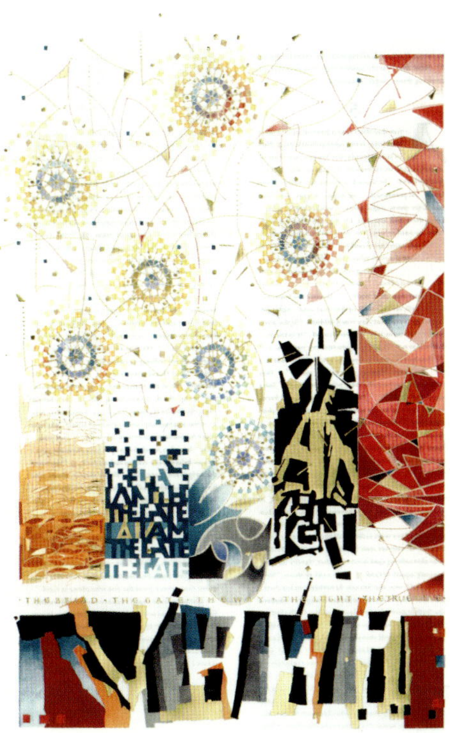

"wealth." These soft letters reflect the warm, maternal comfort of God's message. Ingmire created this shadow effect by wiping the letters with a wet cloth after writing them.[30] They also remind me of the graffiti Ingmire surely sees in his hometown of San Francisco. In graffiti art, letters are frequently made less legible for the sake of design. These soft letters evoke the exuberant hope of Isaiah's message.

Other times, the calligrapher can conceal the letters' forms for theological effect, or to make a point about the nature of language. Ingmire conceals the name of God in his visual anthology of the "I am" sayings in John. Beneath Jesus' proclamations that he is the bread, the gate, the way, the light, and the true vine, Ingmire creates a jagged and hidden "YHWH" using negative space. Many viewers do not catch this at first. The concealed divine name may allude to the Jewish tradition that the Tetragrammaton (God's four-letter name in Hebrew) is unpronounced and unpronounceable. Or perhaps this image suggests that God is hidden and mysterious, that we should be careful to proclaim what we see with too much confidence.[31] Ingmire again obscures letterforms in his illumination of Wisdom of Solomon 1:16–2:24, which tells of the folly of wicked men oppressing the poor righteous man. At top and bottom, Ingmire writes the orderly, rational words of Wisdom in elegant Roman capitals. But most of the image is taken up with those words' contrast: the folly of the unjust who do not follow God's teaching. Their words, "Let us lie in wait for the righteous

30. Thomas Ingmire, personal communication, June 1, 2017.

31. Daniel Train, "Picturing Words: The Gospel as Imaged Word in Thomas Ingmire's Illuminations," in *The Saint John's Bible and Its Tradition: Illuminating Beauty in the Twenty-First Century*, ed. Jack R. Baker, Jeffrey Bilbro, and Daniel Train (Eugene, OR: Pickwick, 2018), 111.

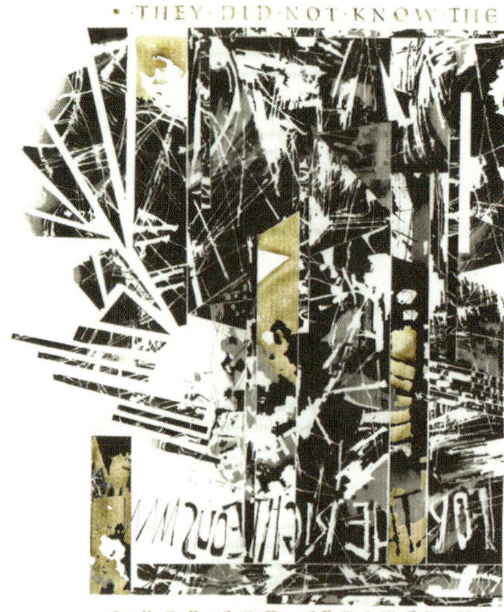

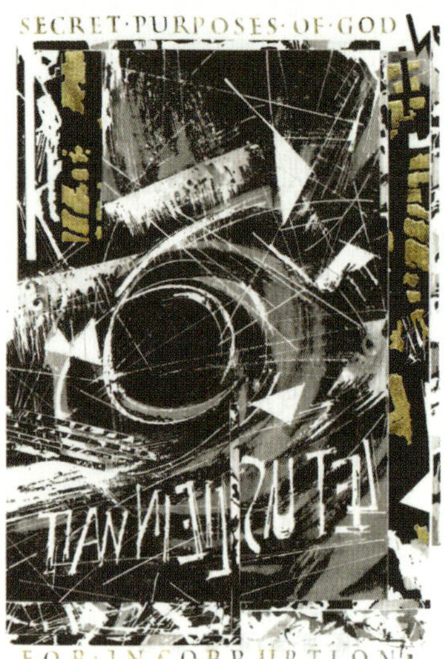

man" (Wis 2:21a), are written backwards, in cruel, jagged letters that appear more scratched than lovingly written. The backward letters may represent that these men see the world backward, or that they are the reversal of goodness. The image also plays on another line in Wisdom, a praise of Wisdom herself:

> For she is a reflection of eternal light,
> a spotless mirror of the working of God,
> and an image of his goodness. (7:26)

Perhaps these letters are backward because they are in a mirror. But this mirror is broken, a dirty reflection of wickedness rather than a clear one of wisdom. Ingmire's backward letters suggest the truth of their content.

Letters, like clothes, both reveal and conceal. Usually we want letters that reveal their meaning, that are legible and clear. Other times, letters serve best by artfully concealing their shapes. In doing so they force the viewer to look a second time, to ponder more, to slow down. The reader must use their imagination, just as the Song's man must use his imagination to peer beneath his clothed lover's garments. In both cases, the visuals are simultaneously revealed and concealed,

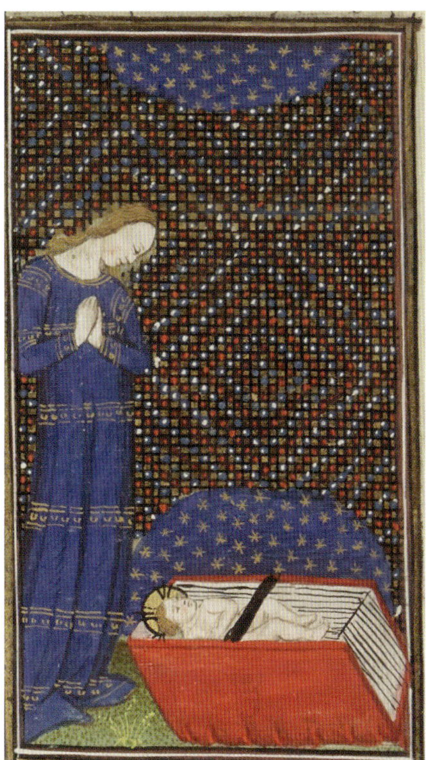

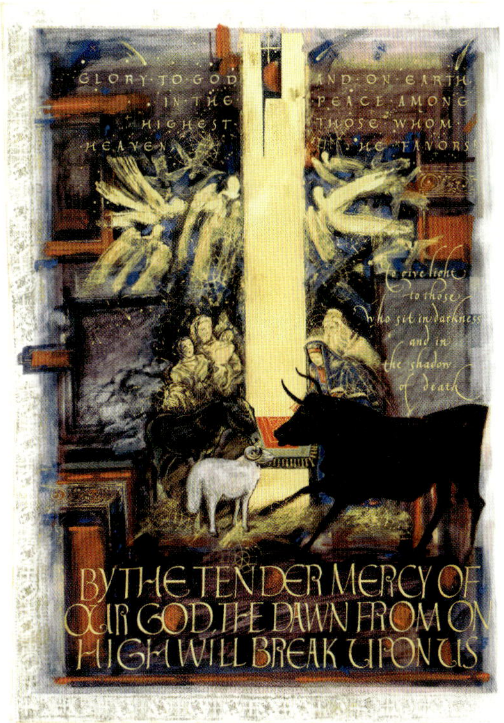

seducing the viewer's attention and perception. As one viewer puts it, "skimming for sense is stymied."[32]

MARY AS PARCHMENT, READER, AND SCRIBE AND BABY JESUS AS BOOK

So far we have seen Mary as a weaver, and that weaving is a metaphor for writing. It should not surprise us, then, to find that the child whom Mary knits in her womb is born as a book or in a book. Michael Patella explains that "in monastic culture, the Word becomes flesh in the *book*, and as such, it becomes an allegory for Christ's incarnation in Mary's womb, and the allegory is but one reason why the Bible is venerated."[33] Jesus is Word made Flesh made book, even in the womb. Mary, too, is wrapped in scribal metaphors.

32. George Greenia, personal communication, September 30, 2021.

33. Patella, *Word and Image*, 13.

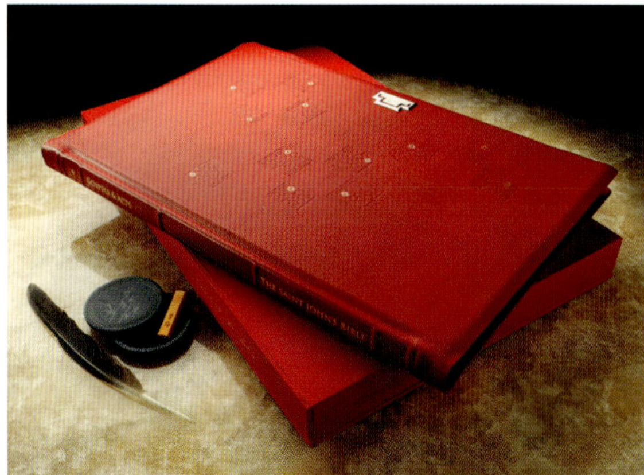

One medieval image of the baby Jesus as a book strangely parallels Donald Jackson's illumination of Christ's Nativity—to me, one of the most enigmatic images in *The Saint John's Bible*. This painting is found in an early fifteenth-century French Book of Hours, a small manuscript for private ownership designed for daily prayer.[34] The baby Jesus lies not in a manger (really, a trough) but in a book. As the Word he is, of course, to be found in a book; or perhaps the image suggests that he is the book. Perhaps this also explains the absence of the baby Jesus in Donald Jackson's illumination of Luke's nativity scene. Here the baby is not obviously present. Some suggest that we are to spiritually place him there ourselves. Yet to me, the empty manger's red square suggests one of the volumes of the Heritage Edition, the full-size reproduction of the original pages of this Bible.[35] Each volume of the Heritage Edition is bound in a bright red similar to that here. Jackson's nativity image suggests that the book is the physical presence of Christ; Christ is a book. Since Jackson created this illumination early in the Bible project, before the Heritage Edition really got off the ground, he may not have intended this image to suggest those bound volumes. Yet to me and to others, the resemblance is there, even if Jackson did not intend it.

Though Jesus is a book, Christian traditions rarely depict Mary as a scribe. More often she is the passive writing surface on which the Father or the Holy Spirit writes.[36] Bernard of Clairvaux depicts Mary's womb as the parchment upon which the Holy Spirit pens the Word made Flesh. In one homily on Mary, he reads Mary's "let it be with

34. Rohan Hours, Paris, France, BnF, MS lat. 9471, fol. 133r; see Laura Saetveit Miles, *The Virgin Mary's Book at the Annunciation: Reading, Interpretation, and Devotion in Medieval England* (Cambridge: D. S. Brewer, 2020), 17–18.

35. Susan Sink, *The Art of* The Saint John's Bible*: The Complete Reader's Guide* (Collegeville, MN: Liturgical Press, 2013), 244.

36. See Martha Driver, "Reading Images of Reading," *The Ricardian* 13 (2003): 186–96; Miles, *The Virgin Mary's Book at the Annunciation*.

me according to your word" (Luke 1:38) through the lens of physically writing words:

> May the Word who in the beginning was with God, become flesh of my flesh, according to your word. . . . Let it be to me, [a Word] not only audible to the ear, but visible to the eyes, one which hands can touch and arms carry. And let it not be to me a written and mute word, but one incarnate and living, that is to say, not [a word] scratched by dumb signs on dead skins, but one in human form truly graven, lively, within my chaste womb, not by the tracings of a dead pen, but by the workings of the Holy Spirit.[37]

Here, Mary's "your word" is not interpreted as "your will" but literally as "your writing." Bernard echoes a much earlier author, fourth-century hymnographer Ephrem the Syrian, for whom the tabernacle containing the tablets of the law prefigures Mary's womb:

> . . . The priest serves
> in the presence of Your Ark because of Your holiness.
> Moses bore the tablet of stone
> that His Lord had written. And Joseph escorted
> the pure tablet in whom was dwelling
> the Son of the Creator. The tablets were left behind
> since the world was filled with Your teaching.[38]

37. Bernard of Clairvaux, *Homilies in Praise of the Blessed Virgin Mary*, trans. Marie-Bernard Saïd, Cistercian Fathers 18A (Kalamazoo, MI: Cistercian Publications, 1979), 57.

38. Ephrem the Syrian, Hymn on the Nativity 16, strophes 16b–17, translated in Ephrem the Syrian, *Ephrem the Syrian: Hymns*, trans. Kathleen E. McVey, Classics of Western Spirituality (New York/Mahwah: Paulist Press, 1989), 151–52. See also Sebastian P. Brock, "Mary as a 'Letter': And Some Other Letter Imagery in Syriac Liturgical Texts," *Hugoye: Journal of Syriac Studies* 21 (2019). A special thanks to Jillian Marcantonio for suggesting these sources to me.

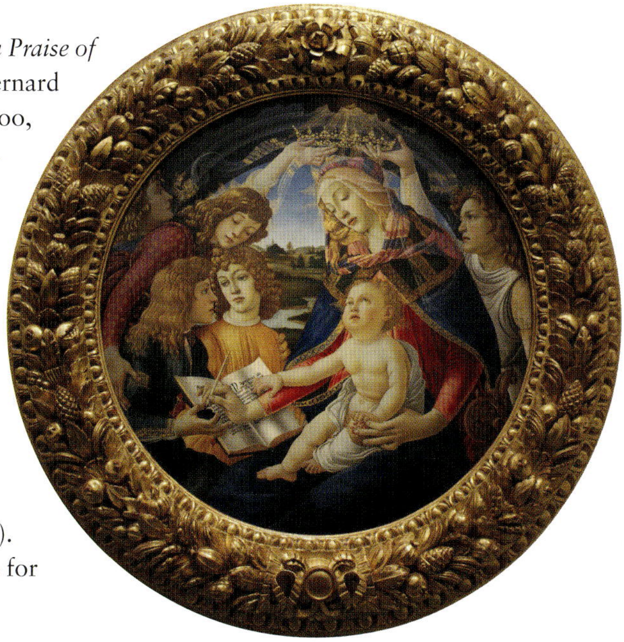

If Mary's womb is the tabernacle, then Jesus is, typologically, the tablets of the Torah given at Sinai. Mary's role is mere container. By contrast, a more active Mary appears in Sandro Botticelli's *Madonna del Magnificat* (ca. 1483), which puts the pen in Mary's hand.[39] This time Mary holds the pen and writes the Magnificat. Jesus holds her arm as if to guide her, suggesting that Mary's song of praise stems from divine inspiration; she is not author but copyist. This image of Mary as scribe is relatively rare in Western art, and as far as we know, Botticelli was the first to paint it. Modern readers may resonate best with this image.[40] It highlights Mary's agency as mother and her voice in singing the Magnificat.

Mary is thus not only parchment but scribe. She is a scribe who weaves words just as she weaves the child in her womb. We can now answer one question viewers of this Bible often ask: Why does a Catholic Bible such as this give so little visual attention to Mary? Outside the Nativity illumination in Luke, she does not appear again in the images. But in her connection with the Song of Songs and her imagery as a weaver, Mary can in fact be discerned in many places in this Bible. Mary weaves and writes the text, the Word made Flesh, the words that are written in the right kind of texture. Like a textile reveals and conceals, so Mary is concealed in images that reveal her at a closer look. And just as Mary is both concealed and revealed, so Mary Magdalene finds herself caught in the interplay between touching and not touching her Lord, her Word made Flesh.

39. Susan Schibanoff, "Botticelli's *Madonna del Magnificat*: Constructing the Woman Writer in Early Humanist Italy," *Proceedings of the Modern Language Association* 109, no. 2 (1994).

40. See Cynthia L. Rigby, "Mary and the Artistry of God," in *Blessed One: Protestant Perspectives on Mary*, ed. Beverly Roberts Gaventa and Cynthia L. Rigby, 145–58 (Louisville, KY: Westminster John Knox Press, 2002).

Chapter Five

MARY MAGDALENE TOUCHING THE WORD

The lace imagery in the Song of Songs illuminations alludes not only to Mary, mother of Jesus, but also to Mary Magdalene and her post-resurrection encounter with Christ in the garden in John. Mary's desire to touch him, to embrace him, is also a desire to understand his true nature. Just as she desires to grasp the Word, so we, touching the pages of manuscripts both medieval and contemporary, can clasp the feelings and bodily movements of the scribe writing the words. We can follow their gestures, their heartbeat and breath, their presence behind the page. Mary Magdalene's touch thus provides an analogy for how we touch and engage calligraphic art both medieval and contemporary.

MARY MAGDALENE AND THE SONG

Previously, we saw that the lace pattern in these illuminations connects the Song to the crucifixion illumination in Luke, and to the women present at the cross: Mary, mother of Jesus, and Mary Magdalene. In *The Saint John's Bible*, Mary Magdalene is visualized most prominently in an illumination of her post-resurrection scene in John. Both John's telling of this scene and Donald Jackson's image of it suggest that the Song's cries of love may accurately voice the sorrow and joy of Mary Magdalene finding her Lord.

Alongside the lace, the vibrant red palette of this double-page spread (and the previous) suggests Mary Magdalene. In this Bible and in Christian art, red often recalls Mary Magdalene, who is traditionally

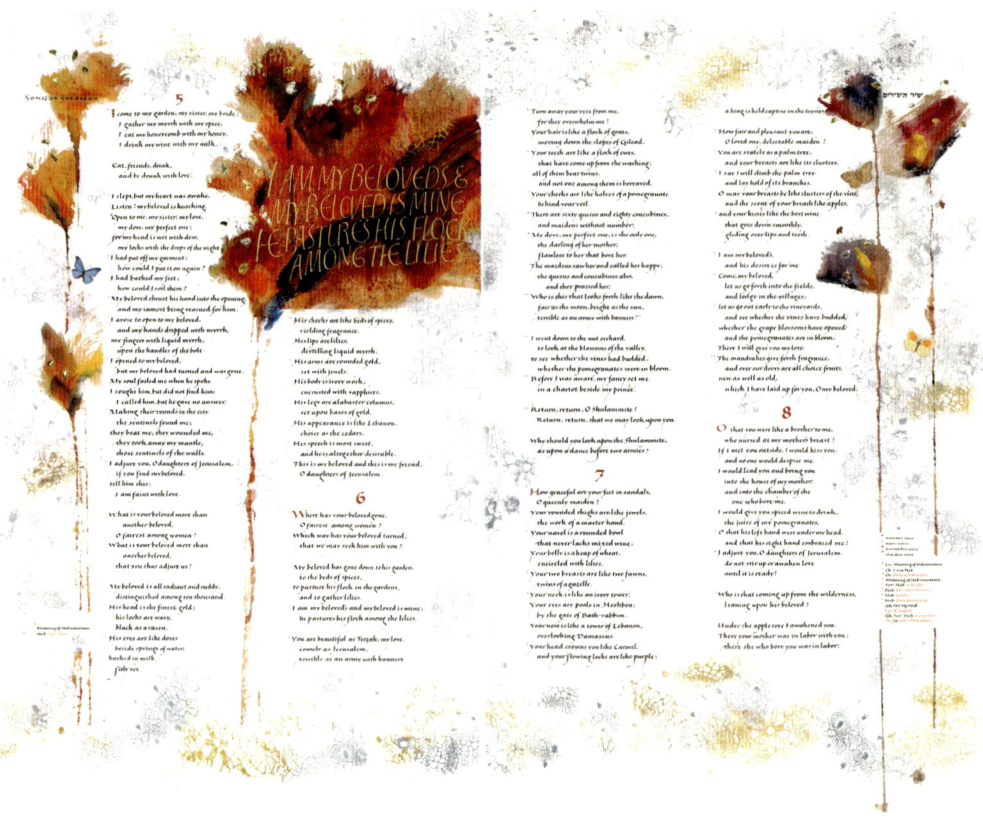

painted with red hair. The largest lily on the left-hand page evokes the red of Mary Magdalene in the illumination of her post-resurrection encounter with Jesus (John 20:11-18). Jackson's image of this scene reveals far more of Mary Magdalene to the viewer than of Jesus. Mary Magdalene is already marked here as a strange, outsider woman, with wild hair and red dress in vivid patterns. She is literally unable to touch Jesus. Her hand becomes translucent the closer it gets to him, "less solid and thus less suitable for clinging and control."[1] Just as Mary

1. James S. Cutsinger, "Patterns of the Glory: Christophanic Reflections on The Saint John's Bible" (lecture, The Frederick Sheffer Memorial Lecture, Colorado College, 19 October 2011), 20, http://www.cutsinger.net/pdf/patterns_of_the_glory.pdf. Jackson comments on his artistic process in creating this illumination, along with images of his drafts, in "Facing the Demons" (lecture, The Society for Calligraphy, 25 September 2021), https://youtu.be/Xk_5Xo09p_k. See also

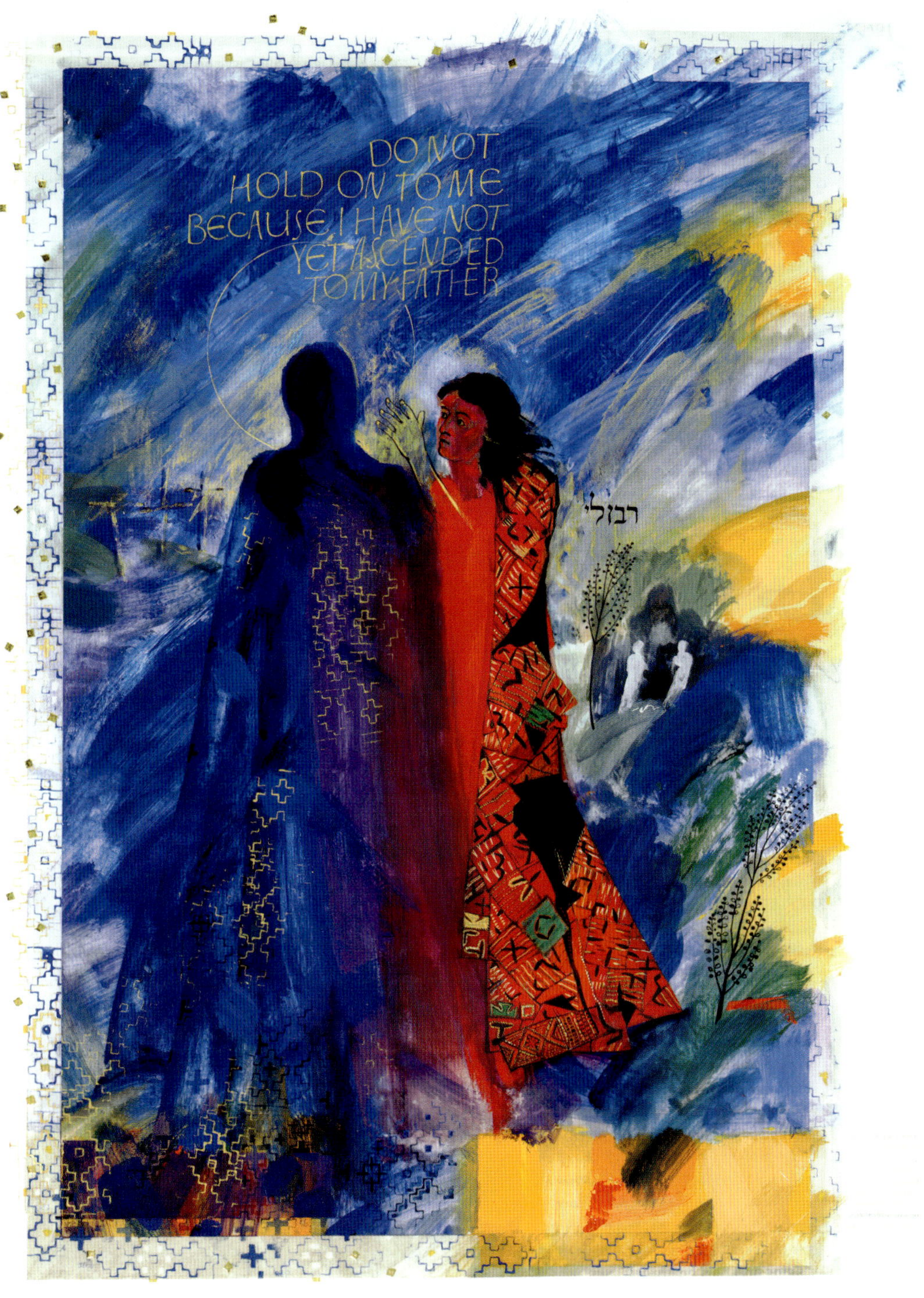
DO NOT
HOLD ON TO ME
BECAUSE I HAVE NOT
YET ASCENDED
TO MY FATHER
רבולי

cannot touch Jesus, we cannot see him. We espy only a silhouette from behind, its colors blending into the background. Christian artists have depicted this scene for centuries, in a genre of paintings known as the *noli me tangere* ("touch me not"), the Latin translation of John 20:17's "Do not hold onto me."[2] Like his predecessors painting this scene, Jackson visually depicts the tension between Mary and Jesus, her desire to touch him and her obedience to his puzzling demand not to.

Like Jackson's image, John's telling of Mary Magdalene encountering the risen Christ in the garden already alludes to the Song of Songs:

> But Mary stood weeping outside the tomb. As she wept, she bent over to look into the tomb; and she saw two angels in white, sitting where the body of Jesus had been lying, one at the head and the other at the feet. They said to her, "Woman, why are you weeping?" She said to them, "They have taken away my Lord, and I do not know where they have laid him." When she had said this, she turned around and saw Jesus standing there, but she did not know that it was Jesus. Jesus said to her, "Woman, why are you weeping? Whom are you looking for?" Supposing him to be the gardener, she said to him, "Sir, if you have carried him away, tell me where you have laid him, and I will take him away." Jesus said to her, "Mary!" She turned and said to him in Hebrew, "Rabbouni!" (which means Teacher). Jesus said to her, "Do not hold on to me, because I have not yet ascended to the Father. But go to my brothers and say to them, 'I am ascending to my Father and your Father, to my God and your God.'" Mary Magdalene went and announced to the disciples, "I have seen the Lord"; and she told them that he had said these things to her. (John 20:11-18)

Not only does the garden setting suggest the Song in general, but John's text alludes to the seeking and finding scene in Song of Songs 3:1-4:

> Upon my bed at night
>   I sought him whom my soul loves;
> I sought him, but found him not;
>   I called him, but he gave no answer.
> "I will rise now and go about the city,
>   in the streets and in the squares;

Jonathan Homrighausen, *Illuminating Justice: The Ethical Imagination of* The Saint John's Bible (Collegeville, MN: Liturgical Press, 2018), 64–66.

2. For a superb selection and discussion, see Barbara Baert and others, Noli Me Tangere*: Mary Magdelene; One Person, Many Images* (Leuven: Peeters, 2006).

I will seek him whom my soul loves."
    I sought him, but found him not.
The sentinels found me,
    as they went about in the city.
"Have you seen him whom my soul loves?"
Scarcely had I passed them,
    when I found him whom my soul loves.
I held him, and would not let him go
    until I brought him into my mother's house,
    and into the chamber of her that conceived me.

Both scenes involve a woman seeking her beloved by night. John's language of touching and grasping echoes the woman of the Song: "I held him, and would not let him go" (3:4c). John's allusion to the Song fits more broadly in that Gospel's portrayal of Jesus as Bridegroom (John 3:29).[3] However, unlike the woman in the Song, Mary Magdalene cannot hold him, cannot refuse to let him go. Jesus' words "do not hold onto me," which could also be translated "do not touch me," do not refer to mere touching. If so, why would he have invited Thomas to touch his side later in the same chapter? Rather, Jesus invites Mary Magdalene to let go of the relationship she had with the pre-Easter Jesus and open herself to a new kind of relationship with the post-resurrection Christ.[4] She must let go of the man she thought she knew.

Later Christian exegetes built on John's allusions to the Song, using the emotive language of the Song to voice Mary Magdalene's feelings in the garden. Gregory the Great (540–604) preaches on John 20:11-18:

> But Mary, *while she was weeping, stooped down and looked into the sepulchre*. It is true that she had already seen that the sepulchre was empty, and had already reported that the Lord had been taken away. Why did she stoop down again, why did she again long to see?

3. Ann Roberts Winsor, *A King Is Bound in the Tresses: Allusions to the Song of Songs in the Fourth Gospel*, Studies in Biblical Literature 6 (New York: Peter Lang, 1999), 35–48; David M. Carr, *The Erotic Word: Sexuality, Spirituality, and the Bible* (New York: Oxford University Press, 2005), 163–67; Adele Reinhartz, "John," in *The Jewish Annotated New Testament*, ed. Amy-Jill Levine and Marc Zvi Brettler, 168–218, 2nd ed. (Oxford: Oxford University Press, 2017), 216–17.

4. Brendan Byrne, *Life Abounding: A Reading of John's Gospel* (Collegeville, MN: Liturgical Press, 2014), 250–52; Marianne Meye Thompson, *John: A Commentary*, New Testament Library (Louisville, KY: Westminster John Knox Press, 2015), 413–18.

> It is not enough for a lover to have looked once, because the force of love intensifies the effort of the search. She sought a first time and found nothing; she persevered in seeking, and so it happened that she found him. It came about that her unfulfilled desires increased, and as they increased they took possession of what they had found.

Gregory takes an easily overlooked detail in John's story and interrogates it to discern Mary's motive. He finds in her persistent search a virtue for his flock to emulate. He continues:

> This is the reason the Church says of this person, her own spouse, in the Song of Songs: *Upon my bed during the night I sought him whom my soul loves; I sought him and did not find him. I will rise and go about the city, through its squares and streets; I will seek him whom my soul loves* [Song 3:1-2]. In her failure to find him she redoubled her efforts saying, *I sought him and did not find him.* But since discovery is not long delayed if the search is not abandoned, *The watchmen who guard the city found me, 'Have you seen him whom my soul loved?' Scarcely had I passed by when I found him whom my soul loves* [Song 3:4].[5]

5. Gregory the Great, *Homilies on John*, 25, translated in Gregory the Great, *Forty Gospel Homilies*, trans. David Hurst, Cistercian Studies 123 (Kalamazoo, MI: Cistercian Publications, 1990), 188–89. The Mary Magdalene–Song connection also appears in Song homilies and commentaries, such as those of Hippolytus, *On the Song of Songs*, 24–25, and Bernard of Clairvaux, *Sermon on the Song of Songs*, 7.8, 12.6. Translations in Hippolytus of Rome, *The Mystery of Anointing: Hippolytus' Commentary on the Song of Songs in Social and Critical Contexts; Texts, Translations, and Comprehensive Study*, ed. Yancy Smith, Gorgias Studies in Early Christianity and Patristics (Piscataway, NJ: Gorgias, 2015), 526–35. See also E. Ann Matter, *The Voice of My Beloved: The Song of Songs in Western Medieval Christianity* (Philadelphia: University of Pennsylvania Press, 1992), 167; Lydia Hayes, "The Experience of Touching Christ: Imitating the Virgin Mary and Mary Magdalene in High Medieval Biblical Commentaries," in *Sensual and Sensory Experiences in the Middle Ages: On Pleasure, Fear, Desire and Pain*, ed. Carme Muntaner Alsina, David Carrillo Rangel, and Delfi I. Nieto-Isabel, 33–44 (Cambridge: Cambridge Scholars Publishing, 2018); Ann W. Astell, "The Song of Songs in Aelred of Rievaulx's Liturgical Preaching," in *A Companion to the Song of Songs in the History of Spirituality*, ed. Timothy Robinson, Brill's Companions to the Christian Tradition 98 (Leiden: Brill, 2021), 161. For examples from the history of Christian art, see Susan Haskins, *Mary Magdalen: Myth and Metaphor* (New York: Riverhead Trade, 1995), 66, 219; Bobbi Dykema Katsanis, "Meeting in the Garden: Intertextuality with the Song of Songs in Holbein's *Noli Me Tangere*," *Interpretation* 61, no. 4 (2007).

Gregory uses the Song's effusive emotional language to flesh out Mary Magdalene's deep confusion and sorrow. He exhorts his hearers to be like Mary: persist in searching for Christ, and you will find him.

MARY AND THOMAS, GRASPING THE WORD

Gregory the Great ponders the Gospels using the language of the whole Christian Bible, bringing their scripturally shaped imagination to the text. Other medieval Christians read Mary's act of touching Christ, as well as Thomas's, as touching the Word made Book. For them, the Word made Book could be the Gospel codex or the tablets at Sinai. Like Moses, once Thomas grasps the Word of God, he can preach it to the people of God. The connection between the Song and Mary Magdalene's yearning to touch the Word made Flesh also suggests the scriptural significance of touching as understanding.

In the eleventh-century Bernward Gospels, made for Bishop Bernward of Hildesheim (modern Germany), a full-page illumination juxtaposes the *noli me tangere* scene at top with an image of Peter charging Mark to write his Gospel in a codex below. In the visual language of medieval Christian art, two images side-by-side often suggest a typology. Here, the illuminator parallels Mary Magdalene's touching Jesus with Mark touching the Gospel book. In this unexpected image, Mary Magdalene actually does touch Jesus, even as his touch pushes her away. This kind of touch-without-touching, art historian Jennifer Kingsley argues, reflects Jesus' dual corporeal and incorporeal nature—that even if one does touch Jesus' body, one cannot fully grasp Christ's divine nature through the senses alone.[6]

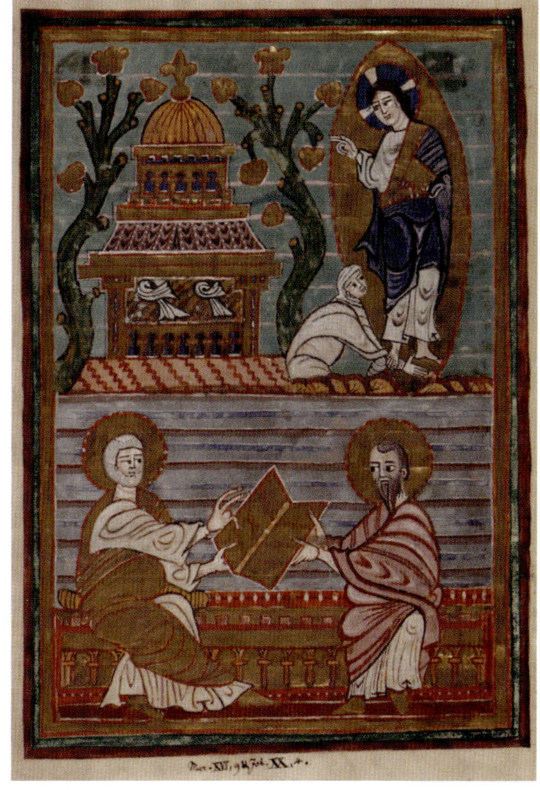

6. Hildesheim, Dom und Diözesanmuseum, Domschatz 18, fol. 75v. Jennifer P. Kingsley, *The Bernward Gospels: Art, Memory and the Episcopate in Medieval Germany* (University Park: Pennsylvania State University Press, 2014), 81–92.

(Ancient New Testament manuscripts themselves vary: some actually say that Mary did touch Jesus.[7]) Similarly, at bottom, Mark's touch of the book, the Gospel that is the Word made Book, reflects Mary's touch at top. Both Mary with her grasp and Mark with his pen take their own agency to touch Christ, whether Christ is present in human body or textual body. Mark's touch also reflects the somatic experience of books for medievals. Whether creating, handling, or reading such books, one could never quite forget their animal origins, even down to the hair follicles present on the parchment.

Other Christian readers juxtapose Mary Magdalene's touch and the touch of material Holy Writ through a third story: Thomas's touch of Jesus' wounds:

> But Thomas (who was called the Twin), one of the twelve, was not with them when Jesus came. So the other disciples told him, "We have seen the Lord." But he said to them, "Unless I see the mark of the nails in his hands, and put my finger in the mark of the nails and my hand in his side, I will not believe."
>
> A week later his disciples were again in the house, and Thomas was with them. Although the doors were shut, Jesus came and stood among them and said, "Peace be with you." Then he said to Thomas, "Put your finger here and see my hands. Reach out your hand and put it in my side. Do not doubt but believe." Thomas answered him, "My Lord and my God!" Jesus said to him, "Have you believed because you have seen me? Blessed are those who have not seen and yet have come to believe." (John 20:24-29)

Paradoxically, it is through Thomas's doubting demand for proof that we get his line "My Lord and my God," one of the loftiest christological credos in John. (You may recognize this as a line from eucharistic prayers in some churches.) This narrative comes later in the same chapter as Mary Magdalene's encounter with the risen Christ in the garden—so even the Gospel of John itself parallels Mary's desired touch with Thomas's actual touch.[8] Sixth-century Byzantine hymnographer and poet Romanos the Melodist connects Thomas's touch with

7. Elizabeth Schrader and Brandon Simonson, "'Rabbouni,' Which Means *Lord*: Narrative Variants in John 20:16," *TC: A Journal of Biblical Textual Criticism* 26 (2022).

8. Later Christian artists draw the same parallel; see, e.g., Haskins, *Mary Magdalen*, 179.

the physical form of manuscripts in "On Doubting Thomas," assigned to Thomas Sunday (the first Sunday after Easter):

> For the definition of this faith was signed surely for me
> through Thomas's hand. By touching Christ
> it became like a pen of a swiftly writing scribe [Ps 45:1]
> writing for believers the place from where faith springs up.[9]

Romanos suggests that Thomas touching Jesus' blood is like a pen dipping into an inkwell. The blood becomes the ink that writes a new covenant between God and the new Israel. Romanos further alludes to the psalmist's "my tongue is like the pen of a ready scribe" (Ps 45:1). The psalm compares scribing and speaking; here Thomas dips his finger into the inkwell of blood so he can preach.

An ivory-carved diptych made in Echternach in the late 900s parallels Thomas's touch with Moses grasping the tablets of Torah at Sinai. The diptych, an artform composed of two panels joined together by hinges, was an ideal vessel for Christian typological interpretation because it could juxtapose an Old Testament scene with a New.[10] This diptych juxtaposes Thomas's act of putting his finger in Jesus' wound with Moses touching the tablets of stone Torah written with a finger: "When God finished speaking with Moses on Mount Sinai, he gave him the two tablets of the covenant, tablets of stone, written with the finger of God" (Exod 31:18; cf. Deut 9:10). In both cases, a human is allowed to touch divine presence, whether in body or in stone. Just as Moses is famously an imperfect servant, striking the stone at Meribah without asking God for

9. Translation and comments in Derek Krueger, *Writing and Holiness: The Practice of Authorship in the Early Christian East* (Philadelphia: University of Pennsylvania Press, 2011), 179. Another example, this one visual, of a typological connection between Thomas touching Christ's wound and the believer touching the material Bible, can be found in David Ganz, "Touching Books, Touching Art: Tactile Dimensions of Sacred Books in the Medieval West," in *Sensing Sacred Texts*, ed. James W. Watts, 81–113, Comparative Research on Iconic and Performative Texts (Bristol: Equinox, 2018), 86–88.

10. William J. Diebold, "'Except I Shall See . . . I Will Not Believe' (John 20:25): Typology, Theology, and Historiography in an Ottonian Ivory Diptych," in *Objects, Images, and the Word: Art in the Service of the Liturgy*, ed. Colum Hourihane, 257–73 (Princeton, NJ: Index of Christian Art and Princeton University Press, 2003); Christopher Hughes, "Visual Typology: An Ottonian Example," *Word & Image* 17, no. 3 (2001).

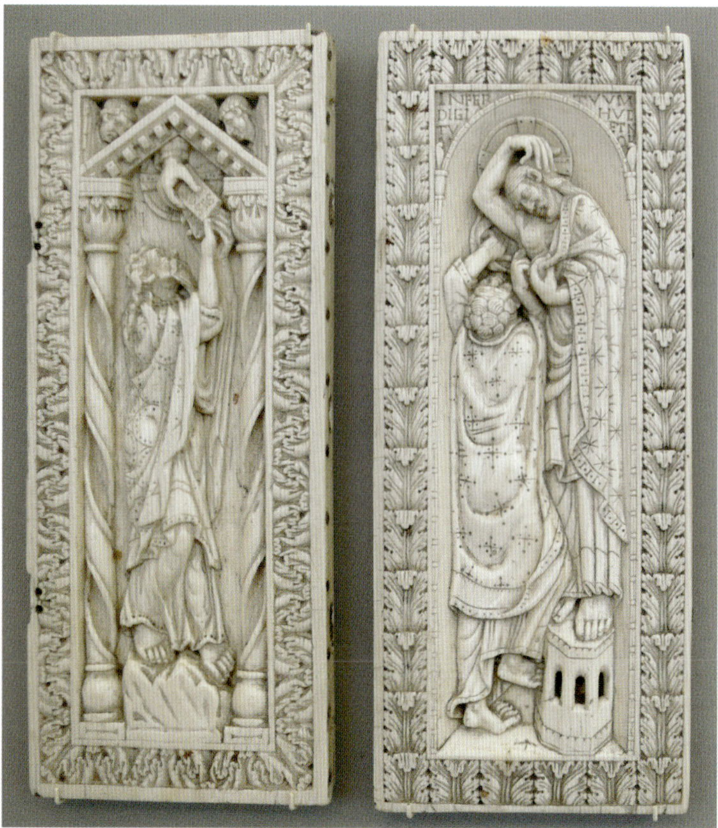

aid, so Thomas has often been chastised for his lack of faith in asking to touch the wound. In the ivory carver's theological reading, even though Thomas is doubtful, the fact that he *can* touch God's body displays the greater divine intimacy and mercy in the new covenant. The carver likely draws inspiration from Paul, who juxtaposed the Mosaic covenant written on "tablets of stone" with the new covenant written on "tablets of human hearts" (2 Cor 3:3). Thomas touches not a tablet of stone but a tablet of flesh. Though John does not name this detail, we can imagine he touched the blood (the ink) that flowed to and from Jesus' heart.

Just as Jackson's illuminations suggest that Mary Magdalene seeking Jesus is like the woman of the Song seeking her beloved, so these medieval traditions suggest that to touch Jesus is to touch the material form of sacred word, whether that form is book or tablet. Biblical metaphors draw an analogy between touching a tangible object and understanding an intangible idea:

Do not ignore the discourse of the aged,
for they themselves learned from their parents;
from them you grasp [*tiqakh*] insight
and to give an answer when the need arises. (Sir 8:9)[11]

The Hebrew verb here is commonly used for grasping or taking physical items. Biblically, grasping is understanding. In English we say we "grasp an idea." Touching a person is more intimate than merely seeing or hearing them. It requires us to place our own body at risk.[12] Mary Magdalene takes this risk and involves her whole self when she reaches out to Jesus, just as the Song uses images of taste and scent far more than the Hebrew Bible's usual sensory focus on sight and sound.[13] Like Mary's touching Jesus, like the woman of the Song's grasping her beloved, so touching a sacred text involves many senses. This holds true whether those sacred texts were Gospel books used in Christian communities or the stone tablets of Torah known only through the scriptures of Israel.

SEEING, HEARING, AND TOUCHING THE MEDIEVAL SCRIBE

Just as Mary Magdalene's desire to touch Jesus echoes Mark's touch of the Gospel book and Moses's touch of the tablets at Sinai, so medieval manuscripts mediate their own varieties of touch. Handwritten books allow us to reach out and touch the scribe. Many who have spent

11. Hebrew text from Pancratius C. Beentjes, *The Book of Ben Sira in Hebrew: A Text Edition of All Extant Hebrew MSS and a Synopsis of All Parallel Hebrew Ben Sira Texts*, Supplements to Vetus Testamentum 68 (Leiden: Brill, 1997), 32. Translation modified from NRSV. See discussions in Nicole L. Tilford, *Sensing World, Sensing Wisdom: The Cognitive Foundation of Biblical Metaphors*, Ancient Israel and Its Literature 31 (Atlanta: SBL Press, 2017), 105–6; Yael Avrahami, *The Senses of Scripture: Sensory Perception in the Hebrew Bible*, The Library of Hebrew Bible/Old Testament Studies 545 (New York: T&T Clark, 2012), 159–60.

12. Tilford, *Sensing World, Sensing Wisdom*, 95–98.

13. Annette Schellenberg, "Senses, Sensuality, and Sensory Imagination: On the Role of the Senses in the Song of Songs," in *Sounding Sensory Profiles in Antiquity: On the Role of Senses in Ancient Israel, Mesopotamia, and Egypt*, ed. Annette Schellenberg and Thomas Krüger, 199–216, Ancient Near East Monographs 25 (Atlanta: SBL Press, 2019).

time with a medieval manuscript can attest to the feeling that the writer is in the room too. An astute viewer can discern a great deal about a book's production from its script. After an afternoon spent looking at one manuscript, calligrapher Christopher Calderhead surmises:

> I suspect the scribe was working at speed. His writing indicates as much. Although the writer was experienced and skillful, his upright strokes are often not quite parallel. He has a tendency to lean backwards at times. I don't think this reflects a lack of ability. I think instead that the scribe was churning out pages on deadline.[14]

This scribe's hurried letters tell us about his stressed state and enable us to imagine his life. The scribe puts something of his essence on the page. Donald Jackson writes that when looking at a work of calligraphy, "each letter betrays both person and prejudice—the unique fingerprints of the scribe."[15] For medieval Christian scribes, writing the Gospels was often seen as a devotional act. Even anonymous Gospels copyists were seen at times as proteges of Mark, Matthew, Luke, and John. Though the vast majority of medieval Christian scribes remain anonymous, at times the twenty-first-century reader can find glimpses of their presence. The same is true for *The Saint John's Bible*, which supplies hints of its creators on the pages.

Although most medieval scribes remain unnamed, at times texts or images in manuscripts make them present and remind us of their labor. Sometimes a scribe added a colophon, an appendix that often supplies historical details of when, where, and by whom a manuscript was copied. Other scribes leave personal notes or prayers, such as the scribe Rodulfus (in chapter 2) who compares his line of writing to furrows in a field. Another comes from a manuscript of Gregory's *Moralia in Job* from Spain, copied in 945 by one Florentius:

> At Valeránica, in the honor, namely, of its patrons, saints Peter and Paul, great apostles and martyrs, I, Florentius, inscribed this book, at the command of the whole monastery represented in abbot Silvanus, when I had accomplished twice ten and two or nearly five and

14. Christopher Calderhead, "An Afternoon Spent Looking at a Manuscript," *Alphabet* 32, no. 3 (Summer 2007): 21.

15. Donald Jackson, "The Elemental Flow," in *Celebration of Calligraphy. Seventy-Five Years of the Society of Scribes & Illuminators*, ed. Society of Scribes and Illuminators, 4 (London: Crafts Council, 1996).

> double ten years of my little life. These things certainly being done, I copiously pray and amply request that you who shall read this codex might direct your frequent prayer to the Lord for me, miserable Florentius, that we might deserve to please Lord Jesus Christ. Amen. . . . Indeed it may be that this work will snatch me out of the fire so that I may deserve to gain the blessed kingdoms of the sky. Amen.[16]

In his prayer, Florentius thanks God for the strength to complete the work, beseeches the Lord to count his scribal labor as pious merit, and asks the reader to pray for his soul. As one medievalist surmises, "The names [of the scribes] are recorded [in the colophons], not for their own sake, but so that they will ultimately be inscribed in the *liber vitae*, the Book of Life."[17] The reader is reminded that in reading this manuscript, he is engaging not only the work of the author, Gregory, but of the scribe whose physical labor is less famed but just as necessary.

At times, carefully written letterforms praise the scribe and suggest that his superior care demonstrates broader spiritual virtue and sanctity. Fourth-century ascetic theologian Evagrius Ponticus writes:

> It is clear then, that he who is far apart from his friend can sense that one's intention through hand, finger, pen, ink, paper and all the other instruments which are at our disposition. . . . Just as someone who reads letters, by their beauty senses the power and ability of the hand and the finger which wrote them together with the intention of the writer, thus he who looks upon creation with understanding, perceives the hand and the finger of its Creator as well as his intention, that is, his love.[18]

Evagrius suggests that the written word speaks not only through what it says. Written words divulge something of the character of their

16. Translated in Catherine Brown, "Remember the Hand: Bodies and Bookmaking in Early Medieval Spain," *Word & Image* 27, no. 3 (2011): 271.

17. Jeffrey Hamburger, "The Hand of God and the Hand of the Scribe: Craft and Collaboration at Arnstein," in *Die Bibliothek des Mittelalters als dynamischer Prozess*, ed. Michael Embach, Claudine Moulin, and Andrea Rapp, 55–80 (Wiesbaden: Reichert, 2012), 64.

18. Quoted in Claudia Rapp, "Holy Texts, Holy Men and Holy Scribes: Aspects of Scriptural Holiness in Late Antiquity," in *The Early Christian Book*, ed. William E. Klingshirn and Linda Safran, 194–224, CUA Studies in Early Christianity (Washington, DC: Catholic University of America Press, 2008), 215.

authors. A scribe who is rushed, sloppy, lazy, or uninterested in their work will produce letters that do not glorify God. This elevation of the role of the scribe departed from pre-Christian Roman attitudes in which authoring texts was seen as lofty work, but the actual act of scribing them down and copying them was seen as menial slave labor. Early Christians took this trope as a sign of the evangelists' humility: those men did not make slaves write their dictation but actually penned their Gospels themselves.[19] But in their humble and difficult physical labor, evangelist and copyist alike displayed virtues of precision, piety, care, and even holiness.

The Lindisfarne Gospels likewise display the character of its scribe, Bishop Eadfrith of Lindisfarne (d. 721). Michelle Brown compares the scribe laboring in solitude on his writing to the hermit fighting spiritual battles in the desert. Eadfrith, who likely spent at least five years writing this book amidst episcopal duties, monastic daily life, and limited daylight, emulated the spiritual battle of St. Cuthbert, the solitary hermit whom he revered.[20] Ewan Clayton, taking stock of the many cultural and visual styles of the Lindisfarne Gospels, discerns an ethic of cultural reconciliation, empathy, and openness to change. The viewer can discern this value of mediating between cultural traditions in the Anglo-Saxon runic writing, the Latin text, and the further Mediterranean influences on this manuscript's visual styles. Such values are embedded in Eadfrith's Christian framework and inspired by Cuthbert's life. But for Clayton, they also hold value for all peoples and religious traditions.[21] As Jackson states:

> When we make things with our hands we put into them energy which comes from our innermost self. When we see and feel objects which were made by craftsmen long dead I believe we can still sense their energy lying beneath each brush-stroke or sweep of the pen, and we can respond to this energy as much as to the object's surface beauty or ingenuity of design.[22]

19. Krueger, *Writing and Holiness*, 33–62.

20. Michelle P. Brown, *The Lindisfarne Gospels: Society, Spirituality and the Scribe* (London: British Library, 2003), 396–408; Michelle P. Brown, *"In the Beginning Was the Word": Books and Faith in the Age of Bede*, Jarrow Lecture 2000 (Jarrow, UK: St. Paul's Church, 2000).

21. Ewan Clayton, *Embracing Change: Spirituality and the Lindisfarne Gospels* (Brighton, UK: Ewan Clayton, 2003).

22. Donald Jackson, *The Story of Writing* (New York: Taplinger, 1981), 13.

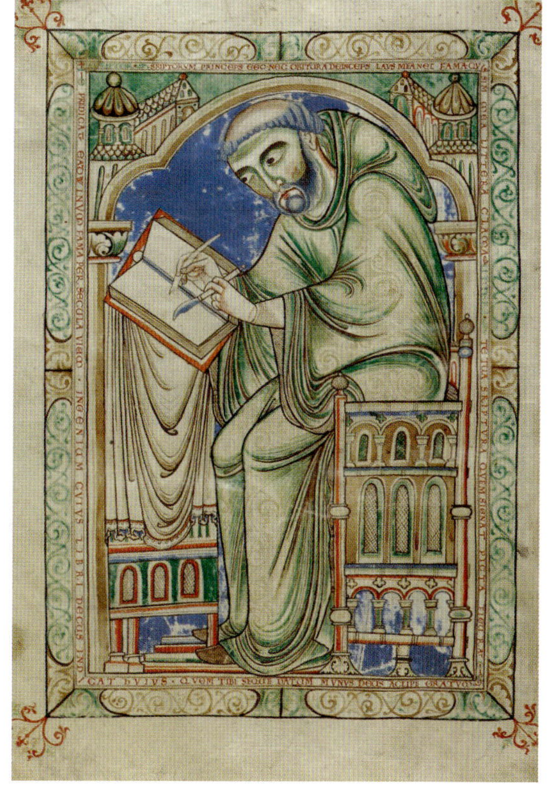

Manuscripts such as the Lindisfarne Gospels tell the stories of those who created them, those scribes' and monasteries' values and spirituality, just as much as their words tell the story of ancient Israel and of the early Christians.

Finally, at times the scribe's virtue echoes that of the evangelists who wrote the Gospels, as in the full-page portrait of Eadwine the scribe in the Anglo-Norman Eadwine Psalter (ca. 1150). Around the portrait of the monk-scribe is an inscription praising and praying for him:

> O scribe: I am the chief of scribes, and neither my praise nor fame shall die; shout out, oh my letter, who I may be, O Letter: By its fame your script proclaims you, Eadwine, whom the painted figure represents, alive through the ages, whose genius the beauty of this book demonstrates. Receive, O God, the book and its donor as an acceptable gift.[23]

Whether written by Eadwine himself or by a later hand, the dialogue between the scribe and his letters reminds the reader of the presence of the scribe on every page. The letters praise the scribe, just as biblically, God's creation praises God (Ps 145). Eadwine's scribal portrait is in turn based on an early medieval convention, found in both Latin and Greek manuscripts, of painting a portrait of each evangelist before

23. Cambridge, Trinity College, MS R.17.1, fol. 283v. Translation modified from Catherine Karkov, "The Scribe Looks Back: Anglo-Saxon England and the Eadwine Psalter," in *The Long Twelfth-Century View of the Anglo-Saxon Past*, ed. M. Brett and D. A. Woodman, 289–306 (London: Routledge, 2015), 302. Thanks to George Greenia for help with the Latin. More broadly, see Michael Gullick, "Self-Referential Portraits of Artists and Scribes in Romanesque Manuscripts," in *Pen in Hand: Medieval Scribal Portraits, Colophons and Tools*, ed. Michael Gullick, 97–114 (London: Red Gull Press, 2006).

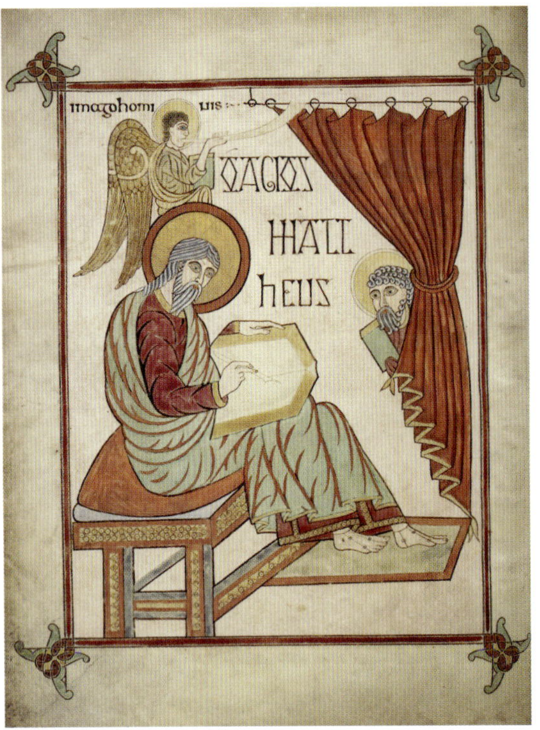

his respective Gospel.[24] For example, the Lindisfarne Gospels opens each Gospel with an evangelist portrait, such as the famed image of Matthew with quill and codex.[25] As Matthew writes, an angel above him trumpets divine inspiration; at his left is written "Saint Matthew" in runic letters. In the Eadwine Psalter, then, the scribe copying Holy Writ is seen as a reflection of the human authors who first penned it, who are in turn a reflection of God writing at Sinai (Exod 31:18; Deut 9:10).[26] Just as we would not have the Word of God without the authorial labor of evangelist and psalmist, so we would not have gospels and psalms without the scribal labor of copyists such as Eadwine and Eadfrith.

The monks of Saint John's Abbey hope that their manuscript will be viewed and admired in a millennium, just as the Lindisfarne Gospels are today. Future viewers will also find hints of the scribes and creators of this Bible in its pages. They may learn that each volume visually hints the names of this Bible's major donors.[27] They will see images of buildings from Saint John's University and its sister school, the College of

24. Dorothy Shepard, "The Latin Gospelbook, c. 600–1200," in *The New Cambridge History of the Bible: Volume 2, From 600 to 1450*, ed. E. Ann Matter and Richard Marsden, 338–62 (Cambridge: Cambridge University Press, 2012); Kathleen Maxwell, "Illustrated Byzantine Gospel Books," in *A Companion to Byzantine Illustrated Manuscripts*, ed. Vasiliki Tsamakda, 270–86 (Leiden: Brill, 2017).

25. See discussion in Brown, *The Lindisfarne Gospels*, 364–66.

26. Joachim Schaper, "A Theology of Writing: The Oral and the Written, God as Scribe, and the Book of Deuteronomy," in *Anthropology and Biblical Studies: Avenues of Approach*, ed. Louise J. Lawrence and Mario I. Aguilar, 97–111 (Leiden: Deo, 2004); Krueger, *Writing and Holiness*, 8.

27. Christopher Calderhead, *Illuminating the Word: The Making of* The Saint John's Bible, 2nd ed. (Collegeville, MN: Liturgical Press, 2015), 185, 201, 209, 223, 237, 249, 261.

Saint Benedict.[28] They will see oscillographs of the monks of Saint John's chanting the psalms in daily prayer.[29] They will view, in the margins, flora and fauna that are native to Minnesota, including the butterflies in the Song illuminations.[30] They will also see the scribes' errors, many of which the scribes chose to correct not through erasure but through creative illustrations. This lemur playfully holds the missing line of writing, as if about to hoist it back into place. Like the medieval manuscripts' colophons and scribal portraits, these visual details bring the circumstances of the manuscript's creation to the fore. *The Saint John's Bible* reminds its readers not only of the scribes' presence, but also of the monks who commissioned it and the donors who funded it. The Word made Flesh incarnates as a book in a concrete time and place, both timeless and timebound. We can reach out and touch that history.

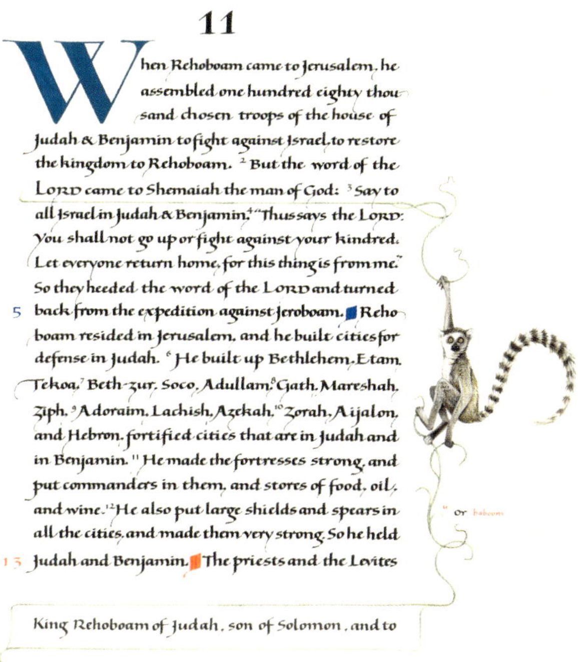
11

When Rehoboam came to Jerusalem, he
assembled one hundred eighty thou
sand chosen troops of the house of
Judah & Benjamin to fight against Israel, to restore
the kingdom to Rehoboam. [2] But the word of the
LORD came to Shemaiah the man of God: [3] Say to
all Israel in Judah & Benjamin, [4] "Thus says the LORD:
You shall not go up or fight against your kindred.
Let everyone return home, for this thing is from me."
So they heeded the word of the LORD and turned
5 back from the expedition against Jeroboam. Reho
boam resided in Jerusalem, and he built cities for
defense in Judah. [6] He built up Bethlehem, Etam,
Tekoa, [7] Beth-zur, Soco, Adullam, [8] Gath, Mareshah,
Ziph, [9] Adoraim, Lachish, Azekah, [10] Zorah, Aijalon,
and Hebron, fortified cities that are in Judah and
in Benjamin. [11] He made the fortresses strong, and
put commanders in them, and stores of food, oil,
and wine. [12] He also put large shields and spears in
all the cities, and made them very strong. So he held
13 Judah and Benjamin. The priests and the Levites

King Rehoboam of Judah, son of Solomon, and to

[11] or baboons

28. Homrighausen, *Illuminating Justice*, 8.

29. Calderhead, *Illuminating the Word*, 202–9; Susan Sink, *The Art of* The Saint John's Bible: *The Complete Reader's Guide* (Collegeville, MN: Liturgical Press, 2013), 154–56.

30. Sink, *The Art of* The Saint John's Bible, 12; Larry Haeg, ed., *The Nature of Saint John's: A Guide to the Landscape and Spirituality of Saint John's Abbey Arboretum* (Collegeville, MN: Saint John's University Press, 2015), 11.

THE SCRIBE'S DANCES AND GESTURES

A book or document written by hand lets us touch the writer in another way. When looking at *The Saint John's Bible* and other works of calligraphy, we can see and touch the presence of the scribe behind the page, reaching out to them through the inky record of their hand's motion on the parchment. Medieval art historian David Ganz describes peering at one manuscript:

> When I gaze at this, I imagine the inhale and exhale of the scribe: the exhale as she moves the pen downward in a confident vertical line, the inhale as she rides up the corner of her quill to make the delicate hairline exit strokes. I see a quill held confidently, with great precision. In the words of one anonymous thirteenth-century scribe, "three are the fingers that write but the whole body is laboring."[31]

Ganz's eyes follow the lines, recreating the scribe's feelings and bodily motions. In a lecture given in the late 1980s, summed up by Christopher Calderhead, Jackson, too, speaks of these inhales and exhales:

> We were to take one piece and dissect it. Starting at one corner of the piece we were to imagine ourselves in the position of the scribe, to picture ourselves making the strokes with the pen. We were to feel whether the pen was used confidently, or tentatively. We were to see the rhythm of writing, where it flowed freely, and where it broke down. As we looked, we were to participate in the making of the piece.[32]

When Jackson lectures to large audiences about calligraphy, he often invites them into the energy and motion of the artform by asking them to draw letters in the air, to feel the dashes and swoops of a flourished capital *A*.[33] Jackson speaks from experience: a core part of his artistic training was copying pages of medieval writing and miniatures directly from manuscripts, retracing the movements of the medieval scribes.[34] When we view calligraphy as Jackson suggests, we imagine writing

31. Ganz, "Touching Books," 81.

32. Christopher Calderhead, "Painting with Words," *The Scribe* 46 (1988): 4.

33. Donald Jackson, "Donald Jackson, Calligrapher" (lecture, EG Conference, Monterey, CA, February 1, 2007), https://vimeo.com/295077919.

34. For examples of this kind of work done by Jackson, see David Harris, *Calligraphy: Modern Masters—Art, Inspiration & Technique* (New York: Crescent, 1991), 52; Jackson, *The Story of Writing*, 90–91.

it all over again. We touch the scribe's body through the page and reenact her motions.

Through this lens, all handwriting belies the scribe's touch. Even the copyists of this Bible look back at their work and see their past mental states and struggles. Scribe Susan Hufton recounts:

> As we look back at the early pages [of the Bible], we can see quite noticeable changes. There are places where the writing is heavier or lighter in weight than is ideal. There are also pages that tell a story, in that they reflect the stresses and strains of life that we thought were successfully put to one side, before we wrote. As we look through the pages, we see a human document that changes and grows.[35]

As Hufton says elsewhere, "Handwriting exposes the inner person even when that is not the intention."[36] Her account recalls the metaphors of a garden that grows, or a pilgrimage that transforms the pilgrim over time. I am struck by the vulnerability with which she admits seeing flaws and frustrations that she did not even realize she had put into her writing.

Though every page enables the viewer to touch the scribe's presence, we can sense the scribes even more acutely in the expressive scripts of this Bible's special text treatments. Thomas Ingmire's treatment of God's disappointed accusation in Numbers 20 renders God's displeasure in jagged inky lines. At left, he writes the key phrase "You did not trust in me" (20:12) in rapid gestures, likely using a ruling pen. Ingmire recounted that after a few weeks sketching and drafting this

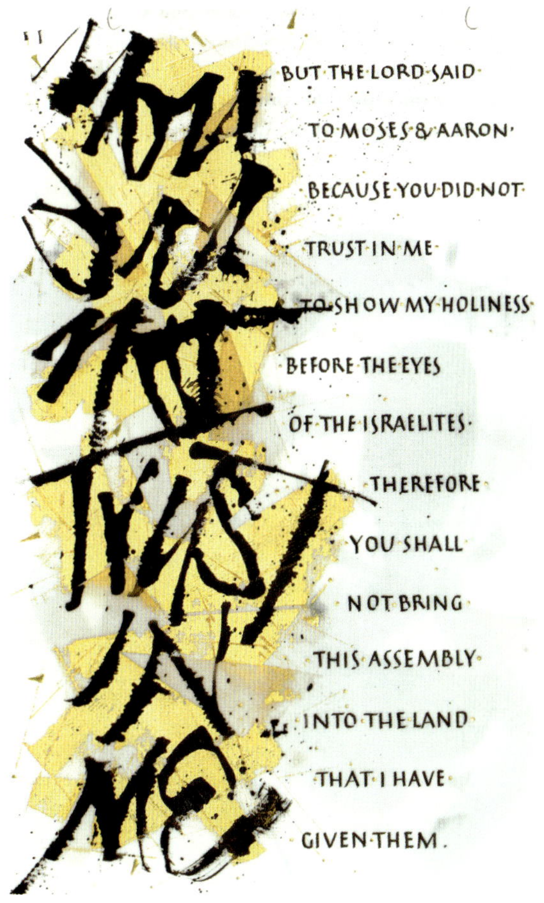

35. Susan Hufton, "Behind the Scenes: The Making of the St John's Bible," *Alphabet* 27, no. 1 (2001): 20–21.

36. Susan Hufton, "Writing by Hand," in *Pen & Print: The Legacy of Edward Johnston, 1906–2006* (Cambridge: The Edward Johnston Foundation and the Society of Scribes and Illuminators, 2006), 25.

work over and over, he did not feel he had gotten it right. Fed up with this, one morning he got up and first thing went to his studio, scratched it out in a few minutes, and then went out for his morning coffee.[37] In this piece I can see the vigor, the openness of a mind still fresh from sleep, the confidence to just get the piece done. The ink splatters around the letters, suggesting his arm's rapid and firm gestures.

For contemporary calligraphers whose works emphasize gesture, the aesthetic pull of letters lies not solely in their formal, precise perfection, but in the human touch, the emotion conveyed by each line, and the rhythmic dance of the pen recorded on the page. Many lettering artists who do this kind of work credit East Asian calligraphy as a major influence.[38] Ewan Clayton explains his gleanings from his art practice and from Chinese calligraphy:

> Calligraphy is a gestural art. In the hand of a master it appears spontaneously on the page, running 'with the freedom of a channeled stream'. Calligraphy is a skill, like that of the dancer and musician, which is developed over time by constant rehearsal. It does not arrive fully formed. The whole body must be apprenticed to this practice, so one develops a felt understanding of movement, a sensitivity of touch.[39]

For Clayton, writing is the transcript of the calligrapher's dance on the page: "Letters are the visible trace of invisible movement."[40] It is not surprising to see a similar inspiration from Chinese calligraphy in the work of Susie Leiper, one of the scribes of *The Saint John's Bible* who also created special text treatments. Many of Leiper's formative

37. Thomas Ingmire, personal communication, June 1, 2017.

38. Ewan Clayton, *The Calligraphy of the Heart* (Brighton, UK: Ewan Clayton, 1996); Izzy Pludwinski, *Mastering Hebrew Calligraphy* (Jerusalem: Koren, 2012); Gina Jonas, *Calligraphy as Art and Meditation: A New Approach* (St. Augustine, FL: Calligraphic Arts Press, 2019); John Stevens, *Scribe: Artist of the Written Word* (Greensboro, NC: John Neal Books, 2013), 87–90; Hans-Joachim Burgert, *The Calligraphic Line: Thoughts on the Art of Writing*, ed. Konrad Bauer, trans. Brody Neuenschwander, 2nd ed. (Berlin: Hans-Joachim Burgert, 2002).

39. Clayton, *The Calligraphy of the Heart*, 4. See also Ewan Clayton, *The Golden Thread: A History of Writing* (Berkeley: Counterpoint, 2014), 348–55.

40. Clayton, *The Calligraphy of the Heart*, 6.

years as a calligrapher were spent in Hong Kong.[41] She shows this sensibility in her treatment of Wisdom 7:26, found next to Sirach 35. Leiper writes with a pointed brush used for Chinese calligraphy.[42] I am particularly enthralled by the swoosh of the *g* in "goodness" and the bold contrast and angularity of the *n* in "reflection." She blurs the line between formal calligraphy and handwriting in this piece, which captures the skill of the former with the speed and personality of the latter.

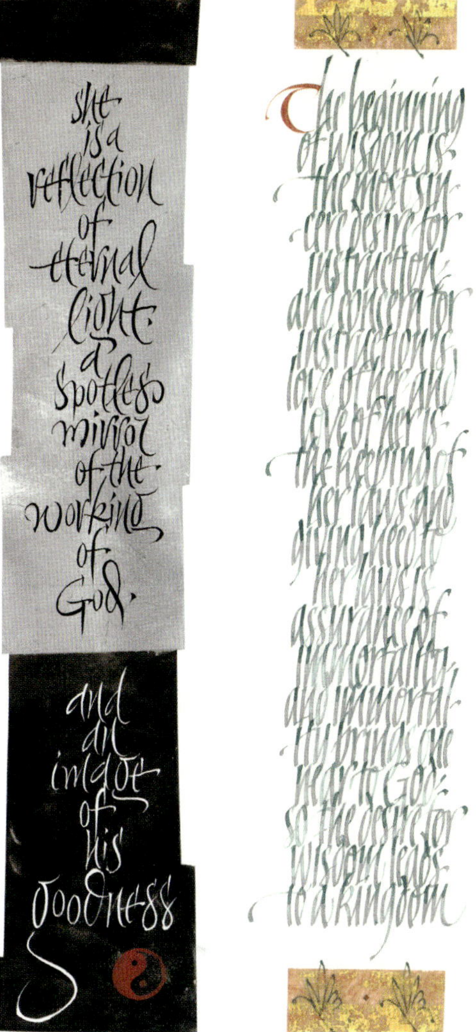

Often, scribes who want to emphasize their gestures employ thinner, more translucent ink to make their movements visible. Sally Mae Joseph does so in her treatment of Wisdom 6:17-20. Joseph's ink allows the viewer to see pools of pigment left behind in the darker areas of letters. Take the letters *m* in "wisdom" and "kingdom" in the last two lines. The tops of the letters are darker. I imagine Joseph writing these rhythmic verticals with speed, slowing as she came to the top of the letter to change direction, to move from the delicate thin push upwards to the bold thick downstroke. Alternately, I imagine that she perhaps lifted the pen to begin each downstroke, and the pool of ink at the top of the vertical line is the inky rush of a quill just touching parchment. Though I am not certain exactly what her *ductus* was for these letters, even imagining the possibilities focuses me on Joseph's gestures suggested by the lighter and darker patches of ink. The wet ink recalls the Song's garden fountain, well of living

41. Sink, *The Art of* The Saint John's Bible, 105; Calderhead, *Illuminating the Word*, 277.

42. Susie Leiper, personal communication, December 27, 2021.

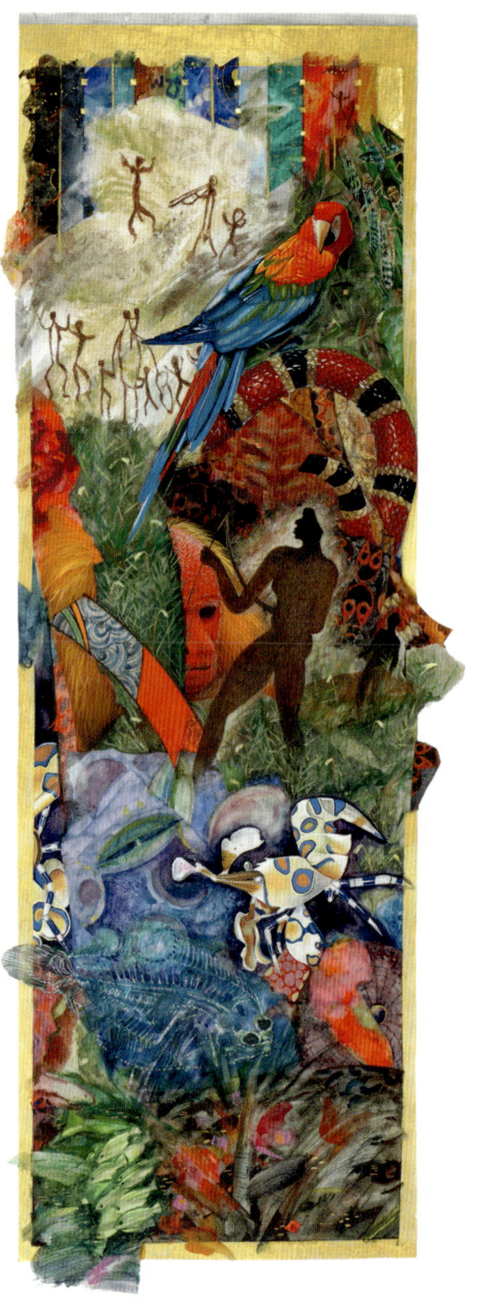

water, and flowing streams from Lebanon (4:15). Here, the ink flows from the fountain of the quill.

Finally, Donald Jackson places his body onto the page in a more unexpected way: his fingerprint on the vellum. In an image meditating on the Garden of Eden in Genesis, Jackson places his finger into the image several times around the prehistoric cave paintings at top left.[43] Jackson explains that he wanted to put something basic, simple, like the cave paintings, which themselves may well have been painted by hand. His prints contrast with Chris Tomlin's sophisticated portrait of the parrot. Elsewhere, Jackson states that the goal of the artist is "to put into each piece of work something of the joyful spirit which a child brings to painting and drawing."[44] What better childlike form of art than painting with humanity's most obvious brush?

Finally, like Mary Magdalene unable to grasp Jesus, we cannot touch this Bible. Many viewers of *The Saint John's Bible* certainly want to. In heavily gilded images such as the opening illumination of the Gospel of John and the crucifixion illumination in Luke, Jackson creates three-dimensional hills and valleys of gold leaf on the page. Jackson, a master gilder, creates this effect by building up layers of

43. Donald Jackson, "The Saint John's Bible: A Lifetime's Dream" (lecture, St. Mary's University, November 18, 2021).

44. Donald Jackson, "Gilding," in *The Calligrapher's Handbook*, ed. Heather Child, 177–98, 2nd ed. (New York: Taplinger, 1986), 177.

gesso (a binding agent) under the gold.[45] These images invite touch. We want to feel the bumps. But very few people get to touch this particular manuscript. When original pages from the Bible travel on exhibition, they always rest safely behind glass. Just as Christian tradition typically sees Mary Magdalene as unable to touch Christ—able only to imagine that touch through her visual and aural encounter with Jesus' visage and voice—in the same way, the viewer of this Bible can only imagine the tactility of the page. The conservationist's glass is our own *noli me tangere*.

As Donald Jackson once described an exhibit of his works: "Each piece was made from a feeling with a feeling; try and touch that and it will touch you."[46] Touching the manuscript is not just metaphorically touching the Word made Flesh. It is also touching the physical presence of the scribe, her "invisible sweat" on the page.[47] We appreciate calligraphy more deeply through following the scribe's hand, the dance of her body. We see her movement and her touch. We see her joy and her strain. But another layer of flesh comes between our hand and the scribe's: the dead skin of the dead animal comprising the page.

45. Jonathan Homrighausen, "Words Made Flesh: Incarnational, Multisensory Exegesis in Donald Jackson's Biblical Art," *Religion and the Arts* 23, no. 3 (2019): 259–60.

46. Jackson, "The Elemental Flow," 4.

47. Brown, "Remember the Hand," 273.

Chapter Six

CREATING LOVE AND CREATING DEATH

In Donald Jackson's final illumination in the Song of Songs, the woman of the Song declares that "love is strong as death, passion fierce as the grave" (Song 8:6b). Just as the woman speaks of love and death, so does *The Saint John's Bible*. In this chapter we turn to the matter of this Bible: its carbon ink made with flame, and its parchment pages made from dead animals. Donald Jackson and the monks' labor of love required death, flames, and skins, just as, in Christian theology, Jesus died for his friends out of love (John 15:13) and his death enabled God's love to be made known in the resurrection. Easter Sunday cannot happen without Good Friday. Death and love are always intertwined. The very parchment matter of this Bible is as much a part of its meaning as its words and images. And the love imbued into this Bible enables it to be set as a seal on its viewers' hearts.

SEALING LOVE AND DEATH

Turning to the final page of the Song of Songs in *The Saint John's Bible*, we encounter Jackson's text treatment of the climactic verse of the Song of Songs: the woman's weighty words on the power of love.

> Set me as a seal upon your heart,
> as a seal upon your arm;
> for love is strong as death,
> passion fierce as the grave.

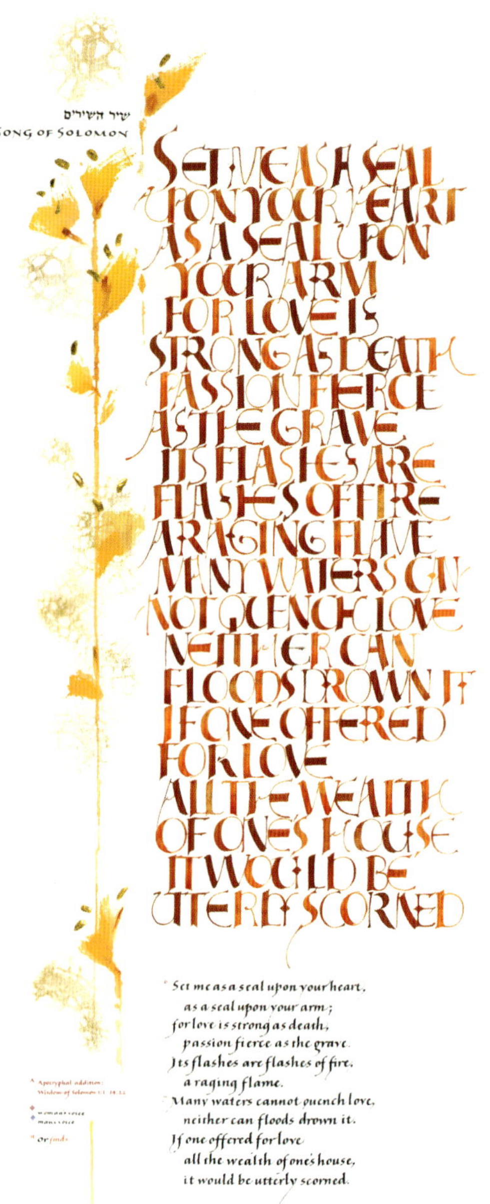
שיר השירים
SONG OF SOLOMON
SET ME AS A SEAL
UPON YOUR HEART
AS A SEAL UPON
YOUR ARM
FOR LOVE IS
STRONG AS DEATH
PASSION FIERCE
AS THE GRAVE
ITS FLASHES ARE
FLASHES OF FIRE
A RAGING FLAME
MANY WATERS CAN
NOT QUENCH LOVE
NEITHER CAN
FLOODS DROWN IT
IF ONE OFFERED
FOR LOVE
ALL THE WEALTH
OF ONE'S HOUSE
IT WOULD BE
UTTERLY SCORNED

Set me as a seal upon your heart,
as a seal upon your arm;
for love is strong as death,
passion fierce as the grave.
Its flashes are flashes of fire,
a raging flame.
Many waters cannot quench love,
neither can floods drown it.
If one offered for love
all the wealth of one's house,
it would be utterly scorned.

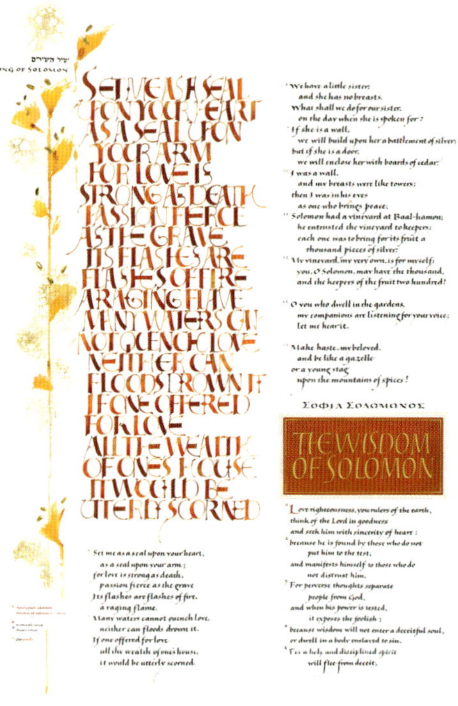
שיר השירים
SONG OF SOLOMON
SET ME AS A SEAL
UPON YOUR HEART
AS A SEAL UPON
YOUR ARM
FOR LOVE IS
STRONG AS DEATH
PASSION FIERCE
AS THE GRAVE
ITS FLASHES ARE
FLASHES OF FIRE
A RAGING FLAME
MANY WATERS CAN
NOT QUENCH LOVE
NEITHER CAN
FLOODS DROWN IT
IF ONE OFFERED
FOR LOVE
ALL THE WEALTH
OF ONE'S HOUSE
IT WOULD BE
UTTERLY SCORNED

Set me as a seal upon your heart,
as a seal upon your arm;
for love is strong as death,
passion fierce as the grave.
Its flashes are flashes of fire,
a raging flame.
Many waters cannot quench love,
neither can floods drown it.
If one offered for love
all the wealth of one's house,
it would be utterly scorned.

We have a little sister,
and she has no breasts.
What shall we do for our sister,
on the day when she is spoken for?
If she is a wall,
we will build upon her a battlement of silver;
but if she is a door,
we will enclose her with boards of cedar.
I was a wall,
and my breasts were like towers;
then I was in his eyes
as one who brings peace.
Solomon had a vineyard at Baal-hamon;
he entrusted the vineyard to keepers;
each one was to bring for its fruit a
thousand pieces of silver.
My vineyard, my very own, is for myself;
you, O Solomon, may have the thousand,
and the keepers of the fruit two hundred!

O you who dwell in the gardens,
my companions are listening for your voice;
let me hear it.

Make haste, my beloved,
and be like a gazelle
or a young stag
upon the mountains of spices!

ΣΟΦΙΑ ΣΟΛΩΜΟΝΟΣ

THE WISDOM OF SOLOMON

Love righteousness, you rulers of the earth,
think of the Lord in goodness
and seek him with sincerity of heart;
because he is found by those who do not
put him to the test,
and manifests himself to those who do
not distrust him.
For perverse thoughts separate
people from God,
and when his power is tested,
it exposes the foolish;
because wisdom will not enter a deceitful soul,
or dwell in a body enslaved to sin.
For a holy and disciplined spirit
will flee from deceit,

Its flashes are flashes of fire,
a raging flame.
Many waters cannot quench love,
neither can floods drown it.
If one offered for love
all the wealth of one's house,
it would be utterly scorned. (8:6-7)

These lines have been called the theological thesis statement of the Song, its *raison d'être*.[1] No doubt this is why *The Saint John's Bible* gives it special treatment. The colors of these letters match the "flashes of fire," in various shades of red. Rather than the quill he

1. Ellen F. Davis, *Proverbs, Ecclesiastes, and the Song of Songs*, WC (Louisville, KY: Westminster John Knox Press, 2000), 296–98; J. Cheryl Exum, *Song of Songs*, Old Testament Library (Richmond: Westminster John Knox Press, 2005), 3.

uses for most of the Bible, here Jackson uses a reed, a traditional tool in both Arabic and Hebrew calligraphy. The reed gives lines with a softer edge than the quill. Both the colors and the soft edges convey the "earthly, primitive feel" of this climactic statement.[2] Just as the poet evokes wild contrasts—love and death, flame and water—so Jackson creates wildly contrasting thicks and thins to give the piece the energy and life of a flickering flame. The letters hold and touch one another, themselves representing the tight bonds of love. The verses are paired with another flower, this time all in gold, with more blooms, and with more gilded flecks—suggesting, as gold always does in *The Saint John's Bible*, the divine presence infused in these verses about love.

The woman's proclamation that "love is strong as death, passion fierce as the grave" carries a double meaning. On the one hand, her words could mean: love is as strong as death, if not stronger. One might think of the poet's immortality through their words, words strong enough to imprint upon their hearer's heart.[3] The medieval liturgical theologian William Durand relates this verse to the durable metals and jewels used in wedding rings: "Just as diamond is unbreakable, so too is love unconquerable, and this love is even as strong as death."[4] In a Christian theological reading, love (Christ) has defeated death (hell), and those who are "set as a seal" in baptism have gained life beyond death.[5] Another take: seals persist in the archaeological record, because their material does not break down over time like papyri and parchment do. "Set me as a papyrus sheet upon your heart" would not be so effective. It is possible that the Song's poet was thinking about

2. Christopher Calderhead, *Illuminating the Word: The Making of* The Saint John's Bible, 2nd ed. (Collegeville, MN: Liturgical Press, 2015), 234; Susan Sink, *The Art of* The Saint John's Bible*: The Complete Reader's Guide* (Collegeville, MN: Liturgical Press, 2013), 126.

3. Exum, *Song of Songs*, 3. The idea of the Song as imprinting on its hearers' hearts was mentioned in a lecture by Jean-Pierre Sonnet.

4. Durand, *Rationale Divinorum Officiorum*, 9.11, translated in William Durand, *The* Rationale Divinorum Officiorum *of William Durand of Mende: A New Translation of the Prologue and Book One*, ed. Timothy M. Thibodeau, Records of Western Civilization (New York: Columbia University Press, 2007), 103.

5. Jean Daniélou, *The Bible and the Liturgy* (Notre Dame, IN: University of Notre Dame Press, 1956), 201–2; Karl Shuve, *The Song of Songs and the Fashioning of Identity in Early Latin Christianity* (Oxford: Oxford University Press, 2016), 40, 153; Paul J. Griffiths, *Song of Songs*, Brazos Theological Commentary on the Bible (Grand Rapids: Brazos Press, 2011), 162–65.

ancient practices of burying the dead with their seal, or a belief that seals warded off illness and death.[6] Whether erotic human love or the love of God, love outmatches and conquers death.

"Strong as death" and "fierce as the grave" could, however, mean something quite different: love is like death in its ability to cause human pain and agony. The woman of the Song certainly suffers when she cannot find her beloved, when the watchmen of the city beat her (5:7). This partly explains why she warns the young women of Jerusalem to "not stir up or awaken love until it is ready!" (2:7). The Hebrew terms in 8:6-7 echo both God's wrath as fire and God's jealousy of Israel worshipping other gods:

> for love is strong as death,
> passion (*qinah*) fierce as the grave (*sheol*). (Song 8:6b)

> They made me jealous (*qin'uni*) with what is no god,
> provoked me with their idols.
> So I will make them jealous (*'aqni'em*) with what is no people,
> provoke them with a foolish nation.
> For a fire (*'esh*) is kindled by my anger,
> and burns to the depths of Sheol;
> it devours the earth and its increase,
> and sets on fire the foundations of the mountains. (Deut 32:21-22)[7]

The Song's "passion" (*qinah*) and Deuteronomy's "jealous" (*qin'uni*) and "make them jealous" (*'aqni'em*) are all from the same root. The Song also uses the odd term *sheol*, the place of the dead, which the Hebrew Bible leaves remarkably undefined. God's love is not impersonal or vague, but intimate and jealous. God has staked a claim on Israel. Israel's prophets, most notably Hosea (1–2), elaborate at great length that God is Israel's husband, furious at his wife's adultery with other gods and other nations. Just as a seal closes a letter or legal contract, so this love seals off each lover from all others, making the woman "a garden locked, a fountain sealed" (4:12b). Psychologically, love's con-

6. William W. Hallo, "For Love Is Strong as Death," *Journal of the Ancient Near Eastern Society* 22 (1993); William W. Hallo, "'As the Seal upon Thine Arm': Glyptic Metaphors in the Biblical World," in *Ancient Seals and the Bible*, ed. Leonard Gorelick and Elizabeth Williams-Forte, 7–17 (Malibu, CA: Undena Publications, 1983).

7. Davis, *Proverbs, Ecclesiastes, and the Song of Songs*, 298.

suming passion dissolves the boundaries between lover and beloved, itself a kind of a death of the individual.[8] Perhaps love's flame is so dangerous and all-consuming that it must be a seal made of clay or stone to survive the heat that would destroy papyrus or parchment.[9] Like the Song's seal, the very parchment matter of *The Saint John's Bible* is as much a part of its meaning as its words and images.

FLAMES OF LOVE AND DEATH

If Jesus is theologically the Word made Flesh, then *The Saint John's Bible*, like its medieval parchment predecessors, is Flesh made Word: the flesh of animals, slaughtered for the sake of the Gospel. Medieval authors suggested many allegories around the materiality of parchment and the process of preparing it and writing on it.[10] Though the metaphor of Christ as a book derives from biblical sources (for example, John 1:1-18; 2 Cor 3:2-3), it is only made explicit in later Christian authors; over time, the metaphor's mappings become more detailed and graphic. Jesus is Word made Flesh made book, and that book requires more death than just his.

Writing a Bible on animal skins requires much quantity of death. Cattle skins that are made into high-quality writing vellum must come from cows who died young; older cows have skin that bears the blemishes of old age, skin that is often too thick for a book. In finding skins, Jackson and his team had to find the right balance: calves old enough to supply skins large enough for the pages of this Bible but

8. Francis Landy, *Paradoxes of Paradise: Identity and Difference in the Song of Songs*, 2nd ed. (Sheffield: Sheffield Academic Press, 2011), 115–28.

9. I am indebted to Marc Brettler for this point, made in his Song of Songs seminar at Duke University in 2020.

10. There are many medieval primary sources here, from which I draw only a few. Useful surveys can be found in Sarah Noonan, "Bodies of Parchment: Representing the Passion and Reading Manuscripts in Late Medieval England" (PhD diss., Washington University in St. Louis, 2010); Martha Driver, "Reading Images of Reading," *The Ricardian* 13 (2003); Marlene V. Hennessy, "The Social Life of a Manuscript Metaphor: Christ's Blood as Ink," in *The Social Life of Illumination: Manuscripts, Images, and Communities in the Late Middle Ages*, ed. Joyce Coleman, Mark Cruse, and Kathryn A. Smith, 17–52, Medieval Texts and Cultures of Northern Europe 21 (Turnhout: Brepols, 2013); Jager, *The Book of the Heart*.

young enough that the skins were still unblemished and smooth.[11] While I do not know how many calves had to be slaughtered for this Bible, estimates have been made for similarly large medieval Bibles. Codex Amiatinus, with its 1,030 leaves each roughly 19 × 13 inches, required, by one estimate, slightly over five hundred sheep's deaths.[12] *The Saint John's Bible* has 1,050 pages, each measuring roughly 24 × 12 inches. While contemplating such vast numbers, consider, too, this Anglo-Saxon riddle appearing in a tenth-century anthology, which speaks in the voice of a personified page:

> I am the scalp of myself, skinned by my foeman:
> robbed of my strength, he steeped and soaked me,
> dipped me in water, whipped me out again,
> set me in the sun. I soon lost there
> the hair I had had.
> The hard edge
> of a keen-ground knife cuts me now,
> fingers fold me, and a fowl's pride
> drives its treasure trail across me,
> bounds again over the brown rim,
> sucks the wood-dye, steps again on me,
> makes his black marks.
> A man then hides me
> between stout shield-boards stretched with hide,
> fits me with gold. There glows on me
> the jewelsmith's handiwork held with wires.

After describing the horrors it has endured, the animal skin hopes that its death was not to no end:

> Let these royal enrichments and this red dye
> and splendid settings spread the glory
> of the Protector of peoples—and not plague the fool.[13]

11. Mark L'Argent, "On the Surface: Preparing the Vellum for the St John's Bible," *Alphabet* 27, no. 3 (2002): 7.

12. Bruce Holsinger, "Of Pigs and Parchment: Medieval Studies and the Coming of the Animal," *Proceedings of the Modern Language Association* 124, no. 2 (2009): 619.

13. This is only an excerpt from the full riddle. Michael Alexander, ed., *The Earliest English Poems*, 3rd ed., Penguin Classics (London: Penguin Books, 1991), 72. See discussion in Holsinger, "Of Pigs and Parchment," 621–22.

This riddle reminds the reader that every page was once an animal skin. Today's viewers of these medieval manuscripts tend to overlook this fact, focusing on the text over its matter, as did many medievals.[14] At the same time, many today, out of a concern for the treatment of animals, feel ethically squeamish with the practice of writing on vellum. Whatever your conclusions on the ethics of writing on animal skin, one cannot deny the reality that a great deal of slaughter and death lies behind this labor of love.

Death lurks elsewhere. Birds must also give to this Bible, though losing a few feathers to make quills is hardly the sacrifice a calf must offer. Jackson recalls one unlikely source of feathers:

> I found a swan's wings under a power line. The whole carcass was there. It must have flown into the power line; if a fox had killed it, it would have eaten the feathers. I brought back the wings, which were intact.[15]

Certainly, many quills were purchased, but this was not the only story of quills found in fields. Many were left behind from molting birds. Even in those cases, there is some hint of death in the bird's molting as it ages. The gesso used to bind Jackson's delicate gilding to the page also hints at death: gesso contains white lead. Today's gesso users, like their medieval predecessors, know that lead kills.[16] This lethal chemical enables many of this Bible's most stunning gilded pages.

Many medieval Christians connected the death required to make a manuscript with the death of Christ. In their eyes, the tools, processes, and materials of book production were an allegory of the crucifixion. Fourteenth-century Benedictine monk Pierre Bersuire homes in on the bodily suffering of the skin:

> Christ is a certain book written on the Virgin's skin and in the womb of the glorious Virgin by the fingers of the Holy Spirit. That so-called book was dictated in the Father's design, written in the conception of Christ, set forth in words in the manifestation of his birth, corrected

14. Anne F. Elvey, *The Matter of the Text: Material Engagements between Luke and the Five Senses*, Bible in the Modern World 37 (Sheffield: Sheffield Phoenix Press, 2011), 29–43; Sarah Kay, "Legible Skins: Animals and the Ethics of Medieval Reading," *Postmedieval* 2, no. 1 (2011).

15. Calderhead, *Illuminating the Word*, 145.

16. Raymond Clemens and Timothy Graham, *Introduction to Manuscript Studies* (Ithaca: Cornell University Press, 2007), 33–34.

> in his passion, erased in his flagellation, punctuated in the imprint of his wounds, placed on top of the pulpit in the crucifixion, illuminated in the effusion of blood, bound in the resurrection, and debated in the ascension.[17]

Here the Latin for "punctuated," the verb *pungere*, suggests both the piercing of Jesus' skin and pricking holes in a parchment page.[18] (Note also the familiar reference to Mary as parchment.) Scribes pricked holes in parchment to create the guidelines on which they wrote, and to ensure that those guidelines would remain consistent from page to page. Similarly, twelfth-century scholar Peter Comestor preached in one sermon:

> You know the scribe's work. First, with the knife he begins to clean the parchment of fat and to remove all gross filth. Next with the pumice stone he smooths away all hair and sinews, without which the script will not be legible or durable. Then he applies the ruler to serve as a guide for writing. All of which you also must do if you want to have the book I have described. This parchment book shall be your heart.[19]

Here the process of scraping the parchment to receive words allegorically suggests the sinner cleansing their inner self. Comestor also draws on the monastic concept of the "inner library," the words of revelation metaphorically written on the believer's heart, actualized in the monastic practice of memorizing Scripture.

Christian writers and artists also suggest that Christ's blood is the ink of the new covenant. In a hymn by Romanos the Melodist, "On Peter's Denial," Jesus tells Peter:

> Look, I am now telling you the cock crows, you will three times
> disown me,

17. Translated in Hennessy, "Christ's Blood as Ink," 23–24.

18. At times holes in parchment were typologically seen as Christ's wounds; see Elina Gertsman, *The Absent Image: Lacunae in Medieval Books* (University Park: Penn State University Press, 2021), 137–48.

19. Jager, *The Book of the Heart*, 52–53. See also Mary A. Rouse and Richard Hunter Rouse, "From Flax to Parchment: A Monastic Sermon from Twelfth-Century Durham," in *New Science out of Old Books: Studies in Manuscripts and Early Printed Books in Honour of A. I. Doyle*, ed. Richard Beadle and Alan J. Piper, 1–13 (Aldershot, UK: Scolar Press, 1995).

> and, as if the waves of the sea were submerging and drowning
> your mind, will three times deny me.
> The first time you cried out, but now as you weep, you will not
> find me
> giving you my hand as before,
> because, having taken in it a reed [as a pen], I am starting to write
> a pardon for all Adam's descendants.
> My flesh, which you see, becomes for me like paper
> and my blood like ink, where I dip my pen and write
> as I distribute an unending gift to those who cry.[20]

Romanos plays on Matthew's account of the Roman soldiers placing a reed in Jesus' right hand on the cross (Matt 27:29). In the Gospel, Jesus was not writing; but since pens made from reeds were a common writing tool of that time, Romanos drew that imaginative association. Richard Rolle, a fourteenth-century English monk, writes in a meditation on Christ's passion:

> Moreover, sweet Jesus, your body is like a book written entirely with red ink: just so is your body entirely written with red wounds. Now, sweet Jesus, allow me to read upon your book, and to understand somewhat the sweetness of that writing, and to enjoy that reading continuously and studiously, and give me grace to understand somewhat the peerless love of Jesus Christ, and to learn by that example to love God in return as I should.[21]

Rolle draws on the convention of using red ink to write initials and rubrics in medieval Latin manuscripts. These bright red pigments echo the color of Christ's blood. In an early fifteenth-century English meditation on the passion, the quill becomes the nails and spears used to torment Jesus on the cross:

20. Romanos the Melodist, *On the Life of Christ: Kontakia*, stanza 7, trans. Ephrem Lash (San Francisco: HarperCollins, 1995), 132; see discussion in Derek Krueger, *Writing and Holiness: The Practice of Authorship in the Early Christian East* (Philadelphia: University of Pennsylvania Press, 2011), 160–62. I am indebted to Jillian Marcantonio and Jenny Knust for these sources.

21. Meditation B, lines 1185–86, rendered into modern English by Lisa Manter, "Rolle Playing: 'And the Word Became Flesh,'" in *The Vernacular Spirit: Essays on Medieval Religious Literature*, ed. Renate Blumenfeld-Kosinski, Duncan Robertson, and Nancy Bradley Warren, 15–37, The New Middle Ages (New York: Palgrave Macmillan US, 2002), 15.

For though my heart be hard as stone,
Thy writing makes it all thine own;
The nail or spear, a stylus keen,
Shall make the letters all be seen.[22]

Jesus is the parchment this time, but not always. The Roman-senator-turned-monk Cassiodorus (485–580) praises the work of the scribe: "For Satan receives as many wounds as the scribe writes words of the Lord."[23] Here Satan is the parchment. Cassiodorus implies that the ink is the blood of Christ, which, in Christian belief, defeats Satan and death.

These medieval allegories may seem strange to modern ears, but they remind us that the materials used to make *The Saint John's Bible* require a great deal of death. These authors knew firsthand how many animals needed to be slaughtered to make a book; and as they wrote, they meditated on the mysteries of their faith.[24] The English language severs parchment from living animal. Just as pigs become bacon and cows become steak, we write not on "cattle flesh" but on parchment or vellum. Yet in the scriptorium, this euphemistic dividing line dissolves in the face of the side of the parchment that was the outside of the animal's skin:

> Parchment is rendered neutral, made white, yet it still retains the imprint of the skin. Some traces of the animal remain: the flecks and grains, pores, the shadows of its pigmentation. The skin is still visible in the writing surface.[25]

These hair follicles, scars, blemishes, and even holes remind the scribe that the parchment was once a living creature. The most expensive manuscripts avoid them by using uterine calfskin. Even so, every skin is different. As Mark L'Argent, vellum preparer for the Bible, quips:

22. Jager, *The Book of the Heart*, 108–11; see also Noonan, "Bodies of Parchment," 58–59.

23. Cassiodorus, *Institutions*, 1.30, translated in Cassiodorus, *Cassiodorus:* Institutions of Divine and Secular Learning *and* On the Soul, trans. James W. Halporn, Translated Texts for Historians 42 (Liverpool: Liverpool University Press, 2003), 163.

24. See description, with illustrations, in Clemens and Graham, *Introduction to Manuscript Studies*, 9–13.

25. Kathryn James, "Skin," *Inscription* 1 (2020).

"Each animal and each skin is an individual."[26] And in becoming a book, the animals enjoy longer lives than nature permits.

Those who work with vellum attest that it has a sense of being alive. Paper tends to stay still, to lie flat. Vellum has personality. It does not like to lie flat.[27] It expands and contracts with humidity. When I visited Thomas Ingmire, he told me how he had to ready every parchment sheet he worked on for the Bible. As an illuminator, he did his work after the scribes. Each sheet of written parchment arrived in a tube, dried up, stiff, unable to be laid flat for artistic work. To smooth it out, he laid each sheet out in his bathroom and ran a hot bath. The humidity made the sheet workable.

Flame, too, has its place in the creation of *The Saint John's Bible*. In the Song, the woman compares love to flames: "Its flashes are flashes of fire, / a raging flame" (Song 8:6c). Jackson's treatment of Song 8:6-7 depicts these flames as golden flowers. Biblically, fire is a potent image—a presence in biblical stories, an essential part of temple ritual, and a vivid metaphor used by poets and prophets.[28] Fire signifies God's presence, as in the pillar of fire guiding Israel in the desert (Exod 13:21-22). Fire's presence is welcomed on a more prosaic level, such as the value of flames to provide warmth in the cold (Acts 28:2-5) or to cook meat (Exod 12:8-10). Other times, flames can burn cities to the ground (Josh 6:24) or kill people, such as Nadab and Abihu (Lev 10:1-2). The remnant of a burnt fire is also the material with which this Bible was written. The black ink found on every page gets its pigment from soot, the carbon remnant of flames. In Jewish tradition, the Torah is called "black fire on white fire." This saying refers to a reading of Deuteronomy 33:2, Moses' retelling of the Sinai theophany: "From his [God's] right, a fiery law [i.e., Torah] unto them [Israel]."[29] But one can also read it as a reference to the Torah scroll's white vellum with black lettering—which, in the ink used by many Torah scribes today, has a shiny quality that makes it glimmer under shifting light, like (very muted) gold leaf or flames. Flames can burn books, but flames also

26. L'Argent, "On the Surface," 7.

27. Calderhead, *Illuminating the Word*, 141–43.

28. Kristin Helms, "Fire: II. Hebrew Bible/Old Testament," *EBR* 9: 68–69; Deena E. Grant, "Fire and the Body of Yahweh," *Journal for the Study of the Old Testament* 40, no. 2 (2015).

29. Translation my own. Mark Verman, "The Torah as Divine Fire," *Jewish Bible Quarterly* 35, no. 2 (2007).

create the ink to write books. Flames can both create life and destroy it, just as love can both create life and, when twisted or betrayed, can become the most bitter hatred.

LOVE, DEATH, AND THE EUCHARIST

In Christian theology, the phrase "love is strong as death" ultimately comes to life in the death and resurrection of Christ, whose body is ritually given up in the Eucharist. In his comments on the draft of the Song illuminations he sent to the Committee on Illumination and Text, Donald Jackson wrote that the layout and chaotic, abundant feel of Song's art reminded him of his highly eucharistic illumination of the two feeding stories in Mark (6:33-44; 8:1-10). It is not a far leap to connect the multiplication of bread to the Eucharist, and Jackson's illumination does so, through the golden circles with crosses (loaves of bread and eucharistic hosts) and the golden breadcrumbs scattered around the columns of text. Anasazi basket designs abound, baskets to hold the bread. Jackson chose these designs for their geometric patterns:

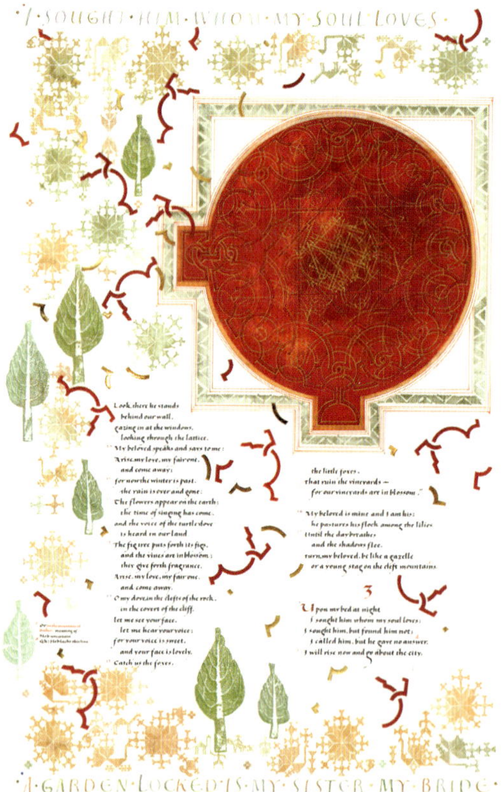

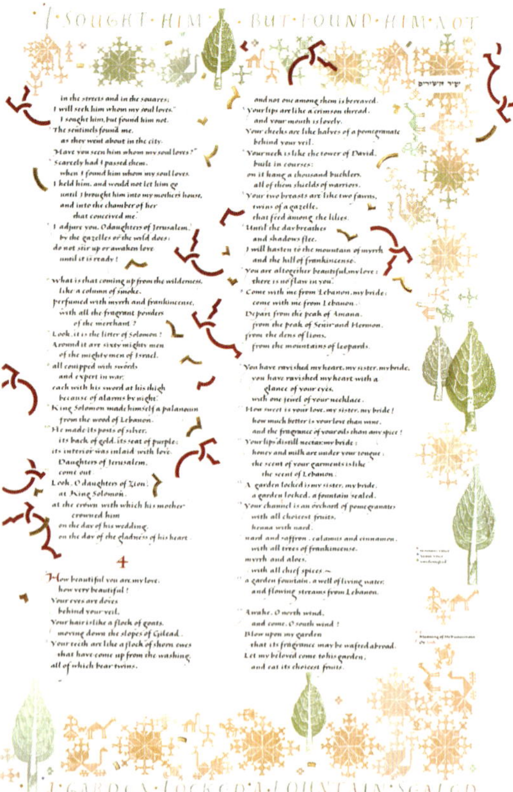

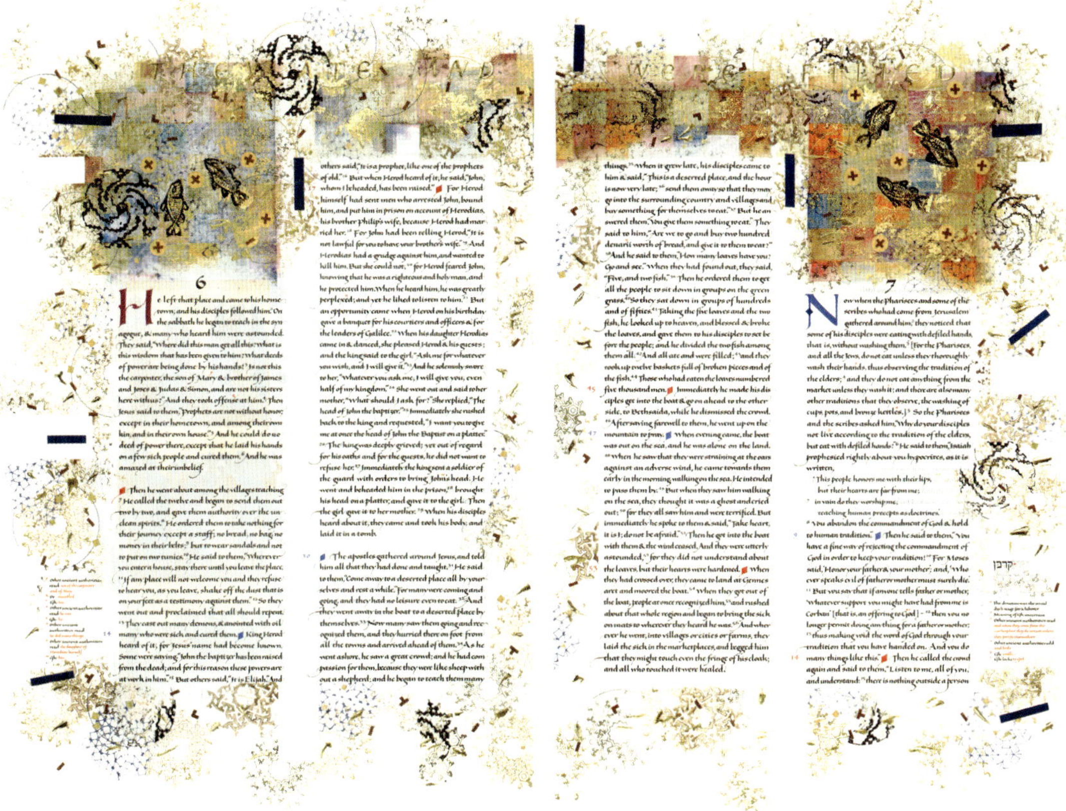

> The basket shapes started to spin, a dizzy feeling. The baskets themselves have a geometric shape. The arithmetic of love is exponential. One act of love begets another.[30]

Love abounds just as bread abounds. Jackson's images suggest several parallels between the Song and the Eucharist. In Mark, the square patterns at top right and top left suggest the temple square motif found in the Song of Songs. Returning to the Song illumination in light of possible eucharistic imagery, one may also see the pomegranate as a chalice of wine viewed from above. Both two-page spreads, rather unusually for *The Saint John's Bible*, intermingle their riot of illumination between and around the text, creating a visual sense of chaos amid order.

30. Calderhead, *Illuminating the Word*, 172.

Jackson's illuminations suggest several textual connections between Mark's feeding stories, the Eucharist, and the Song of Songs. The description of the garden in the Song suggests agrarian abundance and sensory delight, as does the abundance of food in the Gospels' feeding stories. Both gather an array of food beyond belief: Jesus' mysterious multiplication of bread, and the Song's combination of flora (4:12-16), which does not occur naturally anywhere.[31]

While sight and sound are overwhelmingly the central sensory modes in the Hebrew Bible, the Song offers far more imagery of taste and scent:

> Eat, friends, drink,
>   and be drunk with love. (Song 5:1b)

In the Song, taste and eating, much more physically close than sight and sound, suggest the physical closeness of sex, and specific sex acts.[32] In the feeding stories, they suggest not sex but bodily nourishment and God's lavish care.

The Song's language of taste also explains why some patristic and medieval exegetes connected the Song to the Eucharist, such as Bishop Ambrose of Milan (339–397).[33] In a catechetical work for the newly baptized, he writes:

> "I have eaten my bread with my honey" [Song 4:16a]. You see that in this bread there is no bitterness, but there is all sweetness. "I have drunk my wine with my milk" [4:16b]. You see that such is the glad-

31. Elaine T. James, *Landscapes of the Song of Songs: Poetry and Place* (Oxford: Oxford University Press, 2017), 68.

32. Annette Schellenberg, "Senses, Sensuality, and Sensory Imagination: On the Role of the Senses in the Song of Songs," in *Sounding Sensory Profiles in Antiquity: On the Role of Senses in Ancient Israel, Mesopotamia, and Egypt*, ed. Annette Schellenberg and Thomas Krüger, 199–216, Ancient Near East Monographs 25 (Atlanta: SBL Press, 2019).

33. *The Mysteries*, 55–58; *The Sacraments*, 5.2-3, both translated in Ambrose of Milan, *Theological and Dogmatic Works*, trans. Roy J. Deferrari, Fathers of the Church 44 (Washington, DC: Catholic University of America Press, 1963). See commentary in Daniélou, *The Bible and the Liturgy*, 202–5; Shuve, *The Song of Songs*, 150–56.

> ness that it is polluted by the filth of no sin. For as often as you drink, you receive the remission of sins and you are inebriated in spirit.[34]

Ambrose's sacramental reading of the Song also draws on theological concepts of the Eucharist as a nuptial feast between the church and God, found in the New Testament (for example, in Eph 5:22-23), in turn drawing on Hebrew prophetic literature's use of marriage as a metaphor for the relationship between God and Israel (such as in Hos 1–2). The nuptial metaphors and the sensation of taste also figure strongly in Teresa of Ávila's commentary on the Song. Though Teresa (1515–1582) is most famed as the Spanish nun who cofounded the Discalced Carmelite order, she was also the first woman to write a commentary on the Song of Songs. Teresa comments on the woman's description of her beloved, "his fruit was sweet to my taste" (2:3b):

> Here she compares Him to the apple tree, and she says its fruit is sweet to her taste. O souls that practice prayer, taste all these words! How many ways there are of thinking about our God. He is manna, for the taste we get from him conforms to the taste we prefer.[35]

Likewise, commenting on the Song's opening desire—"let him kiss me with the kisses of his mouth!" (1:2)—Teresa asks: "Do we not approach the most Blessed Sacrament?" (1.10). Her language draws on a longer tradition of the Song as a key text for nuptial eucharistic spirituality among late medieval women mystics.[36] While most of the Song commentaries shy away from overly sensory or overly personal

34. *The Sacraments*, 5.4, translated in Ambrose of Milan, *Theological and Dogmatic Works*, 314.

35. *Meditations*, 5.2, translated in Teresa of Avila, "Meditations on the Song of Songs," in *The Collected Works of St. Teresa of Avila*, trans. Kieran Kavanaugh and Otilio Rodriguez (Washington, DC: ICS Publications, 1980), 2:248. See also Bernard McGinn, "'One Word Will Contain within Itself a Thousand Mysteries': Teresa of Avila, the First Woman Commentator on the Song of Songs," *Spiritus* 16 (2016); Ann W. Astell and Catherine Rose Cavadini, "The Song of Songs," in *The Wiley-Blackwell Companion to Christian Mysticism*, ed. Julia A. Lamm, 25–40 (Malden, MA: Wiley-Blackwell, 2012), 32–34.

36. Caroline Walker Bynum, *Holy Feast and Holy Fast: The Religious Significance of Food to Medieval Women* (Berkeley: University of California Press, 1986), 150–64.

engagements with the erotic sensuality of the Song, Teresa and other women mystics are often more frank.

By connecting the Song of Songs to the Eucharist, *The Saint John's Bible*, like Ambrose and Teresa, brings to the fore a network of metaphors found in the Bible (both Hebrew Bible and New Testament) and continued in medieval monastic traditions. God is not merely seen and heard but also tasted. But this tasting requires the death of Jesus, just as the writing of the Word of God on the page requires the death of animals.

LOVE OVERCOMES DEATH

When the woman of the Song declares that "love is strong as death" (8:6b), she is not merely speaking of the risks of love, the self-annihilation, like the death required for the resurrection. Her weighty words also bespeak love that overcomes death, that meets its match. All the death, all the fire and animal skin used to create *The Saint John's Bible*—all of this has a point. These materials become the vessel of a project that shows forth with love, with care, and with intention. This Bible shows a humanity that a mass-produced printed Bible cannot convey. And in its very incarnate materiality, it enables its words to be sealed upon the hearts of its readers.

The woman's demand of her lover to "set me as a seal upon your heart" invokes the power of writing to convey immortality on its author. The writer can speak through his words long after his own death. The written object can persist much longer than the human body, including the seal that the Song invokes. Ancient Israelites used the seal, a small piece of stone with the owner's name carved into it, to authenticate legal documents and letters; the seal would be pressed onto a piece of soft clay on the string holding the document closed. (These clay impressions are called *bullae*.) Unlike papyri and parchment, both used for writing in ancient Israel, stone seals and clay bullae persist well in the archaeological record, and several hundred of them have been found from ancient Israel before the Babylonian exile.[37] Such seals were kept close to one's person, often on a ring or a necklace. Their authenticating power could serve as a proxy for their owner's presence, a "virtual

37. Christopher A. Rollston, *Writing and Literacy in the World of Ancient Israel: Epigraphic Evidence from the Iron Age*, Archaeology and Biblical Studies 11 (Atlanta: SBL Press, 2010), 75–79.

extension of the self in society."[38] Judah discovered this to his dismay when Tamar tricked him into giving her his seal (Gen 38:18).

The seal's physical presence of its owner's name also ties it to the owner, since, in the Hebrew Bible, names often express something of a person's essence.[39] Take, for example, the many babies in Genesis named for something they will do or the circumstances around their birth:

> When Lamech had lived for one hundred and eighty-two years, he became the father of a son; he named him Noah (*noakh*), saying, "Out of the ground that the LORD has cursed this one shall bring us relief (*yenakhameinu*) from our work and from the toil of our hands." (5:28-29)

Here the wordplay is between the name "Noah" and the verb "bring us relief," which both play with the same consonants *n* and *kh*. Other times in Genesis, God assigns someone a new name to signify a new status:

> Then the man said, "You shall no longer be called Jacob, but Israel (*yisra'el*), for you have striven (*sarita*) with God and with humans, and have prevailed." (32:28)

God's wordplay, lost in translation, puns on the consonants *s* and *r* in the verb for "to strive." The people of Israel are people who strive (*yisra'*) with God (*el*). What's in a name? In the Bible, often a great deal.

The woman uses the image of the seal with her name upon it to speak of her imprint upon her beloved's heart—symbolically, upon his reason, intelligence, conscience. Ancients may have worn such seals on a necklace next to the heart.[40] Her name on the seal is physically close to him. No two lovers can be together all day, every day, but her

38. F. Scott Spencer, *Song of Songs*, Wisdom Commentary (Collegeville, MN: Liturgical Press, 2017), 212.

39. William M. Schniedewind, *How the Bible Became a Book: The Textualization of Ancient Israel* (Cambridge: Cambridge University Press, 2005), 29–30; Jeffrey L. Cooley, "Judean Onomastic Hermeneutics in Context," *Harvard Theological Review* 112 (2019); Herbert Marks, "Biblical Naming and Poetic Etymology," *Journal of Biblical Literature* 114 (1995); Moshe Garsiel, "Homiletic Name-Derivations as a Literary Device in the Gideon Narrative: Judges VI–VIII," *Vetus Testamentum* 43, no. 3 (1993).

40. Silvia Schroer and Thomas Staubli, *Body Symbolism in the Bible*, trans. Linda M. Maloney (Collegeville, MN: Michael Glazier, 2001), 43–49; Exum, *Song of Songs*, 250–54.

name can be with him all day. She is also a seal on her beloved's arm, a body part that symbolizes action in the Bible: "The Lord brought us out of Egypt with a mighty hand and an outstretched arm, with a terrifying display of power, and with signs and wonders" (Deut 26:8).[41] His love for her drives his deeds, not merely his thoughts. Instead of the man's name upon her—what we would expect from a patriarchal society such as ancient Israel—her name claims him.

If the woman of the Song desired her love to overcome death, she has succeeded. Over two millennia since this poem was written, we still read it, and read, chant, and sing her words. Just as a clay seal persists in the dirt, so the monks of Saint John's Abbey describe this Bible as "America's Book of Kells." The monks hope that this Bible, too, will last a thousand years. Long after the artists and monks have passed, their work will persist. Viewers in centuries to come can feel Donald Jackson's and the other scribes' heartbeats and breath through the page.

The woman's call to "set me as a seal upon your heart" also invites readers to imprint the Song, and the rest of Scripture, onto their own hearts. Both Hebrew Bible and New Testament suggest that to deeply internalize words of wisdom, one must take them into one's own body.[42] We must eat the Word. Typically, the words are sweet like honey. The Psalms adjure the reader to "taste and see that the Lord is good" (34:8a), and to keep in mind that the precepts of Torah are "sweeter also than honey, and drippings of the honeycomb" (19:10b). Proverbs instructs:

> Pleasant words are like a honeycomb,
> sweetness to the soul and health to the body. (16:24)
>
> My child, eat honey, for it is good,
> and the drippings of the honeycomb are sweet to your taste.

41. Schroer and Staubli, *Body Symbolism in the Bible*, 43–49, 171–73.

42. Nicole L. Tilford, *Sensing World, Sensing Wisdom: The Cognitive Foundation of Biblical Metaphors*, Ancient Israel and Its Literature 31 (Atlanta: SBL Press, 2017), 184–91; Yael Avrahami, *The Senses of Scripture: Sensory Perception in the Hebrew Bible*, The Library of Hebrew Bible/Old Testament Studies 545 (New York: T&T Clark, 2012), 157–63; Tova Forti, "Bee's Honey: From Realia to Metaphor in Biblical Wisdom Literature," *Vetus Testamentum* 56, no. 3 (2006): 333–36; Pierre Van Hecke, "Tasting Metaphor in Ancient Israel," in *Sounding Sensory Profiles in Antiquity: On the Role of Senses in Ancient Israel, Mesopotamia, and Egypt*, ed. Annette Schellenberg and Thomas Krüger, 99–118, Ancient Near East Monographs 25 (Atlanta: SBL Press, 2019).

> Know that wisdom is such to your soul;
> if you find it, you will find a future,
> and your hope will not be cut off. (24:13-14)

Words are also sweet in the Song of Songs:

> His speech is most sweet,
> and he is altogether desirable.
> This is my beloved and this is my friend,
> O daughters of Jerusalem. (5:16)

Divine words are sweet to Ezekiel's palate as well:

> But you, mortal, hear what I say to you; do not be rebellious like that rebellious house; open your mouth and eat what I give you. I looked, and a hand was stretched out to me, and a written scroll was in it. He spread it before me; it had writing on the front and on the back, and written on it were words of lamentation and mourning and woe. He said to me, O mortal, eat what is offered to you; eat this scroll, and go, speak to the house of Israel. So I opened my mouth, and he gave me the scroll to eat. He said to me, Mortal, eat this scroll that I give you and fill your stomach with it. Then I ate it; and in my mouth it was as sweet as honey. (2:8–3:3)

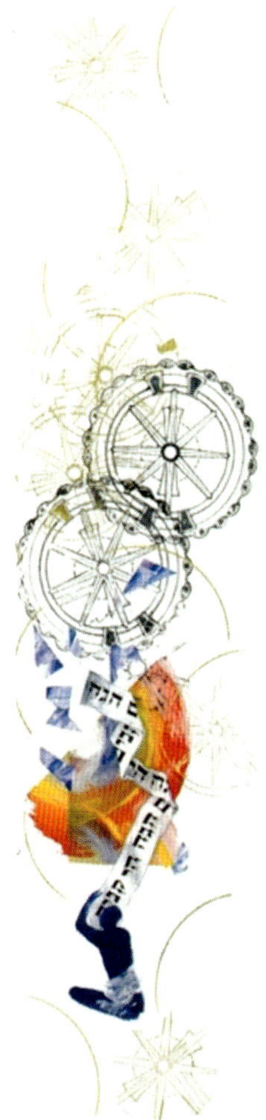

By ingesting the scroll, Ezekiel takes it into his very person. The honey-sweet scroll leads to a bitterly difficult prophetic message to deliver. Like us, the ancients appreciated honey for its taste and medicinal value. Unlike us, they had to work much harder for its sweet taste than those of us living in an age of cheaply available added sugar. Getting honey required some danger: the bees. Donald Jackson illuminates Ezekiel's call. In this image Ezekiel eats a scroll reading, in Hebrew, "words of lamentation and mourning and woe" (Ezek 2:10). After eating the scroll, its words are inside his body. In the parlance of other biblical authors, they are written on the tablet of his heart (cf. Prov 3:3; 7:2; Deut 11:18).[43] John of Patmos undergoes a similar trial:

43. Nili Shupak, "'Eat This Scroll' (Ezekiel 3:1): Writing as Symbol and Metaphor in the Hebrew Bible in the Light of Ancient Near Eastern Sources," *Bibliotheca Orientalis* 70 (2013).

> Then the voice that I had heard from heaven spoke to me again, saying, "Go, take the scroll that is open in the hand of the angel who is standing on the sea and on the land." So I went to the angel and told him to give me the little scroll; and he said to me, "Take it, and eat; it will be bitter to your stomach, but sweet as honey in your mouth." So I took the little scroll from the hand of the angel and ate it; it was sweet as honey in my mouth, but when I had eaten it, my stomach was made bitter (Rev 10:8-10)

Like Ezekiel's scroll, John's is sweet to the taste. Just as Ezekiel's scroll inaugurated a tough, traumatizing prophetic mission, so John's scroll aches his stomach. One commentator quips: "John's message of justice may be sweet but the judgment with which it is accomplished is hard to stomach."[44] For both Ezekiel and John, eating the scroll inaugurates the eater's transformation and the acquisition of new knowledge.[45] These words are both read and eaten. They are material, fleshly, written on flesh, and tasted, ingested, digested, and made into the prophet's flesh.

Later Christian authors, especially those in the monastic tradition out of which *The Saint John's Bible* comes, developed these parallels between the metaphor of ingesting words of wisdom and the ritual of the Eucharist. Bernard of Clairvaux describes his love of the Song's honeyed words: "Enjoying their sweetness, I chew them over and over, my internal organs are replenished, my insides are fattened up, and all my bones break out in praise."[46] Elsewhere, commenting on the Song's opening "let him kiss me with the kisses of his mouth," Bernard compares the sweetness of that erotic kiss to the sweet words of Scripture that nourish the believer and the sweet smell of the sacrifice of prayer as it rises to God: "And when they smell this sweet fragrance in the heavens, they will surely say of you too: 'What is this coming up from the desert like a column of smoke, breathing of myrrh and frankincense

44. David L. Barr, *Tales of the End: A Narrative Commentary on the Book of Revelation*, 2nd ed. (Salem, OR: Polebridge Press, 2011), 159.

45. Meredith J. C. Warren, *Food and Transformation in Ancient Mediterranean Literature*, Writings from the Greco-Roman World Supplement Series 14 (Atlanta: SBL Press, 2019), esp. 59–74.

46. Bernard of Clairvaux, *Sermon on the Song of Songs* 16.2. Translated in Ivan Illich, *In the Vineyard of the Text: A Commentary to Hugh's* Didascalicon (Chicago: University of Chicago Press, 1996), 56–57. See also Robertson, *Lectio Divina*; Rachel Fulton, "'Taste and See That the Lord Is Sweet' (Ps. 33:9): The Flavor of God in the Monastic West," *Journal of Religion* 86 (2006).

and every perfume the merchant knows? [Song 3:6]'."[47] Bernard's Latin term for "chew," *ruminare* (whence "ruminate"), suggests a cow chewing the cud, working over the same food again and again—just as Benedictine monks were to ruminate the words of Scripture as they engaged in the manual labor of the community. The metaphor persists. In a collect in the Church of England's *Book of Common Prayer* still prayed to this day, the faithful beseech God: "Blessed Lord, who hast caused all holy Scriptures to be written for our learning; grant us that we may in such wise hear them, read, mark, learn, and inwardly digest them." More recently, Jesuit priest Greg Boyle, who has spent decades helping Los Angeles youth escape violent gangs and build better lives, named his book after what one of his "homies" told him upon hearing a pivotal life insight: "Damn, I'm gonna tattoo that on my heart."[48] To extend the metaphor: once ingested, the words became part of the believer's internal library, written on the tablets of her heart.[49] To eat the Word is to know the Word. To taste something is to bring it into one's body, far more risky and intimate than merely seeing, hearing, or even touching it.

Just as the Word goes down more smoothly when it is sweet as honey, so *The Saint John's Bible* invites us to internalize the Word through its visual delights. This eating echoes in *The Saint John's Bible*—though I do not encourage any readers to eat its pages. In this Bible, images of bees suggest both wise words as honey and a medieval association of bees in their hive with monks in their monastery.[50] One whimsical bee hoists up a line of text accidentally omitted by the scribe:

47. Bernard of Clairvaux, *Sermon on the Song of Songs* 7.4. Bernard employs metaphors of sweet taste and fragrant scent throughout his sermons on the Song; see also *Sermons on the Song of Songs* 1.3, 16.1, 36.3, and 45.1.

48. Gregory Boyle, *Tattoos on the Heart: The Power of Boundless Compassion* (New York: Free Press, 2011), xiv.

49. Isabelle Cochelin, "When the Monks Were the Book," in *The Practice of the Bible in the Middle Ages: Production, Reception, and Performance in Western Christianity*, ed. Susan Boynton and Diane J. Reilly, 61–83 (New York: Columbia University Press, 2011); Eric Jager, *The Book of the Heart* (Chicago: University of Chicago Press, 2000); Michelle P. Brown, "Spreading the Word," in *In the Beginning: Bibles before the Year 1000*, ed. Michelle P. Brown, 77–103 (Washington, DC: Freer Gallery of Art and Arthur M. Sackler Gallery, Smithsonian Institution, 2006).

50. Jonathan Homrighausen, *Illuminating Justice: The Ethical Imagination of* The Saint John's Bible (Collegeville, MN: Liturgical Press, 2018), 73–75.

soon be free from care;
16 because she goes about seeking those worthy of her;
and she graciously appears to them
in their paths,
and meets them in every thought.

17 The beginning of wisdom is the most sincere
desire for instruction,
and concern for instruction is love of her,
18 and love of her is the keeping of her laws,
and giving heed to her laws is assurance
of immortality,
19 and immortality brings one near to God;
20 so the desire for wisdom leads to a kingdom.

21 Therefore if you delight in thrones and
scepters, O monarchs over the peoples,
honor wisdom, so that you may reign forever.
22 I will tell you what wisdom is and
how she came to be,
and I will hide no secrets from you,
but I will trace her course from the
beginning of creation,
and make knowledge of her clear,
and I will not pass by the truth;
23 nor will I travel in the company of sickly envy,
for envy does not associate with wisdom.
24 The multitude of the wise is the
salvation of the world,
and a sensible king is the stability
of any people.
25 Therefore be instructed by my words,
and you will profit.

7 Therefore I prayed, and understanding
was given me;
8 I preferred her to scepters and thrones,
and I accounted wealth as nothing
in comparison with her.
9 Neither did I liken to her any priceless gem,
because all gold is but a little sand in her sight,
and silver will be accounted as clay before her.
10 I loved her more than health and beauty,
and I chose to have her rather than light,
because her radiance never ceases.
11 All good things came to me along with her,
and in her hands uncounted wealth.
12 I rejoiced in them all, because wisdom
leads them;
but I did not know that she was their mother.
13 I learned without guile and I impart
without grudging;
I do not hide her wealth,
14 for it is an unfailing treasure for mortals;
those who get it obtain friendship with God,
commended for the gifts that come
from instruction.

15 May God grant me to speak with judgment,
and to have thoughts worthy of
what I have received;
for he is the guide even of wisdom
and the corrector of the wise.
16 For both we and our words are in his hand,
as are all understanding and skill in crafts.
17 For it is he who gave me unerring knowledge
of what exists,
to know the structure of the world and

[7] I called on God, and the spirit of
wisdom came to me.

Ironically, the bee delivers the line "I called to God, and the spirit of wisdom came to me" (Wis 7:7). The spirit of wisdom is the bee, delivering words sweet as honey. As biblical scholar Carey Ellen Walsh suggests, the experience of reading the Song aloud in its original Hebrew is its own sensory delight: "In reading aloud as the ancients did, mouths move, caress the language. We can think of reading as kissing a text, of reading aloud as kissing with joyful abandon."[51] With

51. Carey Ellen Walsh, "In the Absence of Love," in *Scrolls of Love: Ruth and the Song of Songs*, ed. Peter S. Hawkins and Lesleigh Cushing Stahlberg (New York: Fordham University Press, 2006), 291.

The Saint John's Bible, we not only read and hear the Word, but we touch it, and metaphorically at least, we taste it. The love with which this Bible was made, a love strong as death, invites us in. This must explain why I am still reading, marking, and inwardly digesting this Bible after five years.

AND THE WORD BECAME FLESH

In this book I have suggested several key metaphors and analogies for how we look at calligraphy: the page as a garden; the pilgrimage of the reading eye and the walk of the writing hand; writing as weaving and the textile texture of the text; touching the page as grasping the hand of the scribe; and the dead animal's skin on which the scribes wrote, which suggests the close relationship between love and death in the Christian story. Each of these lenses, metaphors, and analogies draws from the Song, from the Bible, and from medieval visual and textual sources that reflect on scribal craft and calligraphic art. Each helps us to see better how calligraphy works. Each shows how the content of handwritten words resonates with those words' visual and material forms and the artists' creative processes. Each helps us discern just how word is made flesh in *The Saint John's Bible*.

Why does this matter? In our digital age, it is easy to forget just how fundamental writing is to human civilization. We take this magical technology for granted. We forget that in many cultures, the act of writing is invested with deep significance. This book has suggested what writing, especially beautiful writing, has meant and might mean today for Christians. I now attend synagogue rather than church, and admittedly, I feel an odd distance from the overtly Christian and Marian images I have explored in this book. But those metaphors are the thought-world that produced this Bible. They have helped me better understand how to look at it, how its form and process relate to its Christian content, its Word made Flesh.

But this is just one calligraphic tradition. Even as I finish this book, I am turning to Hebrew calligraphy and Jewish manuscripts. Ironically enough, my conversion spurred a crucial insight of this book. Unlike Christians in the West, who by and large have let go of the heritage of major illuminated manuscript Bibles in favor of the printing press, Jews have continued writing the Torah by hand on parchment, as is required by rabbinic practice. Seeing and feeling the materiality of the written Torah scroll in synagogue helped me grasp just what *The Saint John's Bible* was reclaiming in the Christian past: the Word made Flesh made book.

I end this book where I began: Donald Jackson's illumination of Word becoming Flesh opposite the opening words of the Gospel of John: "In the beginning was the Word." Just as Jackson's illumination suggests a Christ in the process of taking on flesh, so this book represents only one step in the ongoing process of looking at images and engaging hallowed texts. The lenses I have fleshed out here hardly exhaust the ways we might look at calligraphy. Another common metaphor is calligraphy as "music on the page"—a metaphor suggested by Jackson himself.[52] We need only look to the oscillographs of the Psalms volume of *The Saint John's Bible* to see this analogy at work.[53] I leave it to others to take up this theme and improvise on it.

Since my focus in this book has been *The Saint John's Bible*, I did not discuss other art. These lenses, however, also resonate with other contemporary calligraphers, artists who did not work on *The Saint John's Bible*. These artists, too, weave words and plant letters. My hope is that like me, you will venture beyond this landmark project into the broad, rich world of contemporary lettering arts. It is a great garden to get lost in, a wonderful labyrinth to lope through.

52. Jonathan Homrighausen, "Words Made Flesh: Incarnational, Multisensory Exegesis in Donald Jackson's Biblical Art," *Religion and the Arts* 23, no. 3 (2019): 251; Lucinda Allen Mosher, "Christian Liturgy and the Music of the Page," *Visual Music: Calligraphy & Sacred Texts, Henry Luce III Center for the Arts & Religion*, 1 September 2021, https://www.luceartsandreligion.org/christian-liturgy-and-the-music-of-the-page; Sophie Verbeek, *Musical Calligraphy / Calligraphie musicale* (Küssnacht, Switzerland: Sophie Verbeek, 2019).

53. Calderhead, *Illuminating the Word*, 205–7; Sink, *The Art of* The Saint John's Bible, 154–56.

BIBLIOGRAPHY

Alan of Lille. "A Concise Explanation of the Song of Songs in Praise of the Virgin Mary." In *Eros and Allegory: Medieval Exegesis of the Song of Songs*, edited by Denys Turner, 291–309. Cistercian Studies 156. Kalamazoo, MI: Cistercian Publications, 1995.

Albenda, Pauline. "Royal Gardens, Parks, and the Architecture Within: Assyrian Views." *Journal of the American Oriental Society* 138, no. 1 (2018): 105–20.

Alexander, Michael, ed. *The Earliest English Poems*. 3rd ed. Penguin Classics. London: Penguin Books, 1991.

Alter, Robert. *The Art of Biblical Poetry*. Rev. ed. New York: Basic Books, 2011.

Ambrose of Milan. *Theological and Dogmatic Works*. Translated by Roy J. Deferrari. Fathers of the Church 44. Washington, DC: Catholic University of America Press, 1963.

Artress, Lauren. *Walking a Sacred Path: Rediscovering the Labyrinth as a Spiritual Practice*. Rev. ed. New York: Riverhead Books, 2006.

Astell, Ann W. "The Song of Songs in Aelred of Rievaulx's Liturgical Preaching." In *A Companion to the Song of Songs in the History of Spirituality*, edited by Timothy Robinson, 157–88. Brill's Companions to the Christian Tradition 98. Leiden: Brill, 2021.

Astell, Ann W., and Catherine Rose Cavadini. "The Song of Songs." In *The Wiley-Blackwell Companion to Christian Mysticism*, edited by Julia A. Lamm, 25–40. Malden, MA: Wiley-Blackwell, 2012.

Avrahami, Yael. *The Senses of Scripture: Sensory Perception in the Hebrew Bible*. The Library of Hebrew Bible/Old Testament Studies 545. New York: T&T Clark, 2012.

Baert, Barbara, Reimund Bieringer, K. Demasure, Karlijn Demasure, and Sabine van den Eynde. Noli Me Tangere*: Mary Magdelene; One Person, Many Images*. Leuven: Peeters, 2006.

Barney, Stephen A. "The Plowshare of the Tongue: The Progress of a Symbol from the Bible to 'Piers Plowman.'" *Mediaeval Studies* 35 (1973): 261–93.

Barr, David L. *Tales of the End: A Narrative Commentary on the Book of Revelation*. 2nd ed. Salem, OR: Polebridge Press, 2011.

Bartal, Ruth. "Medieval Images of 'Sacred Love': Jewish and Christian Perceptions." *Assaph: Studies in Art History* 2 (1996): 93–110.

Barush, Kathryn. "Labyrinths as an Embodied Pilgrimage Experience: An Ignatian Case Study." In *Material Christianity: Western Religion and the Agency of Things*, edited by Christopher Ocker and Susanna Elm, 197–222. Cham, Switzerland: Springer, 2020.

Bede. *On the Song of Songs and Selected Writings*. Translated and edited by Arthur Holder. Classics of Western Spirituality. New York/Mahwah: Paulist Press, 2011.

Beentjes, Pancratius C. *The Book of Ben Sira in Hebrew: A Text Edition of All Extant Hebrew MSS and a Synopsis of All Parallel Hebrew Ben Sira Texts*. Supplements to Vetus Testamentum 68. Leiden: Brill, 1997.

Bernard of Clairvaux. *On the Song of Songs 1*. Translated by Kilian Walsh. Cistercian Fathers 4. Kalamazoo, MI: Cistercian Publications, 1971.

Bernard of Clairvaux. *Homilies in Praise of the Blessed Virgin Mary*. Translated by Marie-Bernard Saïd. Cistercian Fathers 18A. Kalamazoo, MI: Cistercian Publications, 1979.

Bhandari, Vandana. *Costume, Textiles and Jewellery of India: Traditions in Rajasthan*. London: Mercury Books, 2005.

Boyle, Gregory. *Tattoos on the Heart: The Power of Boundless Compassion*. New York: Free Press, 2011.

British Museum. "Paradise on Earth: The Gardens of Ashurbanipal." *British Museum Blog*, 4 October 2018. https://blog.britishmuseum.org/paradise-on-earth-the-gardens-of-ashurbanipal/.

Brock, Sebastian P. "Mary as a 'Letter': And Some Other Letter Imagery in Syriac Liturgical Texts." *Hugoye: Journal of Syriac Studies* 21 (2019): 3–20.

Brown, Catherine. "Remember the Hand: Bodies and Bookmaking in Early Medieval Spain." *Word & Image* 27, no. 3 (2011): 262–78.

Brown, George Hardin. "Patristic Pomegranates, from Ambrose and Apponius to Bede." In *Latin Learning and English Lore: Studies in Anglo-Saxon Literature for Michael Lapidge*, edited by Katherine O'Brien O'Keeffe and Andy Orchard, 132–49. Vol. 1. Toronto: University of Toronto Press, 2005.

Brown, Michelle P. "Images to Be Read and Words to Be Seen: The Iconic Role of the Early Medieval Book." In *Iconic Books and Texts*, edited by James W. Watts, 93–118. Bristol, CT: Equinox, 2013.

Brown, Michelle P. *"In the Beginning Was the Word": Books and Faith in the Age of Bede*. Jarrow Lecture 2000. Jarrow, UK: St. Paul's Church, 2000.

Brown, Michelle P. "Spreading the Word." In *In the Beginning: Bibles before the Year 1000*, edited by Michelle P. Brown, 77–103. Washington, DC: Freer Gallery of Art and Arthur M. Sackler Gallery, Smithsonian Institution, 2006.

Brown, Michelle P. *The Lindisfarne Gospels: Society, Spirituality and the Scribe*. London: British Library, 2003.

Brown, Rachel Fulton. *From Judgment to Passion: Devotion to Christ and the Virgin Mary, 800–1200*. New York; Chichester: Columbia University Press, 2005.

Brown, William P. *Seeing the Psalms: A Theology of Metaphor*. Louisville, KY: Westminster John Knox Press, 2002.

Bucher, Christina. "The Song of Songs and the 'Enclosed Garden' in Paintings and Illustrations of the Virgin Mary." In *Between the Text and the Canvas: The Bible and Art in Dialogue*, edited by J. Cheryl Exum, 96–116. Bible in the Modern World 13. Sheffield: Sheffield Phoenix Press, 2007.

Bülow-Jacobsen, Adam. "Writing Materials in the Ancient World." In *The Oxford Handbook of Papyrology*, edited by Roger S. Bagnall, 3–29. New York: Oxford University Press, 2009.

Burgert, Hans-Joachim. *The Calligraphic Line: Thoughts on the Art of Writing*. Edited by Konrad Bauer. Translated by Brody Neuenschwander. 2nd ed. Berlin: Hans-Joachim Burgert, 2002.

Bynum, Caroline Walker. *Holy Feast and Holy Fast: The Religious Significance of Food to Medieval Women*. Berkeley: University of California Press, 1986.

Byrne, Brendan. *Life Abounding: A Reading of John's Gospel*. Collegeville, MN: Liturgical Press, 2014.

Calderhead, Christopher. "An Afternoon Spent Looking at a Manuscript." *Alphabet* 32, no. 3 (Summer 2007): 1–28.

Calderhead, Christopher. *Illuminating the Word: The Making of* The Saint John's Bible. 2nd ed. Collegeville, MN: Liturgical Press, 2015.

Calderhead, Christopher. "Painting with Words." *The Scribe* 46 (1988): 3–6.

Calderhead, Christopher, and others. "The Poetics of Space." *Letter Arts Review* 32, no. 3 (2018): 4–19.

Calderhead, Christopher, and others. "Text & Textile." *Letter Arts Review* 35, no. 2 (2021): 10–44.

Calderhead, Christopher, and Izzy Pludwinski. "Writing, Argument and Contemplation: A Conversation with Izzy Pludwinski Mostly by e-Mail." *Letter Arts Review* 17, no. 2 (2002): 40–47.

Carr, David M. *The Erotic Word: Sexuality, Spirituality, and the Bible*. New York: Oxford University Press, 2005.

Carr, David M. "The Song of Songs as a Microcosm of the Canonization and Decanonization Process." In *Canonization and Decanonization: Papers Presented to the International Conference of the Leiden Institute for the Study of Religions (LISOR) Held at Leiden 9–10 January 1997*, edited by A. van der Kooij and K. van der Toorn, 173–89. Numen 82. Leiden: Brill, 1998.

Carruthers, Mary. *The Craft of Thought: Meditation, Rhetoric, and the Making of Images, 400–1200*. New York: Cambridge University Press, 1998.

Cassiodorus. *Cassiodorus:* Institutions of Divine and Secular Learning *and* On the Soul. Translated by James W. Halporn. Translated Texts for Historians 42. Liverpool: Liverpool University Press, 2003.

Cavell, Megan. *Weaving Words and Binding Bodies: The Poetics of Human Experience in Old English Literature.* Toronto: University of Toronto Press, 2016.

Child, Heather, ed. *More than Fine Writing: Irene Wellington, Calligrapher (1904–1984).* Woodstock, NY: Overlook Press, 1987.

Clayton, Ewan. *The Calligraphy of the Heart.* Brighton, UK: Ewan Clayton, 1996.

Clayton, Ewan. *Embracing Change: Spirituality and the Lindisfarne Gospels.* Brighton, UK: Ewan Clayton, 2003.

Clayton, Ewan. *The Golden Thread: A History of Writing.* Berkeley: Counterpoint, 2014.

Clemens, Raymond, and Timothy Graham. *Introduction to Manuscript Studies.* Ithaca: Cornell University Press, 2007.

Clifton, James, and Walter S. Melion, eds. *Scripture for the Eyes: Bible Illustration in Netherlandish Prints of the Sixteenth Century.* New York: Museum of Biblical Art, 2009.

Coatsworth, Elizabeth. "Cloth-Making and the Virgin Mary in Anglo-Saxon Literature and Art." In *Medieval Art: Recent Perspectives; A Memorial Tribute to C.R. Dodwell*, edited by Gale R. Owen-Crocker and Timothy Graham, 8–25. Manchester: Manchester University Press, 1998.

Coatts, Margot. "Donald Jackson." *Baseline* 14 (1991): 8–11.

Cochelin, Isabelle. "When the Monks Were the Book." In *The Practice of the Bible in the Middle Ages: Production, Reception, and Performance in Western Christianity*, edited by Susan Boynton and Diane J. Reilly, 61–83. New York: Columbia University Press, 2011.

Cohn, Yehudah B. *Tangled Up in Text: Tefillin and the Ancient World.* Brown Judaic Studies 351. Providence, RI: Brown Judaic Studies, 2008.

Colvin, Stephen. *A Brief History of Ancient Greek.* Hoboken, NJ: Wiley Blackwell, 2014.

Connolly, Daniel Kevin. "At the Center of the World: The Labyrinth Pavement at Chartres Cathedral." In *Art and Architecture of Late Medieval Pilgrimage in Northern Europe and the British Isles*, edited by Sarah Blick and Rita Tekippe, 285–314. Studies in Medieval and Reformation Traditions 104. Leiden: Brill, 2004.

Connolly, Daniel Kevin. "Imagined Pilgrimage in Gothic Art: Maps, Manuscripts and Labyrinths." PhD diss., University of Chicago, 1998.

Constas, Nicholas P. "Weaving the Body of God: Proclus of Constantinople, the Theotokos, and the Loom of the Flesh." *Journal of Early Christian Studies* 3, no. 2 (1995): 169–94.

Cooley, Jeffrey L. "Judean Onomastic Hermeneutics in Context." *Harvard Theological Review* 112 (2019): 184–208.

Curtius, Ernst Robert. *European Literature and the Latin Middle Ages*. Translated by Willard R. Trask. Bollingen 36. Princeton: Princeton University Press, 2013.

Cutsinger, James S. "Patterns of the Glory: Christophanic Reflections on The Saint John's Bible." Lecture presented at the Frederick Sheffer Memorial Lecture, Colorado College, 19 October 2011. http://www.cutsinger.net/pdf/patterns_of_the_glory.pdf.

Daley, Brian E. "The 'Closed Garden' and the 'Sealed Fountain': Song of Songs 4:12 in the Late Medieval Iconography of Mary." In *Medieval Gardens*, edited by Elisabeth B. MacDougall, 254–78. Washington, DC: Dumbarton Oaks Research Library, 1986.

Daniélou, Jean. *The Bible and the Liturgy*. Notre Dame, IN: University of Notre Dame Press, 1956.

Danto, Arthur C. "Weaving as Metaphor and Model for Political Thought." In *The Textile Reader*, edited by Jessica Hemmings, 205–9. New York: Berg Publishers, 2012.

Davis, Ellen F. *Proverbs, Ecclesiastes, and the Song of Songs*. Westminster Bible Companion. Louisville, KY: Westminster John Knox Press, 2000.

Davis, Ellen F. "Reading the Song Iconographically." In *Scrolls of Love: Ruth and the Song of Songs*, edited by Peter S. Hawkins and Lesleigh Cushing Stahlberg, 172–84. New York: Fordham University Press, 2006.

Davis, Ellen F. "Romance of the Land in the Song of Songs." *Anglican Theological Review* 80, no. 4 (1998): 533–46.

Derolez, Albert. "The Nomenclature of Gothic Scripts." In *The Oxford Handbook of Latin Palaeography*, edited by Frank T. Coulson and Robert Gary Babcock, 301–20. New York: Oxford University Press, 2020.

Derolez, Albert. *The Palaeography of Gothic Manuscript Books: From the Twelfth to the Early Sixteenth Century*. Cambridge: Cambridge University Press, 2003.

Diebold, William J. "'Except I Shall See . . . I Will Not Believe' (John 20:25): Typology, Theology, and Historiography in an Ottonian Ivory Diptych." In *Objects, Images, and the Word: Art in the Service of the Liturgy*, edited by Colum Hourihane, 257–73. Princeton, NJ: Index of Christian Art and Princeton University Press, 2003.

Diebold, William J. *Word and Image: An Introduction to Early Medieval Art*. Boulder, CO: Westview Press, 1999.

Donovan, Claire. *The Winchester Bible*. Toronto: University of Toronto Press, 1993.

Driver, Martha. "Reading Images of Reading." *The Ricardian* 13 (2003): 186–96.

Durand, William. *The* Rationale Divinorum Officiorum *of William Durand of Mende: A New Translation of the Prologue and Book One*. Edited by Timothy M. Thibodeau. Records of Western Civilization. New York: Columbia University Press, 2007.

Elvey, Anne F. *The Matter of the Text: Material Engagements between Luke and the Five Senses*. Bible in the Modern World 37. Sheffield: Sheffield Phoenix Press, 2011.

Ephrem the Syrian. *Ephrem the Syrian: Hymns*. Translated by Kathleen E. McVey. Classics of Western Spirituality. New York/Mahwah: Paulist Press, 1989.

Evangelatou, Maria. "The Purple Thread of the Flesh: The Theological Connotations of a Narrative Iconographic Element in Byzantine Images of the Annunciation." In *Icon and Word: The Power of Images in Byzantium; Studies Presented to Robin Cormack*, edited by Antony Eastmond and Liz James, 269–85. Aldershot, UK: Ashgate, 2003.

Exum, J. Cheryl. *Song of Songs*. Old Testament Library. Richmond: Westminster John Knox Press, 2005.

Farr, Carol. "The Lindisfarne Gospels and the Performative Voice of Gospel Manuscripts." In *The Lindisfarne Gospels: New Perspectives*, edited by Richard Gameson, 134–56. Library of the Written Word 57. Leiden: Brill, 2017.

Fishbane, Michael. *Song of Songs*. JPS Bible Commentary. Philadelphia: Jewish Publication Society, 2015.

Flynn, William. "*In Persona Mariae*: Singing the Song of Songs as a Passion Commentary." In *Perspectives on the Passion: Encountering the Bible through the Arts*, edited by Christine Joynes and Nancy Macky, 106–21. The Library of New Testament Studies. London: Bloomsbury T&T Clark, 2008.

Forti, Tova. "Bee's Honey: From Realia to Metaphor in Biblical Wisdom Literature." *Vetus Testamentum* 56, no. 3 (2006): 327–41.

Frey, Nancy Louise. *Pilgrim Stories: On and Off the Road to Santiago, Journeys along an Ancient Way in Modern Spain*. Berkeley: University of California Press, 1998.

Fulton, Rachel. "'Taste and See That the Lord Is Sweet' (Ps. 33:9): The Flavor of God in the Monastic West." *Journal of Religion* 86 (2006): 169–204.

Ganz, David. "Touching Books, Touching Art: Tactile Dimensions of Sacred Books in the Medieval West." In *Sensing Sacred Texts*, edited by James W. Watts, 81–113. Comparative Research on Iconic and Performative Texts. Bristol: Equinox, 2018.

Garsiel, Moshe. "Homiletic Name-Derivations as a Literary Device in the Gideon Narrative: Judges VI–VIII." *Vetus Testamentum* 43, no. 3 (1993): 302–17.

Gault, Brian P. *Body as Landscape, Love as Intoxication: Conceptual Metaphors in the Song of Songs*. Ancient Israel and Its Literature 36. Atlanta: SBL Press, 2019.

Gerhards, Meik. "Clothing and Nudity in the Song of Songs." In *Clothing and Nudity in the Hebrew Bible*, edited by Christoph Berner, Manuel Schäfer, Martin Schott, Sarah Schulz, and Martina Weingärtner, 557–68. London: T&T Clark, 2019.

Gertsman, Elina. *The Absent Image: Lacunae in Medieval Books*. University Park: Penn State University Press, 2021.

Gibson, Gail McMurray. *The Theater of Devotion: East Anglian Drama and Society in the Late Middle Ages*. Chicago: University of Chicago Press, 1989.

Gillow, John, and Nicholas Barnard. *Traditional Indian Textiles*. Reprint edition. London: Thames & Hudson, 1993.

Gluck, Shira H. "Uchtavtam 'and You Shall Write': An Integrative Study and Practice of Safrut STa"M." Rabbinic thesis, Hebrew Union College–Jewish Institute of Religion, 2019.

Grant, Deena E. "Fire and the Body of Yahweh." *Journal for the Study of the Old Testament* 40, no. 2 (2015): 139–61.

Gray, Nicolete. *Lettering as Drawing*. New York: Taplinger, 1982.

Grayer, Jane. "The Saint John's Bible - Jane Grayer." Interview by Saint John's Bible, 21 August 2013. https://www.youtube.com/watch?v=Qn05j5qEy4g.

Green, Deborah. "'Come South Wind, Blow upon My Garden That Its Spices May Flow': Experience in the Ancient Jewish Garden." In *Sound and Scent in the Garden*, edited by D. Fairchild Ruggles, 53–76. Dumbarton Oaks Colloquium on the History of Landscape Architecture 38. Washington, DC: Dumbarton Oaks Research Library and Collection, 2017.

Greenia, George. "The Bigger the Book: On Oversize Medieval Manuscripts." *Revue Belge de Philologie et d'Histoire* 83, no. 3 (2005): 723–45.

Greenia, George. "What Is Pilgrimage?" *International Journal of Religious Tourism and Pilgrimage* 6, no. 2 (2018): 7–15.

Gregory the Great. *Forty Gospel Homilies*. Translated by David Hurst. Cistercian Studies 123. Kalamazoo, MI: Cistercian Publications, 1990.

Griffiths, Paul J. *Song of Songs*. Brazos Theological Commentary on the Bible. Grand Rapids: Brazos Press, 2011.

Gullick, Michael. "Self-Referential Portraits of Artists and Scribes in Romanesque Manuscripts." In *Pen in Hand: Medieval Scribal Portraits, Colophons and Tools*, edited by Michael Gullick, 97–114. London: Red Gull Press, 2006.

Gullick, Michael. *Words of Risk: The Art of Thomas Ingmire*. Norman, OK: Calligraphy Review Editions, 1989.

Haeg, Larry, ed. *The Nature of Saint John's: A Guide to the Landscape and Spirituality of Saint John's Abbey Arboretum*. Collegeville, MN: Saint John's University Press, 2015.

Halliday, Peter, ed. *Holy Writ: Modern Jewish, Christian, and Islamic Calligraphy*. Lichfield: Lichfield Cathedral, 2014.

Hallo, William W. "'As the Seal upon Thine Arm': Glyptic Metaphors in the Biblical World." In *Ancient Seals and the Bible*, edited by Leonard Gorelick and Elizabeth Williams-Forte, 7–17. Malibu, CA: Undena Publications, 1983.

Hallo, William W. "For Love Is Strong as Death." *Journal of the Ancient Near Eastern Society* 22 (1993): 45–50.

Hamburger, Jeffrey. "The Hand of God and the Hand of the Scribe: Craft and Collaboration at Arnstein." In *Die Bibliothek des Mittelalters als dynamischer Prozess*, edited by Michael Embach, Claudine Moulin, and Andrea Rapp, 55–80. Wiesbaden: Reichert, 2012.

Hamel, Christopher de. *Meetings with Remarkable Manuscripts*. London: Penguin, 2016.

Harris, David. *Calligraphy: Modern Masters—Art, Inspiration & Technique*. New York: Crescent, 1991.

Haskins, Susan. *Mary Magdalen: Myth and Metaphor*. New York: Riverhead Trade, 1995.

Hayes, Lydia. "The Experience of Touching Christ: Imitating the Virgin Mary and Mary Magdalene in High Medieval Biblical Commentaries." In *Sensual and Sensory Experiences in the Middle Ages: On Pleasure, Fear, Desire and Pain*, edited by Carme Muntaner Alsina, David Carrillo Rangel, and Delfi I. Nieto-Isabel, 33–44. Cambridge: Cambridge Scholars Publishing, 2018.

Hechle, Ann. "Ann Hechle, Calligrapher: Based on an Interview at Her Home in Somerset with Bridget Wilkins, 15 November 1999." In *Making Their Mark: Art, Craft and Design at the Central School, 1896–1966*, edited by Sylvia Backemeyer, 139–44. London: A & C Black, 2000.

Hechle, Ann, and Ewan Clayton. *Findings: In the Calligraphic Work and Teachings of Irene Wellington, 1904–1984*. Pinner, UK: Irene Wellington Educational Trust, 2021.

Helms, Kristin. "Fire: II. Hebrew Bible/Old Testament." *EBR* 9: 68–69.

Hendel, Ronald. "The Life of Metaphor in Song of Songs: Poetics, Canon, and the Cultural Bible." *Biblica* 100 (2019): 60–83.

Hennessy, Marlene V. "The Social Life of a Manuscript Metaphor: Christ's Blood as Ink." In *The Social Life of Illumination: Manuscripts, Images, and Communities in the Late Middle Ages*, edited by Joyce Coleman, Mark Cruse, and Kathryn A. Smith, 17–52. Medieval Texts and Cultures of Northern Europe 21. Turnhout: Brepols, 2013.

Hippolytus of Rome. *The Mystery of Anointing: Hippolytus' Commentary on the Song of Songs in Social and Critical Contexts; Texts, Translations, and Comprehensive Study*. Edited by Yancy Smith. Gorgias Studies in Early Christianity and Patristics. Piscataway, NJ: Gorgias, 2015.

Hoare, Diana, ed. *Advanced Calligraphy Techniques*. Secaucus, NJ: Chartwell Books, 1989.

Hoffman, Jeffrey. "*Akdamut*: History, Folklore, and Meaning." *Jewish Quarterly Review* 99, no. 2 (2009): 161–83.

Holloway, Julia Bolton. *The Pilgrim and the Book: A Study of Dante, Langland, and Chaucer*. Rev. ed. New York: Peter Land, 1992.

Holsinger, Bruce. "Of Pigs and Parchment: Medieval Studies and the Coming of the Animal." *Proceedings of the Modern Language Association* 124, no. 2 (2009): 616–23.

Homrighausen, Jonathan. "Curator's Statement: Creating Words, Creating Worlds." *Visual Music: Calligraphy & Sacred Texts. Henry Luce III Center for the Arts & Religion*, 1 September 2021. https://www.luceartsandreligion.org/curators-statement.

Homrighausen, Jonathan. "'I Sought Him Whom My Soul Loves': Symbol, Ornament, and Visual Exegesis of the Song of Songs in *The Saint John's Bible*." In *The Art of Biblical Interpretation: Visual Portrayals of Scriptural Narratives*, edited by Heidi J. Hornik, Ian Boxall, and Bobbi Dykema, 67–101. The Bible and Its Reception 3. Atlanta: SBL Press, 2021.

Homrighausen, Jonathan. *Illuminating Justice: The Ethical Imagination of* The Saint John's Bible. Collegeville, MN: Liturgical Press, 2018.

Homrighausen, Jonathan. "Pludwinski Cursive Aleph-Bet." *Visual Music: Calligraphy & Sacred Texts. Henry Luce III Center for the Arts & Religion*. 1 September 2021. https://www.luceartsandreligion.org/pludwinski-cursive-aleph-bet.

Homrighausen, Jonathan. "Words Made Flesh: Incarnational, Multisensory Exegesis in Donald Jackson's Biblical Art." *Religion and the Arts* 23, no. 3 (2019): 240–72.

Honorius Augustodunensis. *The Seal of Blessed Mary*. Translated by Amelia Carr. Peregrina Translations 18. Toronto: Peregrina Publishing, 1991.

Hufton, Susan. "Behind the Scenes: The Making of the St John's Bible." *Alphabet* 27, no. 1 (2001): 19–22.

Hufton, Susan. "Day-by-Day: The Writing of the St John's Bible." *Alphabet* 28, no. 1 (2002): 21–24.

Hufton, Susan. "Getting It Right: The Making of the St John's Bible." *Alphabet* 27, no. 2 (2002): 27–29.

Hufton, Susan. "The Calligraphers: Susan Hufton." *The Scribe* 75 (2002): 41–43.

Hufton, Susan. "Writing by Hand." In *Pen & Print: The Legacy of Edward Johnston, 1906–2006*, 24–27. Cambridge: The Edward Johnston Foundation and the Society of Scribes and Illuminators, 2006.

Hughes, Christopher. "Visual Typology: An Ottonian Example." *Word & Image* 17, no. 3 (2001): 185–98.

Hyer, Maren Clegg. "Text, Textile, Context: Aldhelm and Wordweaving as Metaphor in Old English." In *Textiles, Text, Intertext: Essays in Honour of Gale R. Owen-Crocker*, edited by Maren Clegg Hyer, 121–38. Woodbridge, Suffolk: Boydell & Brewer, 2016.

Illich, Ivan. *In the Vineyard of the Text: A Commentary to Hugh's* Didascalicon. Chicago: University of Chicago Press, 1996.

Ingmire, Thomas, ed. *Codici 1: Volume One, 2003*. San Francisco: Scriptorium Saint Francis, 2003.

Ingmire, Thomas, ed. *Codici 2: Calligraphic Visual Communication Research*. San Francisco: Scriptorium Saint Francis, 2021.

Ingold, Tim. *Lines: A Brief History*. London: Routledge, 2007.

Isidore of Seville. *The Etymologies of Isidore of Seville*. Translated by Stephen A. Barney, W. J. Lewis, J. A. Beach, and Oliver Berghof. New York: Cambridge University Press, 2010.

Jackson, Donald. "An Evening with Donald Jackson." Concordia University, St. Paul, 12 February 2015. https://www.youtube.com/watch?v=HRx_Vm-XNJ8.

Jackson, Donald. "Donald Jackson, Calligrapher." Lecture presented at the EG Conference, Monterey, CA, February 1, 2007. https://vimeo.com/295077919.

Jackson, Donald. "Earning and Luck." Lecture presented at The Society for Calligraphy, September 4, 2021. https://youtu.be/3uHRDpjkdms.

Jackson, Donald. "Facing the Demons." Lecture presented at The Society for Calligraphy, September 25, 2021. https://youtu.be/Xk_5Xo09p_k.

Jackson, Donald. "Gilding." In *The Calligrapher's Handbook*, edited by Heather Child, 177–98. 2nd ed. New York: Taplinger, 1986.

Jackson, Donald. "Irene Wellington in the Context of Her Time: A Personal View." In *More than Fine Writing: Irene Wellington, Calligrapher (1904–1984)*, edited by Heather Child, 28–37. Woodstock, NY: Overlook Press, 1987.

Jackson, Donald. "Preparation of Quills and Reeds." In *The Calligrapher's Handbook*, edited by Heather Child, 15–36. 2nd ed. New York: Taplinger, 1986.

Jackson, Donald. "The Dream and the Realities." *The Scribe* 75 (2002): 3–8.

Jackson, Donald. "The Elemental Flow." In *Celebration of Calligraphy. Seventy-Five Years of the Society of Scribes & Illuminators*, edited by Society of Scribes and Illuminators, 4. London: Crafts Council, 1996.

Jackson, Donald. "The Saint John's Bible: A Lifetime's Dream." Lecture, St. Mary's University, November 18, 2021.

Jackson, Donald. "The Scribe Speaks: Making the St John's Bible." In *The Lion Companion to Christian Art*, edited by Michelle Brown, 410–14. Oxford: Lion, 2008.

Jackson, Donald. *The Story of Writing*. New York: Taplinger, 1981.

Jager, Eric. *The Book of the Heart*. Chicago: University of Chicago Press, 2000.

James, Elaine T. *Landscapes of the Song of Songs: Poetry and Place*. Oxford: Oxford University Press, 2017.

James, Kathryn. "Skin." *Inscription* 1 (2020): 27–35.

John of the Cross. *The Collected Works of St. John of the Cross*. Translated by Kieran Kavanaugh and Otilio Rodriguez. Rev. ed. Washington, DC: ICS Publications, 2010.

Johnston, Edward. *Lessons in Formal Writing*. Edited by Heather Child and Justin Howes. New York: Taplinger, 1986.

Jonas, Gina. *Calligraphy as Art and Meditation: A New Approach*. St. Augustine, FL: Calligraphic Arts Press, 2019.

Joseph, Judith. "Calligraphy as a Long Walk." *Preachy*, 22 March 2021. https://justpreachy.com/calligraphy-as-a-long-walk/.

Joseph, Sally Mae. "About Writing, About Life." *Alphabet* 29, no. 1 (2003): 24–29.

Joseph, Sally Mae. "The Studio Manager." *The Scribe* 75 (2002): 27–34.

Kaese, Anne. "Ink, Quill, and Goal." *Transpositions*, 30 November 2018. http://www.transpositions.co.uk/ink-quill-and-goal/.

Kaplan, Jonathan, and Aren M. Wilson-Wright. "How Song of Songs Became a Divine Love Song." *Biblical Interpretation* 26 (2018): 334–51.

Karkov, Catherine. "The Scribe Looks Back: Anglo-Saxon England and the Eadwine Psalter." In *The Long Twelfth-Century View of the Anglo-Saxon Past*, edited by M. Brett and D. A. Woodman, 289–306. London: Routledge, 2015.

Katsanis, Bobbi Dykema. "Meeting in the Garden: Intertextuality with the Song of Songs in Holbein's *Noli Me Tangere*." *Interpretation* 61, no. 4 (2007): 402–16.

Kay, Sarah. "Legible Skins: Animals and the Ethics of Medieval Reading." *Postmedieval* 2, no. 1 (2011): 13–32.

Keel, Othmar. *The Song of Songs*. Translated by Frederick J. Gaiser. Continental Commentaries. Minneapolis: Fortress, 1994.

Kendrick, Laura. *Animating the Letter: The Figurative Embodiment of Writing from Late Antiquity to the Renaissance*. Columbus: Ohio State University Press, 1999.

Kingsley, Jennifer P. *The Bernward Gospels: Art, Memory and the Episcopate in Medieval Germany*. University Park: Pennsylvania State University Press, 2014.

Kingsmill, Edmée. *The Song of Songs and the Eros of God: A Study in Biblical Intertextuality*. Oxford Theological Monographs. Oxford: Oxford University Press, 2009.

Klepper, Deeana. "Theories of Interpretation: The Quadriga and Its Successors." In *From 1450 to 1750*, edited by Euan Cameron, 418–38. Vol. 3 of *The New Cambridge History of the Bible*. Cambridge: Cambridge University Press, 2016.

Knight, Stan. *Historical Scripts: A Handbook for Calligraphers*. New York: Taplinger, 1986.

Koester, Craig R. *Symbolism in the Fourth Gospel: Meaning, Mystery, Community*. Minneapolis: Fortress, 2003.

Krueger, Derek. *Writing and Holiness: The Practice of Authorship in the Early Christian East*. Philadelphia: University of Pennsylvania Press, 2011.

Landy, Francis. *Paradoxes of Paradise: Identity and Difference in the Song of Songs*. 2nd ed. Sheffield: Sheffield Academic Press, 2011.

L'Argent, Mark. "On the Surface: Preparing the Vellum for the St John's Bible." *Alphabet* 27, no. 3 (2002): 7–10.

Lavin, Marilyn Aronberg, and Irving Lavin. *The Liturgy of Love: Images from the Song of Songs in the Art of Cimabue, Michelangelo, and Rembrandt.* Franklin D. Murphy Lectures 14. Lawrence: Spencer Museum of Art, University of Kansas, 2001.

Leclercq, Jean. *The Love of Learning and The Desire for God: A Study of Monastic Culture.* Translated by Catherine Mizrahi. New York: Fordham University Press, 1982.

Levine, Amy-Jill. *The Misunderstood Jew: The Church and the Scandal of the Jewish Jesus.* San Francisco: HarperSanFrancisco, 2006.

Lieber, Laura S. "*Akdamut Milin*: The Enigma and Perseverance of Tradition." *TheTorah.Com*, 17 May 2014. https://www.thetorah.com/article/akdamut-milin.

Lovett, Patricia. *The Art and History of Calligraphy.* London: British Library Publishing, 2017.

Lowden, John. "The Word Made Visible: The Exterior of the Early Christian Book as Visual Argument." In *The Early Christian Book*, edited by William E. Klingshirn and Linda Safran, 13–47. CUA Studies in Early Christianity. Washington, DC: Catholic University of America Press, 2007.

Manter, Lisa. "Rolle Playing: 'And the Word Became Flesh.'" In *The Vernacular Spirit: Essays on Medieval Religious Literature*, edited by Renate Blumenfeld-Kosinski, Duncan Robertson, and Nancy Bradley Warren, 15–37. The New Middle Ages. New York: Palgrave Macmillan US, 2002.

Marks, Herbert. "Biblical Naming and Poetic Etymology." *Journal of Biblical Literature* 114 (1995): 21–42.

Matter, E. Ann. *The Voice of My Beloved: The Song of Songs in Western Medieval Christianity.* Philadelphia: University of Pennsylvania Press, 1992.

Maxwell, Kathleen. "Illustrated Byzantine Gospel Books." In *A Companion to Byzantine Illustrated Manuscripts*, edited by Vasiliki Tsamakda, 270–86. Leiden: Brill, 2017.

McGinn, Bernard. "'One Word Will Contain Within Itself a Thousand Mysteries': Teresa of Avila, the First Woman Commentator on the Song of Songs." *Spiritus* 16 (2016): 21–40.

Meyvaert, Paul. "The Medieval Monastic Garden." In *Medieval Gardens*, edited by Elisabeth B. MacDougall, 23–54. Washington, DC: Dumbarton Oaks, 1986.

Miles, Laura Saetveit. *The Virgin Mary's Book at the Annunciation: Reading, Interpretation, and Devotion in Medieval England.* Cambridge: D. S. Brewer, 2020.

Mitchell, Victoria. "Textiles, Text, and Techne." In *The Textile Reader*, edited by Jessica Hemmings, 5–13. New York: Berg Publishers, 2012.

Moore, Suzanne. "The Saint John's Bible - Suzanne Moore." Interview by Saint John's Bible, 21 August 2013. https://www.youtube.com/watch?v=h1FCz-Bdog4.

Moser, Matthew A. Rothaus. "Should Bibles Be Beautiful? How Beauty Teaches Us to Pray." In *The Saint John's Bible and Its Tradition: Illuminating Beauty in the Twenty-First Century*, edited by Jack R. Baker, Jeffrey Bilbro, and Daniel Train, 43–58. Eugene, OR: Pickwick Publications, 2018.

Mosher, Lucinda Allen. "Christian Liturgy and the Music of the Page." *Visual Music: Calligraphy & Sacred Texts. Henry Luce III Center for the Arts & Religion*, 1 September 2021. https://www.luceartsandreligion.org/christian-liturgy-and-the-music-of-the-page.

Muller, Marion. "The Scribe Who Renounced the Pen." *Upper & Lower Case: The International Journal of Typographics* 15, no. 4 (1988): 26–29.

Munro, Jill M. *Spikenard and Saffron: The Imagery of the Song of Songs*. Journal for the Study of the Old Testament Supplement Series 203. Sheffield: Sheffield Academic Press, 1995.

Nasr, Seyyed Hossein, Caner Karacay Dagli, Maria Massi Dakake, Joseph E. B. Lumbard, and Mohammed Rustom, eds. *The Study Quran: A New Translation and Commentary*. New York: HarperOne, 2015.

Nelson, Margaret. "America's Book of Kells." *Newsweek*, 6 March 2000.

Nicholas of Lyra. *The Postilla of Nicholas of Lyra on the Song of Songs*. Edited by James George Kiecker. Milwaukee: Marquette University Press, 1998.

Noonan, Sarah. "Bodies of Parchment: Representing the Passion and Reading Manuscripts in Late Medieval England." PhD diss., Washington University in St. Louis, 2010.

Norton, Laura. "Calligraphy with Laura Norton." *The Hidden Village Podcast*, 17 September 2017. https://soundcloud.com/the-holden-village-podcast/calligraphy-with-laura-norton.

O'Brien, Conor. "Tabernacle, Temple or Something in Between? Architectural Representation in Codex Amiatinus, Fols II v –III." *Leeds Studies in English* 48 (2018): 7–20.

O'Keefe, John J., and R. R. Reno. *Sanctified Vision: An Introduction to Early Christian Interpretation of the Bible*. Baltimore: Johns Hopkins University Press, 2005.

Ola, Per, and Emily D'Aulaire. "Inscribing the Word: At a Scriptorium in Wales, Calligraphers Are Applying Medieval Arts to Create the 21st-Century Saint John's Bible." *Smithsonian*, 1 December 2000.

O'Reilly, Jennifer. "The Library of Scripture: Views from Vivarium and Wearmouth-Jarrow." In *Early Medieval Text and Image 2: The Codex Amiatinus, the Book of Kells and Anglo-Saxon Art*, edited by Carol A.

Farr and Elizabeth Mullins, 3–40. Variorum Collected Studies. New York: Routledge, 2019.

Pardes, Ilana. *The Song of Songs: A Biography*. Princeton: Princeton University Press, 2019.

Parmenter, Dorina Miller. "The Iconic Book: The Image of the Bible in Early Christian Rituals." In *Iconic Books and Texts*, edited by James W. Watts, 63–92. Bristol, CT: Equinox, 2013.

Patella, Michael. "The Theology of The Saint John's Bible." *ARTS* 17, no. 1 (2005): 20–28.

Patella, Michael. *Word and Image: The Hermeneutics of* The Saint John's Bible. Collegeville, MN: Liturgical Press, 2013.

Pirotte, Emmanuelle. "Hidden Order, Order Revealed: New Light on Carpet Pages." In *Pattern and Purpose in Insular Art: Proceedings of the Fourth International Conference on Insular Art Held at the National Museum and Gallery, Cardiff 3–6 September 1998*, edited by Mark Redknap, Nancy Edwards, Alan Lane, and Susan Youngs, 203–8. Oxford: Oxbow Books, 2002.

Pludwinski, Izzy. *Mastering Hebrew Calligraphy*. Jerusalem: Koren, 2012.

Pludwinski, Izzy. "The Saint John's Bible - Izzy Pludwinski." Interview by Saint John's Bible, 21 August 2013. https://www.youtube.com/watch?v=ExyyDX_uH4U.

Plummer, William, and Margaret Nelson. "Holy Writ." *People*, 14 June 1999.

Prudentius. *The Poems of Prudentius*. Translated by M. Clement Eagan. Fathers of the Church 43. Washington, DC: Catholic University of America Press, 1962.

Quintilian. *The Orator's Education*: *Books 9–10*. Edited and translated by Donald A. Russell. Vol. 4. Loeb Classical Library 127. Cambridge: Harvard University Press, 2002.

Rapp, Claudia. "Holy Texts, Holy Men and Holy Scribes: Aspects of Scriptural Holiness in Late Antiquity." In *The Early Christian Book*, edited by William E. Klingshirn and Linda Safran, 194–224. CUA Studies in Early Christianity. Washington, DC: Catholic University of America Press, 2008.

Reinhartz, Adele. "John." In *The Jewish Annotated New Testament*, edited by Amy-Jill Levine and Marc Zvi Brettler, 168–218. 2nd ed. Oxford: Oxford University Press, 2017.

Reynolds, Lloyd J. "Comments on Disciplined Freedom." In *Straight Impressions*, 26–28. Woolwich, ME: TBW Books, 1979.

Rigby, Cynthia L. "Mary and the Artistry of God." In *Blessed One: Protestant Perspectives on Mary*, edited by Beverly Roberts Gaventa and Cynthia L. Rigby, 145–58. Louisville, KY: Westminster John Knox Press, 2002.

Robertson, Duncan. *Lectio Divina: The Medieval Experience of Reading*. Cistercian Studies 238. Collegeville, MN: Liturgical Press, 2011.

Robinson, Timothy, ed. *A Companion to the Song of Songs in the History of Spirituality*. Brill's Companions to the Christian Tradition 98. Leiden: Brill, 2021.

Rohrs, Carl. "Raymond F. DaBoll." *Alphabet* 47, no. 2 (2021): 16–35.

Rollston, Christopher A. *Writing and Literacy in the World of Ancient Israel: Epigraphic Evidence from the Iron Age*. Archaeology and Biblical Studies 11. Atlanta: SBL Press, 2010.

Romanos the Melodist. *On the Life of Christ: Kontakia*. Translated by Ephrem Lash. San Francisco: HarperCollins, 1995.

Rouse, Mary A., and Richard Hunter Rouse. "From Flax to Parchment: A Monastic Sermon from Twelfth-Century Durham." In *New Science out of Old Books: Studies in Manuscripts and Early Printed Books in Honour of A. I. Doyle*, edited by Richard Beadle and Alan J. Piper, 1–13. Aldershot, UK: Scolar Press, 1995.

The Saint John's Bible. "AMEN—The Saint John's Bible." 22 November 2011. https://www.youtube.com/watch?v=SY0onA4WAb0.

Sassoon, Rosemary. *The Art and Science of Handwriting*. Oxford: Intellect Ltd, 2001.

Schäfer, Peter. *Mirror of His Beauty: Feminine Images of God from the Bible to the Early Kabbalah*. Princeton: Princeton University Press, 2004.

Schaper, Joachim. "A Theology of Writing: The Oral and the Written, God as Scribe, and the Book of Deuteronomy." In *Anthropology and Biblical Studies: Avenues of Approach*, edited by Louise J. Lawrence and Mario I. Aguilar, 97–111. Leiden: Deo, 2004.

Scheid, John, and Jesper Svenbro. *The Craft of Zeus: Myths of Weaving and Fabric*. Translated by Carol Volk. Cambridge: Harvard University Press, 2001.

Schellenberg, Annette. "Senses, Sensuality, and Sensory Imagination: On the Role of the Senses in the Song of Songs." In *Sounding Sensory Profiles in Antiquity: On the Role of Senses in Ancient Israel, Mesopotamia, and Egypt*, edited by Annette Schellenberg and Thomas Krüger, 199–216. Ancient Near East Monographs 25. Atlanta: SBL Press, 2019.

Schibanoff, Susan. "Botticelli's *Madonna del Magnificat*: Constructing the Woman Writer in Early Humanist Italy." *Proceedings of the Modern Language Association* 109, no. 2 (1994): 190–206.

Schniedewind, William M. *How the Bible Became a Book: The Textualization of Ancient Israel*. Cambridge: Cambridge University Press, 2005.

Schrader, Elizabeth, and Brandon Simonson. "'Rabbouni,' Which Means *Lord:* Narrative Variants in John 20:16." *TC: A Journal of Biblical Textual Criticism* 26 (2022): forthcoming.

Schroer, Silvia, and Thomas Staubli. *Body Symbolism in the Bible*. Translated by Linda M. Maloney. Collegeville, MN: Michael Glazier, 2001.

Sears, Elizabeth. "The Afterlife of Scribes: Swicher's Prayer in the Prüfening Isidore." In *Pen in Hand: Medieval Scribal Portraits, Colophons and Tools*, edited by Michael Gullick, 75–96. London: Red Gull Press, 2006.

Shahn, Ben. *The Shape of Content*. Cambridge: Harvard University Press, 1957.

Shepard, Dorothy. "The Latin Gospelbook, c. 600–1200." In *From 600 to 1450*, edited by E. Ann Matter and Richard Marsden, 338–62. Vol. 2 of *The New Cambridge History of the Bible*. Cambridge: Cambridge University Press, 2012.

Shupak, Nili. "'Eat This Scroll' (Ezekiel 3:1): Writing as Symbol and Metaphor in the Hebrew Bible in the Light of Ancient Near Eastern Sources." *Bibliotheca Orientalis* 70 (2013): 25–42.

Shuve, Karl. *The Song of Songs and the Fashioning of Identity in Early Latin Christianity*. Oxford: Oxford University Press, 2016.

Sink, Susan. *The Art of* The Saint John's Bible: *The Complete Reader's Guide*. Collegeville, MN: Liturgical Press, 2013.

Snodgrass, Klyne R. *Stories with Intent: A Comprehensive Guide to the Parables of Jesus*. Grand Rapids: Eerdmans, 2018.

Solnit, Rebecca. *Wanderlust: A History of Walking*. New York: Penguin Books, 2001.

Soria, Marina. "Weaving Words, Weaving Dreams." *International Exhibition of Calligraphy*, 19 September 2011. http://calligraphy-expo.com/en/about/news/weaving-words-weaving-dreams-by-marina-soria.

Spencer, F. Scott. *Song of Songs*. Wisdom Commentary. Collegeville, MN: Liturgical Press, 2017.

Stevens, John. *Scribe: Artist of the Written Word*. Greensboro, NC: John Neal Books, 2013.

Teresa of Avila. "Meditations on the Song of Songs." In *The Collected Works of St. Teresa of Avila*. Translated by Kieran Kavanaugh and Otilio Rodriguez. Washington, DC: ICS Publications, 1980.

Thompson, Marianne Meye. *John: A Commentary*. New Testament Library. Louisville, KY: Westminster John Knox Press, 2015.

Tilford, Nicole L. *Sensing World, Sensing Wisdom: The Cognitive Foundation of Biblical Metaphors*. Ancient Israel and Its Literature 31. Atlanta: SBL Press, 2017.

Tilghman, Benjamin C. "Pattern, Process, and the Creation of Meaning in the Lindisfarne Gospels." *West 86th: A Journal of Decorative Arts, Design History, and Material Culture* 24 (2017): 3–28.

Train, Daniel. "Picturing Words: The Gospel as Imaged Word in Thomas Ingmire's Illuminations." In *The Saint John's Bible and Its Tradition: Illuminating Beauty in the Twenty-First Century*, edited by Jack R. Baker, Jeffrey Bilbro, and Daniel Train, 104–21. Eugene, OR: Pickwick, 2018.

Trible, Phyllis. *God and the Rhetoric of Sexuality*. Overtures to Biblical Theology. Philadelphia: Fortress, 1978.

Turner, Tom. *Garden History: Philosophy and Design, 2000 BC–2000 AD*. London: Spon Press, 2005.

Turner, Victor, and Edith Turner. *Image and Pilgrimage in Christian Culture*. New York: Columbia University Press, 1978.

Van Hecke, Pierre. "Tasting Metaphor in Ancient Israel." In *Sounding Sensory Profiles in Antiquity: On the Role of Senses in Ancient Israel, Mesopotamia, and Egypt*, edited by Annette Schellenberg and Thomas Krüger, 99–118. Ancient Near East Monographs 25. Atlanta: SBL Press, 2019.

Verbeek, Sophie. *Musical Calligraphy / Calligraphie musicale*. Küssnacht, Switzerland: Sophie Verbeek, 2019.

Verman, Mark. "The Torah as Divine Fire." *Jewish Bible Quarterly* 35, no. 2 (2007): 94–102.

Wachter, Rudolf. "Inscriptions." In *A Companion to the Ancient Greek Language*, edited by Egbert J. Bakker, 47–61. Malden, MA: Wiley-Blackwell, 2010.

Walsh, Carey Ellen. *Exquisite Desire: Religion, the Erotic, and the Song of Songs*. Minneapolis: Fortress, 2000.

Walsh, Carey Ellen. "In the Absence of Love." In *Scrolls of Love: Ruth and the Song of Songs*, edited by Peter S. Hawkins and Lesleigh Cushing Stahlberg, 283–93. New York: Fordham University Press, 2006.

Warren, Meredith J. C. *Food and Transformation in Ancient Mediterranean Literature*. Writings from the Greco-Roman World Supplement Series 14. Atlanta: SBL Press, 2019.

Waters, Sheila. "Calligraphy in the Pursuit of Excellence." Lecture presented at the Washington Calligraphers Guild, 6 August 1988. https://www.calligraphersguild.org/Resources/SheilaLecture1998 .

Weems, Renita J. *What Matters Most: Ten Lessons in Living Passionately from the Song of Solomon*. New York: Warner, 2004.

Wechsler, Judith Glatzer. "A Change in the Iconography of the Song of Songs in 12th and 13th Century Latin Bibles." In *Texts and Responses: Studies Presented to Nahum N. Glatzer on the Occasion of His Seventieth Birthday by His Students*, edited by Michael A. Fishbane and Paul R. Flohr, 73–93. Leiden: Brill, 1975.

Winsor, Ann Roberts. *A King Is Bound in the Tresses: Allusions to the Song of Songs in the Fourth Gospel*. Studies in Biblical Literature 6. New York: Peter Lang, 1999.

ILLUSTRATION CREDITS

All images from The Saint John's Bible: Copyright 2002–2011, The Saint John's Bible, Saint John's University, Collegeville, Minnesota USA. Used by permission. All rights reserved.

Chapter 2:

Rajasthani camel girth: Camel Girth (Pakistan); goat hair; H x W: 269.2 x 9.5 cm (8 ft. 10 in. x 3 3/4 in.); Museum purchase from General Acquisitions Endowment Fund; 2007-20-1. Object ID 18710421. Web entry: http://cprhw.tt/o/2DTXt/. Used by permission: © Cooper Hewitt, Smithsonian Design Museum / Art Resource, NY.

Relief from Ashurbanipal's palace at Nineveh: British Museum, Asset Number 32504001. © The Trustees of the British Museum. Web entry: https://www.britishmuseum.org/collection/object/W_1856-0909-36_1. Image: https://www.britishmuseum.org/collection/image/32504001. Used by permission.

Chapter 3:

Cathedral of Santiago de Compostela: © User:Yearofthedragon / Wikimedia Commons / CC-BY-SA-3.0 / GFD. https://commons.wikimedia.org/wiki/File:Spain.Santiago.de.Compostela.Catedral.Puerta.Meridional.jpg.

Tabernacle in Codex Amiatinus: Wikimedia Commons. https://commons.wikimedia.org/wiki/File:Zeltheiligtum_(Codex_Amiatinus).png.

Lindisfarne Gospels, fol. 2v: via British Library at http://www.bl.uk/manuscripts/FullDisplay.aspx?ref=Cotton_MS_Nero_D_IV. Used by permission.

Chartres Cathedral labyrinth: © User:Maksim / Wikimedia Commons / CC-BY-SA-3.0 / GFD. https://commons.wikimedia.org/wiki/File:Labyrinth_at_Chartres_Cathedral.JPG.

Chapter 4:

Berlin, Staatliche Museen, Gemäldegalerie. Upper Rhine, ca. 1400: Wikimedia Commons. https://commons.wikimedia.org/wiki/File:Master_of_Erfurt,_The_Virgin_Weaving,_Upper_Rhine,_ca_1400_(Berlin).jpg

Textura script in Malmesbury Bible: © Adrian Pingstone / Wikimedia Commons / CC-BY-SA-3.0 / GFD. https://commons.wikimedia.org/wiki/File:Calligraphy.malmesbury.bible.arp.jpg

Rohan Hours: https://archivesetmanuscrits.bnf.fr/ark:/12148/cc77494b. © Bibliothèque nationale de France. Used by permission.

Botticelli, Madonna of the Magnificat: © User:Livioandronico2013 / Wikimedia Commons / CC-BY-SA-3.0 / GFD. https://commons.wikimedia.org/wiki/File:Madonna_of_the_Magnificat.png

Chapter 5:

Bernward Gospels. © Dommuseum Hildesheim. Used by permission.

Ivory Diptych of Moses and Thomas: © User:AndreasPraefcke / Wikimedia Commons / CC-BY-SA-3.0 / GFD. https://commons.wikimedia.org/wiki/File:Trier_10_Jh_Diptychon_Moses_Thomas.jpg.

Portrait in Eadwine Psalter: Image © Master and Fellows of Trinity College, Cambridge and is licensed under a Creative Commons Attribution-NonCommercial 4.0 International License. https://mss-cat.trin.cam.ac.uk/Manuscript/R.17.1

Matthew in Lindisfarne Gospels: Wikimedia Commons. https://en.wikipedia.org/wiki/File:Meister_des_Book_of_Lindisfarne_001.jpg.

SCRIPTURE INDEX

ILLUMINATION INDEX